Select Naval Documents

Edited by Harold Winter Hodges and Edward Arthur Hughes

CAMBRIDGE
UNIVERSITY PRESS

CAMBRIDGE UNIVERSITY PRESS

Cambridge New York Melbourne Madrid Cape Town Singapore São Paolo Delhi

Published in the United States of America by Cambridge University Press, New York

www.cambridge.org
Information on this title: www.cambridge.org/9781108003766

This edition first published 1936
This digitally printed version 2009

ISBN 978-1-108-00376-6

CAMBRIDGE LIBRARY COLLECTION

Books of enduring scholarly value

History

The books reissued in this series include accounts of historical events and movements by eye-witnesses and contemporaries, as well as landmark studies that assembled significant source materials or developed new historiographical methods. The series includes work in social, political and military history on a wide range of periods and regions, giving modern scholars ready access to influential publications of the past.

Select Naval Documents

This illustrated book, first published in 1936, is an edited compilation of source material drawn from some 145 diverse naval documents covering a period of more than three centuries from 1497 to 1805. The editors' intention was to smooth the approach to a highly technical subject, and to use original documents to give concrete illustrations of the limiting conditions of sea warfare, thus removing some common misconceptions such as that the big Spanish ships of the Armada were defeated by cockleshells manned by volunteers. Subjects include the seaworthiness of ships in Elizabethan times; Drake's views on strategy; sea punishments; Kempenfelt's 1782 design for a signal book; victuals; the battle of Kentish Knock (1562); the 1803 defences against invasion; Nelson's watch off Toulon; the coppering of ships; and many other topics giving insights into the history and development of the British navy.

Cambridge University Press has long been a pioneer in the reissuing of out-of-print titles from its own backlist, producing digital reprints of books that are still sought after by scholars and students but could not be reprinted economically using traditional technology. The Cambridge Library Collection extends this activity to a wider range of books which are still of importance to researchers and professionals, either for the source material they contain, or as landmarks in the history of their academic discipline.

Drawing from the world-renowned collections in the Cambridge University Library, and guided by the advice of experts in each subject area, Cambridge University Press is using state-of-the-art scanning machines in its own Printing House to capture the content of each book selected for inclusion. The files are processed to give a consistently clear, crisp image, and the books finished to the high quality standard for which the Press is recognised around the world. The latest print-on-demand technology ensures that the books will remain available indefinitely, and that orders for single or multiple copies can quickly be supplied.

The Cambridge Library Collection will bring back to life books of enduring scholarly value across a wide range of disciplines in the humanities and social sciences and in science and technology.

SELECT NAVAL DOCUMENTS

LONDON
Cambridge University Press
FETTER LANE

NEW YORK · TORONTO
BOMBAY · CALCUTTA · MADRAS
Macmillan

TOKYO
Maruzen Company Ltd

Select Naval Documents

Edited by

H. W. HODGES, M.A., F.R.Hist.S.

Late Exhibitioner of Lincoln College, Oxford
Head of History and English Department,
Royal Naval College, Dartmouth

and

E. A. HUGHES, M.A.

Late Major Scholar of Trinity College, Cambridge
Assistant Master at the Royal Naval College, Dartmouth

Cambridge
at the University Press
1936

First Edition 1922
Reprinted 1927
Second Edition 1936

PRINTED IN GREAT BRITAIN

PREFACE

THE use of 'source-books' in historical studies has been justified by experience: the imagination can hardly fail to be quickened by the living voices of the past. In addition to this purpose—the provision of colour and the heightening of the personal aspect, we have another—the smoothing of the approach to a highly technical subject. Naval History is so different from land History, and sailing ships are so different from steamships, that the subject abounds in pitfalls. The belief is still common that the 'big ships' of the Armada were defeated by 'cockle-shells' manned by volunteers; plans of battles still appear in which ships are shown sailing straight into the wind; the strategy of blockade is frequently discussed in the abstract, apart from its practical problems. The cure for such misconceptions lies in concrete illustrations of the limiting conditions of sea warfare. Many of the points emphasized may at first seem trivial: unless they are made vivid, they are not realized to be vital. If we appear to lay too much stress upon administrative defects, we would remind our readers that they only heighten the fame of the admirals who triumphed in spite of them.

It is obvious that a book of this size can in no sense be exhaustive, but can deal only with certain aspects: there are large gaps which must be filled by the text-book, which this selection is intended to supplement, not to replace. Thus, while conflicting evidence is produced, for example, on the tactics employed at the Chesapeake in September, 1781, no direct mention is made of Lord Howe's tactics on June 1, 1794. Again, a considerable space has been allotted to the work of Kempenfelt, to whose genius scant justice is usually done. Many problems of strategy, tactics and administration are illustrated by the reproduction of a single document, when a dozen would not have been superfluous.

Lack of space, too, has made us avoid such disputed questions as the precise meaning of 'deck' in the sixteenth and early seventeenth centuries, and has led us to make our notes as brief as possible, at the risk of their appearing dogmatic: they are designedly merely introductory or explanatory, to allow more room for Drake, Hawke, Kempenfelt and Nelson.

The papers here printed may be divided into two classes. The first class consists of documents, such as the Fighting Instructions and the Trafalgar Memorandum, which are of great importance in themselves, and which have been frequently printed at length, but not in a single volume: most of these are here reprinted by kind permission of the Navy Records Society, to whose volumes this book is intended to be an elementary introduction, and without which its compilation could not have been attempted. Where there is no *locus classicus*, we have tried to choose the more lively and less accessible illustrations. Many of the passages in this class appear in print for the first time.

In two respects we have not strictly adhered to the rules of scholarship. Since limitations of space have forced us to weigh the claims of almost every sentence, we have made so many omissions (without changing the general sense) that we have thought it best not to indicate them by means of the usual sign. Secondly, though it goes against the grain to alter words like 'bittacle,' 'fadom,' and 'Cales,' we have, except in one or two extracts, modernised the spelling and punctuation for the convenience of readers who are unfamiliar with the older forms.

We are deeply indebted to Mr W. G. Perrin, Admiralty Librarian, for his ready and invaluable help both in suggestion and in the reading of the MS. Our warm thanks are also due to Messrs L. G. Carr Laughton and Edward Fraser, of the Admiralty Library, for valuable assistance and advice.

Acknowledgment is further due to Mr O. F. Morshead, Pepysian Librarian of Magdalene College, Cambridge, to the officials in charge of the Search Room, Public Record Office, and to those of the Manuscripts Room, British Museum, for their invariable courtesy.

Our best thanks are due to Professor G. A. R. Callender for advice on the arrangement of our material, to Messrs P. F. R. Bashford and Arthur Chambers for French translations, and to Mr D. F. Ferguson for help in the preparation of the MS. for the press.

H. W. H.
E. A. H.

Royal Naval College
Dartmouth.

July 1922

FROM the second edition we have omitted the old Nos. 101 and 102, which were mainly of political interest, and No. 121, which has been proved spurious. In their place we print a document relating to the early history of 'Divisions' (which we have numbered 101 and 102 in order to avoid altering the numbering of the others) and an additional one on the reform of the Signal Book.

H. W. H.
E. A. H.

July 1935

CONTENTS

HENRY VIII

ELIZABETH

JAMES I AND CHARLES I

THE COMMONWEALTH AND PROTECTORATE

CONTENTS

THE RESTORATION NAVY

WILLIAM III AND ANNE

THE PEACE PERIOD AND NEED FOR REFORM

REVOLUTIONARY AND NAPOLEONIC WARS

LIST OF PLATES

ILLUSTRATIONS IN THE TEXT

ABBREVIATIONS

P.R.O. = Public Record Office.
S.P. Dom. = State Papers, Domestic (in P.R.O.).
Cal. S.P. Sp. = Calendar of State Papers, Spanish.
Cal. S.P. Ven. = Calendar of State Papers, Venetian.
N.R.S. = Publications of the Navy Records Society.

SELECT NAVAL DOCUMENTS

HENRY VIII

WE choose this reign as our starting-point, not because it is the beginning of English naval history, but because Henry VIII originated a new epoch—that of the broadside sailing ship. The two following lists give the armament of the *Sovereign* in 1497 and in 1509, when she was rebuilt. Before the time of Henry VIII, English warships were armed with a large number of small breech-loading guns, meant to sweep the enemy's deck as a preliminary to capturing him by boarding, and therefore carried high; while their own crews were protected from the enemy's fire by many-storied fore- and stern-castles, in which most of the guns were mounted, the rest being placed in the waist. Retaining the breech-loaders as a secondary armament, Henry VIII introduced a small number of heavy guns, which could penetrate the hull of an enemy, and which would have to be carried on a lower gun-deck. This is the germ of the revolution which converted the warship from a transport, to be attacked and defended by soldiers, into a gun-carriage or floating battery.

The changes in armament involved changes in ship-construction. The old 'round-ship,' besides being top-heavy, was only twice as long as she was broad, and was therefore very slow. Importing Italian ship-wrights, accustomed to build 'galleons' with a length of three times their beam, Henry experimented throughout his reign with a view to building ships which should be more seaworthy, speedier, and better gun-platforms. The last four ships built in his reign—the *Hart, Antelope, Tiger,* and *Bull*—were flush-decked, and without any kind of superstructure. If this was too great a departure from tradition, Henry was only exaggerating a sound principle.

Two further points may be noticed: the publication of a code of laws for the Royal Navy, based largely on 'The Custom of the Sea,' and the establishment, in 1546, of a system of administration which remained essentially unchanged until 1832. The Navy Board (to use its later name) was responsible for the civil administration of the Navy. The 'Principal Officers' were the Treasurer of the Navy, the Comptroller, whose duty was to check the Treasurer's accounts, the Surveyor, who inspected and made inventories of ships and stores, and the Clerk of the Ships (later, of the Acts), who was secretary to the Board.

1. Inventory of the *Sovereign*, Jan. 31, 1497

(As 'delivered to James Finch and other merchants for a voyage to be made into the Levant.' *N.R.S.* VIII, p. 216.)

In the Storehouse of the said Ship

Serpentines[1] of iron in the forecastle above the deck, with miches[2] and forelocks to the same	16
Chambers of iron to the same	48
Serpentines of iron in the forecastle alow, with miches and forelocks of iron	24
Chambers of iron to the same	72
Stone guns[3] of iron in the Waist of the said ship, with miches and forelocks to the same	20
Chambers of iron to the same	60
Serpentines of iron in the summercastle[4], with miches and forelocks to the same	20
Serpentines of brass in the summercastle, with a miche and a forelock	1
Stone guns in the summercastle, with miches and forelocks	11
Chambers to the said serpentines and stone guns	92
Serpentines of iron in the stern, with miches and forelocks	4
Chambers of iron to the same	12
Serpentines of iron in the deck over the summercastle, with miches and forelocks	25
Chambers to the same	75
Serpentines of iron in the poop[5], with miches and forelocks	20
Chambers to the same	60
Bows of yew	200
Chests to the same	4

[1] There is no contemporary description of a serpentine, but it probably weighed about 250 lbs., and was certainly a breech-loader, the powder and shot being placed in a cylinder (the 'chamber'), which locked into the breech.

[2] Mr G. A. R. Callender says (*Mariner's Mirror*, V, 36): 'I believe that Tudor "miches, bolts and forelocks" were simply trunnion-fittings. I think that the "miche" was what today we call the "cap-square."'

[3] Guns for firing stone balls.   [4] Probably the 'poop.'

[5] Probably the 'poop royal.'

Arrows   800 sheaves
Spears   80
Gunpowder   5 barrels
Pellets of lead   400
Dice of iron of inch and a half square   200
Gun hammers of iron   12
Ladles of iron to melt lead in, for making of pellets   1
Moulds of stone for casting of pellets   6

2. ARMAMENT OF THE *SOVEREIGN* IN 1509

Letters and Papers, Henry VIII, No. 5721, f. 229.

Hereafter followeth all the ordnance and artillery and harness
that is in the *Sovereign*.

Item 4 whole Cortos[1] (*sic*) of brass.
Item 3 half cortos of brass
Item 2 falcons of brass
Item 2 culverins of brass
Item one culverin of brass without a stock
Item 4 serpentines of brass

Item 6 }

longing to them 12 chambers
Item 7 great pieces of iron }
longing to them 14 chambers }
Item 4 slings of iron }
longing to them 8 chambers }
Item 42 serpentines of iron, great & small, }
longing to them 126 chambers with their }
miches, bolts, & forelocks. }
Item 2 stone guns for the top
Item 7 harquebuses
Item 7 gavelocks[2] of iron
chambers of iron 209.

The inventory also gives the quantities of iron, stone and lead pellets, gunpowder, harness (*i.e.* armour), bows and arrows, bills, marlin-spikes, and stakes.

[1] The curtow, or curtall, was a short heavy siege gun, weighing 3000 lbs.
The culverin was the long-range heavy gun: at a later period (and possibly
in this reign) it was an 18-pounder. The falcon was a 3-pounder. The sling
was a small breech-loader.
[2] Javelins or crowbars.

3. Henry VIII's Sea Laws

A Book of Orders for the War both by Sea and Land, written by Thomas Audley[1] at the command of King Henry VIII (*c.* 1530). (*Harl. MSS.* 309, f. 10.)

Orders to be used in the King's Majesty's Navy by the Sea

First, the laws which be written what every man ought to do in the ship towards his captain to be set in the main mast in parchment to be read as occasion shall serve.

If any man kill another within the ship, he that doeth the deed shall be bound quick to the dead man, and so be cast into the sea, and a piece of ordnance shot off after they be thrown into the sea.

If any man draw a weapon within the ship to strike his captain, he shall lose his right hand.

If any man within the ship draweth any weapon or causeth tumult or likelihood of murder or bloodshed within the ship shall lose his right hand as is before said.

If any man within the ship steal or pick money or clothes within the ship duly proved, he shall be three times dipped at the bowsprit, and let down two fathoms within the water, and kept on live, and at the next shore towed aland bound to the boat's stern, with a loaf of bread and a can of beer, and banished the King's ships for ever.

If any man within the ship do sleep his watch iiii times and so proved, this be his punishment: the first time he shall be headed at the main mast with a bucket of water poured on his head.

The second time he shall be armed, his hands haled up by a rope, and ii buckets of water poured into his sleeves.

The third time he shall be bound to the main mast with certain gun chambers tied to his arms and as much pain to his body as the captain will.

The fourth time and last punishment, being taken asleep he shall be hanged on the bowsprit end of the ship in a basket, with a can of beer, a loaf of bread, and a sharp knife, choose to hang there till he starve or cut himself into the sea.

[1] Speaker in 1529; afterwards Lord Chancellor.

If any mariner or soldier depart from the King's ships without license of his captain, the same is felony by statute.

The captain shall not permit his boat to go to shore without license from his ship at no time. If the boat must go for necessaries, as water or other needful things, then the boatswain and one of the quarter-masters shall go, and they to choose such men to go to land as be of good rule to come again in time and none to run away as they will answer: the boatswain and the quarter-masters know the conditions best of every mariner.

If any man within the ship be a drunkard, not being content with the victuals of the ship, nor as the rest be of the company, the captain shall imprison him in the bilboes while he think him duly punished that so offendeth.

Orders for Captains to their Admiral

No captain shall take the wind of his admiral, but come under his lee, except necessity require the same.

All captains must be obedient to their admiral. If any be stubborn, the admiral shall set him on shore and put another in his place, and write to the King and his Council of his faults, truly without malice.

Whensoever and at all times the admiral doth shoot off a piece of ordnance and set up his banner of council on starboard buttock of his ship, every ship's captain shall with speed go aboard the admiral to know his will.

When and at all times the admiral will anchor or disanchor, he must shoot a piece that thereby the rest may know to do the same, and that no ship ride in another's wake, for in that is great danger.

The admiral ought to have a swift pinnace always abroad to ascry so far off that he may see the fleet out of his top, and if he seeth any enemies or any other sails give knowledge to the admiral; if they be enemies, let him shoot two or three pieces off.

If they meet with enemies, the admiral must apply to get the wind of the enemy by all the means he can, for that is the advantage[1]. No private captain should board the admiral enemy

---

[1] Though it would be rash to assert that the ships of this period could not beat to windward, they were so clumsily built that they could only do so under favourable conditions.

but the admiral English, except he cannot come to the enemy's, as the matter may so fall out without they both the one seek the other. And if they chase the enemy, let them that chase shoot no ordnance till he be ready to board him, for that will let his ship's way.

Let every ship match equally as near as they can, and leave some pinnaces at liberty to help the overmatched. And one small ship when they shall join battle to be attending upon the admiral to relieve him, for the overcoming of the admiral is a great discouraging of the rest of the other side.

In case you board[1] your enemy enter[2] not till you see the smoke gone and then shoot off all your pieces, your port-pieces, the pieces of hail-shot, [and] cross-bow shot to beat his cage decks, and if you see his deck well rid, then enter with your best men, but first win his top in any wise if it be possible. In case you see there come rescue, bulge[3] the enemy ship, [but] first

[1] In fight, *to board* a ship is to bring the ship to touch the other; where you must note the advantages and disadvantages of every place in boarding, and know that when two ships fight, the defendant may choose whether you shall board him or no, but only in the quarter, which is a bad place to board, for men can worst enter there, in respect that it is the highest part of the ship's hull: and for that there is only the mizen shrouds to enter by; as also for that ships are hottest there, and men being entered there can do little good and are easily scoured off with murderers from the close fights. The best boarding for entering is, if you can, to board on bow, for then you may quickly bring all your broadside to; but the greatest advantage for use of ordnance is to board athwart her hawse, for then you may use all your ordnance on one side and she can only use her chase and her prow pieces.

[2] **Enter.** To enter is to come into a ship, but in fight they must be careful to clear the decks with fire pots or the like, if it be possible, from the trains of powder before men do enter; for it happens many times that there are more men lost in a minute by entering than in long fight board and board; and therefore being so dangerous it is fit that men should be well advised first; though many times if a ship is not well provided of close fights it is the speediest and safest way of taking her.

[3] **Bilge** or **Bulge.** The bilge of the ship, is the breadth of the floor, whereon the ship doth rest when she is aground. A ship is *bilged*, that is, when she strikes on a rock or an anchor or the like, and breaks some of her timbers or planks there, and so springs a leak.

The above definitions are taken from Sir Henry Mainwaring's *Seaman's Dictionary*, written between 1620 and 1623, and printed, in an incomplete and careless form, in 1644.

take heed your own men be retired, [and] take the captain with certain of the best with him, the rest [to be] committed to the bottom of the sea, for else they will turn upon you to your confusion.

No captain presume to send his boat aboard any strange ship without leave of the admiral: if that should be suffered, they would pilfer things from our own nation as well of the King's dear friends.

If the lord admiral take the strange lord admiral enemy, it is indifferent whether he be the King's prisoner or his; but if any other private captain take him, the King shall have him, and reward the captain that takes him.

The admiral ought to have this order before he join battle with the enemy, that all his ships shall bear a flag in their mizen-top, and himself one in the foremast beside the mainmast, that every man may know his own fleet by that token. If he see a hard match with the enemy and be to leeward, then to gather his fleet together and seem to flee, and flee indeed for this purpose till the enemy draw within gunshot. And when the enemy doth shoot, then [he shall] shoot again, and make all the smoke he can to the intent the enemy shall not see the ships, and [then] suddenly hale up his tackle aboard, and have the wind of the enemy. And by this policy it is possible to win the weather-gage of the enemy, and then he hath a great advantage, and this may well be done if it be well foreseen aforehand, and every captain and master made privy to it beforehand at whatsoever time any such disadvantage shall happen.

The admiral shall not take in hand any exploit to land or enter into any harbour enemy with the King's ships, but he call a council and make the captains privy to his device and the best masters in the fleet or pilots, known to be skilful men in that coast or place where he intendeth to do his exploit, and by good advice. Otherwise the fault ought partly to be laid on the admiral if anything should happen but well.

And if he did an exploit without assent of the captains and [it] proved well, the King ought to put him out of his room for purposing a matter of such charge of his own brain, whereby all the fleet might fall into the hands of the enemy to the destruction of the King's people.

ELIZABETH

THE powerful fleet created by Henry VIII was maintained almost at full strength by Edward VI and Mary, but allowed to decline by Elizabeth in the early years of her reign. In the 1570's, however, the views of the experts (especially of Sir John Hawkyns, Treasurer and Comptroller of the Navy) were embodied in a building programme of ships of the 'middle sort.' The existence of two schools of thought among builders and seamen, as illustrated in the first extract, must have led to improvements, one of which is described in the second passage. That this clash of opinion (and the supervision of Sir John Hawkyns) led builders to put good material and workmanship into their ships is proved by the testimony of Howard and Wynter.

4. RACE-BUILT V. LOFTY SHIPS

The Observations of Sir Richard Hawkyns, Knight, in his Voyage into the South Seas, Anno Domini 1593 (Hakluyt Society), p. 199[1].

Here is offered to speak of a point much canvassed amongst carpenters & sea captains, diversely maintained but yet undetermined: that is, whether the race or lofty built ship be best for the merchant, & those which employ themselves in trading. I am of opinion that the race ship is most convenient; yet so as that every perfect ship ought to have two decks, for the better strengthening of her; the better succouring of her people; the better preserving of her merchandise & victual; & for her greater safety from sea & storms.

But for the prince's ships, & such as are employed continually in the wars, to be built lofty I hold very necessary for many reasons. First for majesty & terror of the enemy; secondly, for harbouring of many men; thirdly, for accommodating more men to fight; fourthly, for placing & using more artillery; fifthly, for better strengthening & securing of the ship; sixthly, for over-topping & subjecting the enemy; seventhly, for greater safeguard & defence of the ship & company. For it is plain that the ship with three decks, or with two & a half, shows more pomp than another of her burthen with a deck & a half, or two decks, & breedeth greater terror to the enemy, discovering herself to be a more powerful ship, as she is, than the other; which being indeed a ship of force, seemeth to be but a bark, & with

---

[1] This book was not printed until 1622, the year of Hawkyns's death.

her low building hideth her burthen. And who doubteth that a deck & a half cannot harbour that proportion of men, that two decks, & two decks & a half can accommodate to fight; nor carry the artillery so plentifully, nor so commodiously. Neither can the ship be so strong with a deck & a half as with two decks; nor with two, as with three; nor carry her masts so taunt[1]; nor spread so great a clew[2]; nor contrive so many fights, to answer one another for defence & offence. And the advantage the one hath of the other, experience daily teacheth.

5. THE *TEREDO NAVALIS*

Richard Hawkyns's *Observations*, p. 119.

These *arters* or *broma*, in all hot countries, enter into the planks of ships, and especially where are rivers of fresh water; for the common opinion is that they are bred in fresh water, and with the current of the rivers are brought into the sea; but experience teacheth that they breed in the great seas in all hot climates, especially near the equinoctial line; for lying so long under and near the line, and towing a shalop at our stern, coming to cleanse her in Brazil, we found her all under water covered with these worms, as big as the little finger of a man, on the outside of the plank, not fully covered, but half the thickness of their body, like to a jelly, wrought into the plank as with a gouge. And natural reason, in my judgment, confirmeth this; for creatures bred and nourished in the sea, coming into fresh water die; as those actually bred in ponds or fresh waters die presently, if they come into salt water.

In little time, if the ship be not sheathed, they put all in hazard; for they enter in no bigger than a small Spanish needle, and by little and little their holes become ordinarily greater than a man's finger. The thicker the plank is, the greater he groweth; yea, I have seen many ships so eaten, that the most of their planks under water have been like honey-combs, and especially those betwixt wind and water. If they had not been sheathed, it had been impossible that they could have swum.

[1] High.
[2] 'The clew of a sail is the lower corner of the sail. A ship *spreads a great clew*; that is, hath very broad yards and so spreads much canvas.' (Mainwaring.)

The entering of them is hardly to be discerned, the most of them being small as the head of a pin. Which all such as purpose long voyages are to prevent by sheathing their ships.

And for that I have seen divers manners of sheathing, for the ignorant I will set them down which by experience I have found best.

In Spain and Portugal, some sheath their ships with lead, which, besides the cost and weight, although they use the thinnest sheet-lead that I have seen in any place, yet it is nothing durable, but subject to many casualties[1].

But the most approved of all, is the manner of sheathing used nowadays in England, with thin boards, half inch thick; the thinner the better; and elm better than oak; for it riveth not, it endureth better under water, and yieldeth better to the ship's side.

The invention of the materials incorporated betwixt the plank and the sheathing, is that indeed which availeth; for without it many planks were not sufficient to hinder the entrance of this worm; this manner is thus:

Before the sheathing board is nailed on, upon the inner side of it they smear it over with tar half a finger thick and upon the tar another half finger thick of hair, such as the white-limers use, and so nail it on, the nails not above a span distance one from another; the thicker they are driven, the better.

Some hold opinion that the tar killeth the worm; others, that the worm passing the sheathing, and seeking a way through, the hair and the tar so involve him that he is choked therewith; which methinks is most probable; this manner of sheathing was invented by my father, and experience hath taught it to be the best and of least cost.

6. Seaworthiness of English Ships

(a) Howard to Burghley, February 21, 1588. (N.R.S. I, p. 79.)

I have been aboard of every ship that goeth out with me, and in every place where any may creep, and I do thank God that they be in the estate they be in; and there is never a one of them that knows what a leak means. I have known when an Admiral

---

[1] Hawkyns describes other methods:—double planks, canvas, burnt planks, and in China with varnish.

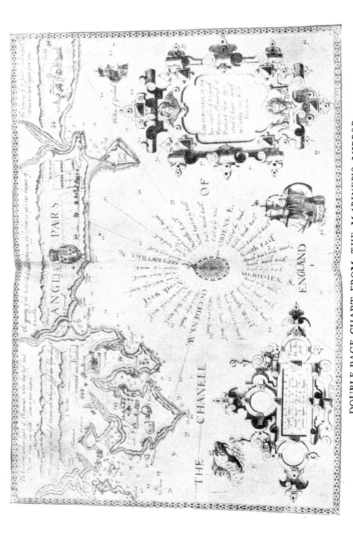

DOUBLE-PAGE CHART FROM *THE MARINER'S MIRROR*

of England hath gone out, and two ships in fleet could not say so. There is none that goeth out now but I durst go to the Rio de la Plata in her.

(b) Same to same, February 29, 1588. (*N.R.S.* I, p. 83.)

I protest before God, and as my soul shall answer for it, that I think there were never in any place in the world worthier ships than these are, for so many. And as few as we are, if the King of Spain's forces be not hundreds, we will make good sport with them. And I pray you tell her Majesty from me that her money was well given for the *Ark Ralegh*[1], for I think her the odd ship in the world for all conditions; and truly I think there can no great ship make me change and go out of her. We can see no sail, great nor small, but how far soever they be off, we fetch them and speak with them.

(c) Sir William Wynter to the Principal Officers, February 28, 1588. (*N.R.S.* I, p. 81.)

Our ships doth show themselves like gallants here. I assure you it will do a man's heart good to behold them; and would to God the Prince of Parma were upon the seas with all his forces, and we in the view of them; then I doubt not but that you should hear that we would make his enterprise very unpleasant to him.

7. Dartmouth Haven

The works from which the following extracts are taken were both published in England in 1588. *The Mariner's Mirror* was Ashley's English translation of a Dutch book of charts and sailing directions.

Extract from sailing directions accompanying plate opposite.

If your course lieth to Dartmouth, you shall discern a red point on the east side of the haven, and a black point at the water's side. In the red point lieth a great white rock: when you have brought this rock right over the black point, you are hard aboard the blind rock that lieth thwart the channel of Dartmouth, yet nearer to the eastward. But when you come to discern the quay of the town that standeth on the east side of the haven, keep amidst the channel, until you may perfectly see the same, then hale inwards until you are within the two castles

---

[1] Bought from Sir Walter Ralegh for £5000, and renamed the *Ark Royal*.

standing on the haven's side, and you shall go clear of the rock. The haven is wide within: you may turn westward and let fall anchor before the town or the brew-houses, where you list.

8. The Properties, Office, and Duty of a Gunner

This passage is from Three Books of Colloquies concerning the art of shooting in great and small pieces of artillery; written in Italian by Nicholas Tartaglia and now translated into English by Cyprian Lucar; whereunto is annexed a Treatise called Lucar Appendix.

A gunner ought to be a sober, wakeful, lusty, hardy, patient, prudent, and quick spirited man; he ought also to have a good eyesight, a good judgment, and perfect knowledge to select a convenient place in the day of service, to plant his ordnance where he may do most hurt unto the enemies, and be least annoyed by them.

Also a gunner in time of service ought to forbid with meek and courteous speeches all manner of persons, other than his appointed assistants, to come near his pieces, to the end that none of his pieces may be choked, poisoned, or hurt; and he ought not for any prayers or reward to lend any piece of his gunmatch to another person, because it may be very hurtful to him in time of service to lack the same.

Also every gunner ought to know that as it is a wholesome thing for him to drink and eat a little meat before he doth discharge any piece of artillery, because the fume of saltpetre and brimstone will otherwise be hurtful to his brains, so it is very unwholesome for him to shoot in any piece of ordnance while his stomach is full.

Every gunner which shall serve upon the sea in any ship ought before his going to sea to write with good advisement in a paper book for the owner or captain of the vessel in which he shall serve, the weight and price of so much gunpowder, and of so many fit pellets, as will be enough to charge all the pieces in his vessel forty times over, and also the price of ten barrels of more gunpowder, which he ought to have for the only making of fireworks.

Some of Lucar's Paragraph Headings

How the makers of gunpowder do mingle together the simples and material things of which they do make gunpowder.

How great pieces of artillery are named; and how, through the intolerable fault of careless or unskilful gun-founders, all our great pieces of one name are not of one length, nor of one weight, nor of one height in their mouths.

How you may cause any great piece of artillery to make in his discharge an exceeding great noise and a marvellous roar.

How you may know what number of feet, yards, paces, or scores, any piece of artillery will shoot in an unsensible crooked line, or (as the gunner's term is) at point blank.

How you may make hollow balls of metal, which, being shot out of great ordnance or mortar pieces, or thrown with slings out of men's hands among soldiers standing or marching in battle ray (*sic*), will suddenly break in many pieces and do great harm.

Another kind of firework which may be shot out of great ordnance, or thrown with men's hands, and will burn in water, armour, stones, and every other thing upon which it shall fall.

How you may make divers sorts of fireworks, which, being shot in a dark night out of a mortar piece, or out of any other piece of artillery, or thrown out of men's hands into an appointed place, will give so great a light as that you may discern by the same light whether or no any enemies are in or near unto that place.

To make rockets or squibs, which, being thrown up into the air, will cast forth flames of fire, and in coming down towards the ground will shew like stars falling from heaven.

The bigness, fashion, and use of an instrument named a Gunner's Semicircle, and of an instrument named a Geometrical Square.

To know, by the help of a Gunner's Semicircle, how many miles, paces, yards, or feet any ship lying at Road in the sea, or tower, or any other mark upon the land in sight, is from you.

9. Drake's Views on Strategy

When it became certain that the long-expected Armada was about to sail, opinions differed widely as to the strategy proper to meet the danger.
Drake to the Council, March 30, 1588. (*N.R.S.* I, p. 123.)

If her Majesty and your Lordships think that the King of Spain meaneth any invasion in England, then doubtless his force is and will be great in Spain; and thereon he will make his groundwork or foundation, whereby the Prince of Parma may have the better entrance, which[1], in mine own judgment, is most to be feared. But if there may be such a stay or stop made by any means of this fleet in Spain, that they may not come through the seas as conquerors—which, I assure myself, they think to do—then shall the Prince of Parma have such a check thereby as were meet.

To prevent this I think it good that these forces here[2] should be made as strong as to your Honours' wisdoms shall be thought convenient, and that for two special causes:—First, for that they are like to strike the first blow; and secondly, it will put great and good hearts into her Majesty's loving subjects both abroad and at home; for that they will be persuaded in conscience that the Lord of all strength will put into her Majesty and her people courage and boldness not to fear any invasion in her own country, but to seek God's enemies and her Majesty's where they may be found; for the Lord is on our side, whereby we may assure ourselves our numbers are greater than theirs. I must crave pardon of your good Lordships again and again, for my conscience hath caused me to put my pen to the paper; and as God in his goodness hath put my hand to the plough, so in His mercy it will never suffer me to turn back from the truth.

My very good Lords, next under God's mighty protection, the advantage and gain of time and place will be the only and chief means for our good; wherein I most humbly beseech your good Lordships to persevere as you have began, for that with fifty sail of shipping we shall do more good upon their own coast, than a great many more will do here at home; and the sooner we are gone[3], the better we shall be able to impeach them.

I have sent unto your good Lordships the note of such powder and munition as are delivered unto us for this great service; which, in truth, I judge to be just a third part of that which is

[1] The antecedent of *which* is meant to be *groundwork or foundation*.
[2] At Plymouth.
[3] In considering Drake's advice, we must take the date into account: at this time he could have been certain of reaching Spain before the departure of the Armada.

needful; for if we should want it when we shall have most need thereof, it will be too late to send to the Tower for it. I assure your Honours it neither is or shall be spent in vain.

10. ELIZABETH AS AN ARMCHAIR STRATEGIST

Walsyngham to Howard, June 9, 1588. (*N.R.S.* I, p. 192.)

My very good Lord:—Her Majesty, perceiving by your Lordship's late letters to me that you were minded to repair to the Isles of Bayona[1], if the wind serve, there to abide the Spanish fleet or to discover what course they meant to take, doubting that in case your Lordship should put over so far the said fleet may take some other way, whereby they may escape your Lordship, as by bending their course westward to the altitude[2] of 50 degrees, and then to shoot over to this realm, hath therefore willed me to let your Lordship understand that she thinketh it not convenient that your Lordship should go so far to the south as the said Isles of Bayona, but to ply up and down in some indifferent place between the coast of Spain and this realm, so as you may be able to answer any attempt that the said fleet shall make either against this realm, Ireland or Scotland. And so &c.

11. HOWARD TAKES THE ADVICE OF EXPERTS

Howard to Walsyngham, June 15, 1588. (*N.R.S.* I, p. 202.)

Sir:—Within three hours after I had written my letter, which herewith I send you, I received your letter of the 9th of this present by a pursuivant. Which letter I do not a little marvel at; for thereby you signify that her Majesty, perceiving by a letter I sent you heretofore, that I was minded to go on the coast of Spain, to the Isles of Bayona, her pleasure is that I should not go so far, but only òff and on, betwixt the coast of Spain and England; lest the Spanish fleet should come into the height of 50, and then should bend their course directly to this realm.

Sir, for the meaning we had to go on the coast of Spain, it was deeply debated by those which I think the world doth judge

----

[1] Off Vigo.   [2] Latitude.

to be men of greatest experience that this realm hath; which are these: Sir Francis Drake, Mr Hawkyns, Mr Frobiser, and Mr Thomas Fenner; and I hope her Majesty will not think that we went so rashly to work, or without a principal and choice care and respect of the safety of this realm.

But now, as by your directions to lie off and on betwixt England and Spain, the South-West wind, that shall bring them to Scotland or Ireland, shall put us to the leeward. The seas are broad; but if we had been on their coast, they durst not have put off, to have left us on their backs; and when they shall come with the south-westerly wind, which must serve them if they go for Ireland or Scotland, though we be as high as Cape Clear, yet shall we not be able to go to them as long as the wind shall be westerly. And if we lie so high, then may the Spanish fleet bear with the coast of France, to come for the Isle of Wight; which, for my part, I think, if they come to England, they will attempt. Then are we clean out of the way of any service against them.

But I must and will obey; and am glad there be such there, as are able to judge what is fitter for us to do, than we here; but by my instructions which I had, I did think it otherwise. But I will put them up in a bag.

Sir, you know it hath been the opinion both of her Majesty and others, that it was the surest course to lie on the coast of Spain. I confess my error at that time, which[1] was otherwise; but I did and will yield ever unto them of greater experience.

12. Wynter on the Strategy of Invasion

Wynter to Walsyngham, June 20, 1588. (*N.R.S.* i, p. 212.)

And whereas it is said the Prince of Parma's strength is 30,000 soldiers, then I assure your Honour it is no mean quantity of shipping that must serve for the transporting of that number and that which doth appertain to them, without the which I do not think they will put forth; 300 sail must be the least; and, one with another, to be counted 60 ton. For I well remember that in the journey made to Scotland, in the Queen's Majesty's father's time, when we burned Leith and Edinburgh,

---

[1] When my opinion.

and there was in that expedition 260 sail of ships; and yet we were not able to land above 11,000 men, and we then in fear of none that could impeach us by sea. It may be said the cut between Flanders and the places named is shorter than out of England to the Frith in Scotland, which is true; but, Sir, men that do come for such a purpose, being so huge an army as 30,000 men, must have a mighty deal of all sorts of provisions to serve them, as your honourable wisdom can well consider.

But, Sir, I take the Prince's case to be far otherwise. For I suppose, if the countries of Holland and Zealand did arm forth but only the shipping which the Lord Admiral at his departing delivered unto our admiral[1] in writing that they would send from those parts to join with us here[2], and that was 36 sail of ships of war, and that it were known to the Prince those did nothing but remain in readiness to go to the seas for the impeaching of his fleet whensoever they did come forth, I should live until I were young again or[3] the Prince would venture to set his ships forth.

And again, if her Majesty's ships, and such others as doth but now remain under our admiral's[1] charge, may be continued in the state we are in, and not to be separated, the Prince's forces, being no other than that which he hath in Flanders at this time (upon whom we mean to keep as good watch for their coming forth as possible we can), dare not come to the seas.

13. SHORTAGE OF VICTUALS

It is clear that shortage of victuals kept the English fleets tethered to their ports.

Howard to the Council, June 22, 1588. (*N.R.S.* I, p. 217.)

I pray your Lordships to pardon me that I may put you in remembrance to move her Majesty that she may have an especial care to draw ten or twelve thousand men about her own person, that may not be men unpractised.

My Lords, our victuals are not yet come, but we hope shortly to hear of them if this wind continue 40 hours, or else we cannot tell what to think of them, or what should become of them; and yet we have sent three or four pinnaces to seek them

---

[1] Lord Henry Seymour.   [2] In the Downs.   [3] =ere.

out. If they come not, our extremity will be very great, for our
victuals ended the 15th of this month; and if that Mr Darell
had not very carefully provided us of 14 days' victuals, and again
with four or five days' more, which now he hath provided, we
had been in some great extremity. Mr Hawkyns hath disbursed
money for all that, and for many other charges more, wherein
Sir Francis Drake hath likewise disbursed some; and therefore
to avoid that danger and inconvenience that may fall out the
thereby, it would do very well that her Majesty would send five
or six thousand pounds hither, for it is likely we shall stand in
great need of it.

Several men have fallen sick, and by thousands fain to be
discharged, and other pressed in their stead, which hath been an
infinite charge with great trouble unto us, the army being so
great as it is, the ships so many in number, and the weather so
extreme foul as it hath been; whereby great charges have risen
and daily do. And yet I protest before God we have been more
careful of her Majesty's charges than of our own lives, as may
well appear by the scantyings which we have made.

14. RALEGH ON STRATEGY

Though Ralegh did not write his *History* until the next reign, his views
on strategy were derived from Elizabethan experience, and may fitly be
introduced here.

Ralegh, *History of the World*, Part I, Book V, Chap. I, Sect. 9.

It is impossible for any maritime country, not having the
coasts admirably fortified, to defend itself against a powerful
enemy that is master of the sea. Let us consider of the matter
itself; what another nation might do, even against England, in
landing an army, by advantage of a fleet, if we had none. This
question, *Whether an invading Army may be resisted at their
landing upon the coast of England, were there no fleet of ours at
the sea to impeach it*, is already handled by a learned gentleman
of our nation, in his observations upon Caesar's Commentaries,
that maintains the affirmative. This he holds only upon supposition, *in absence of our shipping*: and comparatively, as that it
is a more safe and easy course to defend all the coast of England
than to suffer any enemy to land, and afterwards to fight with

him. Surely I hold with him, that it is the best way, to keep our enemy from treading upon our ground; wherein, if we fail, then must we seek to make him wish that he had stayed at his own home. But making the question general, and positive, *Whether England, without help of her fleet, be able to debar an enemy from landing*; I hold that it is unable so to do: and therefore I think it most dangerous to make the adventure. For the encouragement of a first victory to an enemy, and the discouragement of being beaten to the invaded, may draw after it a most perilous consequence.

Our question is, of an army to be transported over sea, and to be landed again in an enemy's country, and the place left to the choice of the invader. Hereunto I say that such an army cannot be resisted on the coast of England, without a fleet to impeach it; no, nor on the coast of France, or any other country: except every creek, port, or sandy bay had a powerful army, in each of them, to make opposition. For let his whole supposition be granted; that Kent is able to furnish twelve thousand foot, and that those twelve thousand be laid in the three best landing places within that country, to wit, three thousand at Margate, three thousand at the Ness, and six thousand at Folkestone, that is somewhat equally distant from them both; as also that two of these troops (unless some other order be thought more fit) be directed to strengthen the third, when they shall see the enemy's fleet to bend towards it: I say that, notwithstanding this provision, if the enemy, setting sail from the Isle of Wight in the first watch of the night, and towing their longboats at their sterns, shall arrive by dawn of day at the Ness, and thrust their army on shore there; it will be hard for those three thousand that are at Margate (twenty and four long miles from thence) to come time enough to reinforce their fellows at the Ness. Nay, how shall they at Folkestone be able to do it, who are nearer by more than half the way? seeing that the enemy, at his first arrival, will either make his entrance by force, with three or four hundred shot of great Artillery, and quickly put the first three thousand, that were entrenched at the Ness, to run; or else give them so much to do that they shall be glad to send for help to Folkestone, and perhaps to Margate, whereby those places will be left bare. Now let us suppose that all the twelve thousand Kentish soldiers arrive at the Ness ere the enemy can be ready to disembark his army, so that he shall find it unsafe to land in the face of so many, prepared to withstand him; yet must we believe that he will play the best of his own game, and (having liberty to go which way he list) under cover of the night, set sail towards the East, where what shall hinder him to take ground, either at Margate, the Downs, or elsewhere, before they at the Ness can be well aware of his departure? Certainly, there is nothing more easy than to do it. Yea the like may be said of Weymouth, Purbeck, Poole, and of all landing places on the South Coast. For there is no man ignorant that ships, without putting themselves out of breath, will easily outrun the soldiers that coast them. *Les Armées ne volent point en poste; Armies neither fly, nor run post*, saith a Marshal of France. And I know it to be true that a fleet of ships may be seen at sunset, and after it, at the Lizard; yet by the next morning they may recover Portland, whereas an army of foot shall not be able to march it in six days.

For end of this digression, I hope that this question shall never come to trial; his Majesty's many movable forts will forbid the experience. And although the English will no less disdain, than any nation under heaven can do, to be beaten upon their own ground, or elsewhere by a foreign enemy; yet to entertain those that shall assail us, with their own beef in their bellies, and before they eat of our Kentish capons, I take it to be the wisest way. To do which, his Majesty, after God, will employ his good ships on the sea, and not trust to any entrenchment upon the shore.

15. English Ships v. Spanish Galleys

When Philip II finally resolved to invade England, he began to collect a fleet consisting of two elements: galleys and galleons. The fighting ship was the galley, which carried five guns in the bows but relied mainly on ramming with its beak, and which, in battle, was propelled by oars. What Drake and Fenner thought of the galley is shown in the following despatches, after the 'singeing of the King of Spain's beard' at Cadiz in 1587.

(a) Drake to Walsyngham, April 27, 1587. (*N.R.S.* XI, p. 107.)

The 19th we arrived into the Road of Cadiz, in Spain, where we found sundry great ships, some laden, some half-laden, and some ready to be laden with the King's provisions for England. We stayed there until the 21st, in which meantime we sank a Biscayan of 1,200 tons, burnt a ship of the Marquess of Santa Cruz of 1,500 tons, and 31 ships more of 1,000, 800, 600, 400 to 200 tons the piece, carried away four with us laden with provisions, and departed thence at our pleasure, with as much honour as we could wish, notwithstanding that during the time of our abode there we were both oftentimes fought withal by twelve of the King's galleys, of whom we sank two, and always repulsed the rest, and were without ceasing vehemently shot at from the shore, but to our little hurt, God be thanked; yet at our departure we were courteously written unto by one Don Pedro, general of those galleys.

(b) Thomas Fenner to Walsyngham, May 17, 1587. (*N.R.S.* XI, p. 134.)

Shipping we take daily which are bound with pipe-boards and hoops for Andalusia which we burn, whereof they will have so great want as to them will be a marvellous offence.

By intelligence we find the greatest provisions of strength out of the Straits, as from Sicily eight galleons and from Naples four galleasses, and divers galleys out of Italy.

The provisions are so overthrown and wasted as is wonderful, for in Cadiz we brought away and burned seven hundred tons of bread.

We hold this Cape[1] so greatly to our benefit and so much to their disadvantage as a great blessing is the attaining thereof. For the rendezvous is at Lisbon, where we understand of some 25 ships and 7 galleys. The rest, we lie between home and them, so as the body is without the members; and they cannot come together by reason that they are unfurnished of their provisions in every degree, in that they are not united together.

I assure your Honour there is no account to be made of his galleys. Twelve of her Majesty's ships will not make account of all his galleys in Spain, Portugal, and all his dominions within the Straits, although there are 150 in number. If it be to their advantage in a calm, we have made such trial of their fights that we perfectly see into the depth thereof.

1 Sagres.

16. Subjection of Spanish Seamen to Soldiers

In point of fact, the four galleys which accompanied the Armada never reached the Channel, so that the issue was fought out by the galleons on both sides. The table on p. 23, compiled from lists given by Laughton, Corbett, and Hale, shows the superiority of English armaments. The armament attributed to the English ships is that fixed as a standard by Wynter in 1569, and apparently still regarded as the ideal in 1585; but there is reason to believe that they were more heavily armed in 1588. The Spanish method of calculating tonnage brought their ships out at anything from a quarter to a half as big again as they would appear if judged by English standards.

The Spaniards still regarded a battle between sailing ships as 'a land fight on sea,' to be decided by boarding, by which means the Spanish superiority in soldiers would counterbalance the English superiority in heavy guns. As, however, their galleons were slower and clumsier than those of the English, the choice of tactics did not rest with them.

Richard Hawkyns's *Observations*.

The Spaniards, in their armadoes by sea, imitate the discipline, order, and officers, which are in an army by land, and divide themselves into three bodies: to wit, soldiers, mariners, and gunners.

Their soldiers ward and watch, and their officers in every ship round, as if they were on the shore; this is the only task they undergo, except cleaning their arms, wherein they are not over curious. The gunners are exempted from all labour and care, except about the artillery. And these are either Almaynes, Flemings, or strangers; for the Spaniards are but indifferently practised in this art. The mariners are but as slaves to the rest, to moil and to toil day and night; and these but few and bad, and not suffered to sleep or harbour themselves under the decks. For in fair or foul weather, in storms, sun, or rain, they must pass void of covert or succour.

The gunners fight not but with their great artillery: the mariners attend only to the tackling of the ship and handling of the sails, and are unarmed, and subject to all misfortunes; not permitted to shelter themselves, but to be still aloft, whether it be necessary or needless. So ordinarily, those which first fail are the mariners and sailors, of which they have the greatest need.

17. ENGLISH AND SPANISH ARMAMENTS

SHIPS		MEN			GUNS¹								
Names	Tons	Sailors	Soldiers	Total	Cannon	Demi-Cannon	Cannon-Perier	Culverin	Basilisk	Demi-Culverin	Saker	Total number of battery guns	Small Pieces
Spanish													
S. Lorenzo²	—	144	244	388	4	8	—	6	—	6	10	34	16
N. S. d. Rosario	1150	119	240	359	—	3	6	4	1	1	6	21	20
San Salvador	958	90	281	371	4	—	4	5	—	1	—	14	11
Annunciada	703	80	186	266	—	—	—	—	—	8	—	8	18
Sta Maria d. Vison	666	93	355	448	—	—	—	—	—	6	—	6	18
English													
Triumph	1100	340	160	500	—	9	4	13	—	7	6	39	28
Victory	800	304	126	430	—	6	4	12	—	8	2	32	32
Nonpareil	500	174	76	250	—	4	2	4	—	6	12	28	24
Foresight	300	130	20	150	—	—	—	4	—	8	8	20	16
Tiger	200	92	8	100	—	—	—	4	—	6	10	16	12

¹ These guns may be described as follows:

Cannon, probably   42-pounder   Basilisk
Demi-cannon   30-   „   Demi-culverin, long   15-pounder
Cannon-perier, light 24-   „   Saker   9-   „
Culverin, long   18-   „   6-   „

² Flagship of the 4 galleasses, the most heavily armed Spanish ships.

18. Philip II warns Medina Sidonia against English Gunnery

Instructions to the Duke of Medina Sidonia, April 1, 1588. (*Cal. S.P. Sp.*)

Above all, it must be borne in mind that the enemy's object will be to fight at long distance, in consequence of his advantage in artillery, and the large number of artificial fires with which he will be furnished. The aim of our men, on the contrary, must be to bring him to close quarters and grapple with him, and you will have to be very careful to have this carried out. For your information a statement is sent to you describing the way in which the enemy employs his artillery, in order to deliver his fire low and sink his opponent's ships; and you will take such precautions as you consider necessary in this respect.

19. Medina Sidonia protests his Unfitness

Duke of Medina Sidonia to Juan de Idiaquez, February 16, 1588. (*Cal. S.P. Sp.*)

I first humbly thank his Majesty for having thought of me for so great a task, and I wish I possessed the talents and strength necessary for it. But, sir, I have not health for the sea, for I know by the small experience that I have had afloat that I soon become sea-sick, and have many humours. Besides this, your worship knows, as I have often told you verbally and in writing, that I am in great need, so much so that when I have had to go to Madrid I have been obliged to borrow money for the journey. My house owes 900,000 ducats, and I am therefore quite unable to accept the command. I have not a single real I can spend on the expedition.

Apart from this, neither my conscience nor my duty will allow me to take this service upon me. The force is so great, and the undertaking so important, that it would not be right for a person like myself, possessing no experience of seafaring or of war, to take charge of it. So, sir, in the interest of his Majesty's service, and for the love I bear him, I submit to you, for communication to him, that I possess neither aptitude, ability, health, nor fortune, for the expedition.

20. Estimates of Neutral Observers

(*a*) Giovanni Mocenigo, Venetian Ambassador in France, to the Doge and Senate, April 8, 1588. (*Cal. S.P. Ven.*)

He (Philip II) very well knows how much consideration ought to be paid to such a fleet as the English fleet, both on account of its size, and also because the English are men of another mettle from the Spaniards, and enjoy the reputation of being, above all the Western nations, expert and active in all naval operations, and great sea dogs.

(*b*) Giovanni Gritti, Venetian Ambassador in Rome, to the Doge and Senate, August 20, 1588. (*Cal. S.P. Ven.*)

'The King' (said the Pope) 'goes trifling with this Armada of his, but the Queen acts in earnest. Were she only a Catholic she would be our best beloved, for she is of great worth. Just look at Drake! Who is he? What forces has he? And yet he burned twenty-five of the King's ships at Gibraltar, and as many again at Lisbon; he has robbed the flotilla and sacked San Domingo. His reputation is so great that his countrymen flock to him to share his booty. We are sorry to say it, but we have a poor opinion of this Spanish Armada, and fear some disaster.'

(*c*) Same to same, September 3.

'The Queen of England,' his Holiness remarked, 'has no need of the Turk to help her. Have you heard how Drake with his fleet has offered battle to the Armada? with what courage! do you think he showed any fear? He is a great captain;' and with that his Holiness went on to recount Drake's enterprises.

21. Tactics which may have been used against the Armada

The English tactical formation against the Armada remains obscure. Sir Julian Corbett, who holds that an elementary line-ahead formation in small groups was used, has produced evidence to show that the following order, issued by Ralegh for his Guiana expedition, may date from before the Armada. It is at least evident, from the Queen's complaint and the passage from Ralegh's *History*, that the English had abandoned boarding tactics. The despatches written by Howard and Drake after the Battle of Gravelines, though silent on the subject of tactics, afford an interesting contrast to each other.

Ralegh's Instructions of 1617. (*N.R.S.* xxix, p. 42.)

29. If we find an enemy to be leewards of us, the whole fleet shall follow the admiral, vice-admiral, or other leading ship within musket shot of the enemy; giving so much liberty to the leading ship as after her broadside delivered she may stay and trim her sails. Then is the second ship to tack as the first ship and give the other side, keeping the enemy under a perpetual shot. This you must do upon the windermost ship or ships of an enemy, which you shall either batter in pieces, or force him or them to bear up and so entangle them, and drive them foul one of another to their utter confusion.

22. Elizabeth as an Armchair Tactician

A memorial for Richard Drake, Esquire, being sent to the Lord Admiral, of such things as her Majesty doth desire to be informed of. (*N.R.S.* i, p. 354. July 31, 1588.)

What causes are there why the Spanish navy hath not been boarded by the Queen's ships? And though some of the ships of Spain may be thought too huge to be boarded by the English, yet some of the Queen's ships are thought very able to have boarded divers of the meaner ships of the Spanish navy.

23. Ralegh on Tactics

Ralegh, *History of the World*, Part I, Book V, Chap. 1, Sect. 6.

Certainly, he that will happily perform a fight at sea, must be skilful in making choice of vessels to fight in: he must believe that there is more belonging to a good man of war, upon the waters, than great daring; and must know that there is a great deal of difference between fighting loose or at large, and grappling. The guns of a slow ship pierce as well, and make as great holes, as those in a swift. To clap ships together, without consideration, belongs rather to a madman than to a man of war: for by such an ignorant bravery was Peter Strozzi lost at the Azores, when he fought against the Marquess of Santa Cruz[1]. In like sort had the Lord Charles Howard, Admiral of England, been lost in the year 1588, if he had not been better

---

[1] In 1582.

advised than a great many malignant fools were, that found
fault with his demeanour. The Spaniards had an army aboard
them; and he had none: they had more ships than he had, and
of higher building and charging; so that, had he entangled himself with those great and powerful vessels, he had greatly
endangered this Kingdom of England. For twenty men upon
the defences are equal to an hundred that board and enter;
whereas then, contrariwise, the Spaniards had an hundred, for
twenty of ours, to defend themselves withal. But our Admiral
knew his advantage, and held it: which had he not done, he had
not been worthy to have held his head. Here to speak in general
of Sea-fight (for particulars are fitter for private hands than for
the press), I say that a fleet of twenty ships, all good sailers,
and good ships, have the advantage, on the open sea, of an
hundred as good ships, and of slower sailing. For if the fleet of
an hundred sail keep themselves near together, in a gross squadron,
the twenty ships, charging them upon any angle, shall force
them to give ground, and to fall back upon their own next
fellows, of which so many as entangle, are made unserviceable
or lost. Force them they may easily, because the twenty ships,
which give themselves scope, after they have given one broadside of artillery, by clapping into the wind and staying, they
may give them the other: and so the twenty ships batter them in
pieces with a perpetual volley; whereas those that fight in a
troop have no room to turn, and can always use but one and the
same beaten side. If the fleet of an hundred sail give themselves
any distance, then shall the lesser fleet prevail, either against
those that are a-rear and hindmost, or against those that by
advantage of over-sailing their fellows keep the wind: and if
upon a lee-shore, the ships next the wind be constrained to fall
back into their own squadron, then it is all to nothing, the whole
fleet must suffer shipwreck, or render itself.

24. GRAVELINES DESPATCHES

(a) Howard to Walsyngham, July 29, 1588. (*N.R.S.* 1, p. 340.)

Sir:—I have received your letter wherein you desire a proportion of shot and powder to be set down by me and sent unto
you; which, by reason of the uncertainty of the service, no man

can do; therefore I pray you to send with all speed as much as you can. And because some of our ships are victualled but for a very short time, and my Lord Henry Seymour with his company not for one day, in like to pray you to dispatch away our victuals with all possible speed, because we know not whether we shall be driven to pursue the Spanish fleet.

This morning we drove a galleass ashore before Calais, whither I sent my long boat to board her, where divers of my men were slain, and my lieutenant sore hurt in the taking of her. Ever since we have chased them in fight until this evening late, and distressed them much; but their fleet consisteth of mighty ships and great strength; yet we doubt not, by God's good assistance, to oppress them; and so I bid you heartily farewell. From aboard her Majesty's good ship the *Ark*, the 29th of July, 1588.

Your very loving friend,
C. HOWARD.

Sir:—I will not write unto her Majesty before more be done. Their force is wonderful great and strong; and yet we pluck their feathers by little and little. I pray to God that the forces on the land be strong enough to answer so present a force. There is not one Flushinger nor Hollander at the seas.

Sir, I have taken the chief galleass this day before Calais, with the loss of divers of my men; but Monsieur Gourdan doth detain her, as I hear say. I could not send unto him, because I was in fight; therefore I pray you to write unto him, either to deliver her, or at leastwise to promise upon his honour that he will not yield her up again unto the enemy.

(*b*) Drake to Walsyngham, July 29, 1588. (*N.R.S.* I, p. 341.)

Right Honourable:—This bearer came aboard the ship I was in in a wonderful good time, and brought with him as good knowledge as we could wish. His carefulness therein is worthy recompense, for that God hath given us so good a day in forcing the enemy so far to leeward as I hope in God the Prince of Parma and the Duke of Sidonia shall not shake hands this few days; and whensoever they shall meet, I believe neither of them will greatly rejoice of this day's service. The town of Calais

hath seen some part thereof, whose Mayor her Majesty is
beholden unto. Business commands me to end. God bless her
Majesty, our gracious Sovereign, and give us all grace to live
in his fear. I assure your Honour this day's service hath much
appalled the enemy, and no doubt but encouraged our army.
From aboard her Majesty's good ship the *Revenge*, this 29th of
July, 1588.

Your Honour's most ready to be commanded,

FRA. DRAKE.

There must be great care taken to send us munition and
victual whithersoever the enemy goeth.

Yours,

FRA. DRAKE.

25. WYNTER'S OPINION OF AUXILIARIES

The Armada was beaten by the Queen's ships, not by the auxiliaries:
mere enthusiasm could not take the place of preparation.

Wynter to Walsyngham, August 1, 1588. (*N.R.S.* II, p. 13.)

I dare assure your Honour, if you had seen that which I
have seen, of the simple service that hath been done by the
merchant and coast ships, you would have said that we had been
little holpen by them, otherwise than that they did make a show.

26. SICKNESS AND MORTALITY

Howard to Burghley, August 10, 1588. (*N.R.S.* II, p. 96.)

My good Lord:—Sickness and mortality begins wonderfully
to grow amongst us; and it is a most pitiful sight to see, here at
Margate, how the men, having no place to receive them into
here, die in the streets. I am driven myself, of force, to come
a-land, to see them bestowed in some lodging; and the best I
can get is barns and such outhouses; and the relief is small that
I can provide for them here. It would grieve any man's heart
to see them that have served so valiantly to die so miserably.

The *Elizabeth Jonas*, which hath done as well as ever any
ship did in any service, hath had a great infection in her from
the beginning, so as of the 500 men which she carried out, by

the time we had been in Plymouth three weeks or a month, there were dead of them 200 and above; so as I was driven to set all the rest of her men ashore, to take out her ballast, and to make fires in her of wet broom, three or four days together; and so hoped thereby to have cleansed her of her infection; and thereupon got new men, very tall and able as ever I saw, and put them into her. Now the infection is broken out in greater extremity than ever it did before, and the men die and sicken faster than ever they did; so as I am driven of force to send her to Chatham. We all think and judge that the infection remaineth in the pitch. Sir Roger Townshend, of all the men he brought out with him, hath but one left alive; and my son Southwell likewise hath many dead.

It is like enough that the like infection will grow throughout the most part of our fleet; for they have been so long at sea and have so little shift of apparel, and so few places to provide them of such wants, and no money wherewith to buy it, for some have been—yea the most part—these eight months at sea. My Lord, I would think it a marvellous good way that there were a thousand pounds worth or two thousand marks worth of hose, doublets, shirts, shoes and such like, sent down; and I think your Lordship might use therein the Controller of the Navy and Waker, Mr Hawkyns his man, who would use all expedition for the providing and sending away of such things; for else, in very short time I look to see most of the mariners go naked. Good my Lord, let mariners be prest and sent down as soon as may be; and money to discharge those that be sick here; and so, in haste, I bid your Lordship farewell. From Margate, the 10th of August, 1588.

Your Lordship's most assured to command,

C. HOWARD[1].

27. A BEGGING LICENCE

The begging licence reproduced in facsimile on the opposite page is in *Lands. MSS.* 144, f. 53.

---

[1] On the question of Elizabeth's responsibility for the shortage of victuals and munitions, see the references given by Oppenheim, *N.R.S.* XXII, p. 175, note 60.

Harles Lord Howard, Baron of Effingham Knight of the
Noble order of the Garter, Lord high Admirall of England, Ireland, and
Wales, and the dominions and Iles of the same, of the towne of Callis
and marches therof, of Normandy, Gascoyne, and Guynes, and Captaine
Generall of her Maiesties Seas and Nauy Royall. To all and singuler
Vizeadmiralls, Iustices of Peace, Maiors, Sherifes, Bayliffes, Constables, Custo-
mers, Comptrowlers, Ministers, Parsons, Vicars, Curats, Churchwardens, Collec-
tors for the poore, and all other her Maiesties Officers, Ministers, and louing subiects,
aswell within the Citie of London, as the dominions of her Maiesties Realme of England, and to euery of them greeting. Wheras this bearer William Browne, of London
gunner, lately serued in her Maiesties seruice against the Spaniards, in the Barke of
Feuersham, and in that seruice was shot through his bodie, and grieuously wounded in
sundry places, and by meanes of the same maimed for euer: In consideration wherof
and for that I vnderstand he is greatly indebted to his Surgeons, in the curing of his
wounds and otherwise brought to extreame pouertie thereby. I haue thought good
to graunt him these presents, and by authority hereof, in her Maiesties name do require
and earnestly entreate you and euery of you, throughout the said Citie of London and
the dominions of her Maiesties Realme of England, to haue a Christian and pitifull regard of the said William Browne and his extreame want and miserie gotten in the seruice of our gracious Prince, and defence of this our Countrye, and to helpe and releiue
him with your charitable beneuolence and almes, towards the supplying of their great
want, and to permit, suffer and assist them, to gather and aske the same in all Churches
and Chappels, and of all well disposed people within the said Citie of London, and her
Maiesties said dominions, without any let, trouble, molestation, or incumbrance what-
soeuer, wherin you shall doo a deed very acceptable in the sight of God, and greatly comfortable to him, his said wife and children in this extremitie, wherin we require you not
to fayle. This presents to indure for the space of twelue moneths, from the date hereof.
Giuen at London in her Maiesties highe Court of Th'admiralty, vnder the great seale
thereof, the seuenteenth of August, 1590. And in the two and thirtith yere of the raigne
of our soueraigne Lady Elizabeth by the grace of God Queene of England, Fraunce
and Ireland, defender of the faith, &c.   Hareward.

C. Howard.

God saue the Queene.

28. An Army Necessary for Offence

The fact that the Navy had saved England from invasion did not delude the sounder school of strategists into the belief that the Navy alone could end the war. Essex was anxious for the joint expedition to proceed to Cadiz.

Essex to the Council, May, 1596. (Birch, Memoirs of Queen Elizabeth, II, 8.)

If it be said, the queen may seem to do somewhat, & send her fleet, but stay her army; I am persuaded, that tho' some ignorant soul both of sea-actions and of the wars, may by the fire-side make such a proposition; yet there cannot any man be found so vain, that will undertake the action. But if there be, I would ask him, where he would save himself; or how he will get a port, if he have not a land-force to command the shore? Next, how he will distress or burn the maritimes of Spain, if he go not to them where they are? or how he dare go into them, or shall be able to take such forts as they make for their defences in the harbours? Lastly, when he hath spent his victuals and must return, after he hath sailed unprofitably up and down some few months, why shall not the Spaniard, that without impeachment prepares all that while, follow him; and when the English ships are laid up, execute any thing upon them that they list?

JAMES I AND CHARLES I

In naval, as in constitutional history, the last years of Elizabeth merge or, rather, decline into the first of James: towards the end of her reign one courtier was appointed Treasurer of the Navy; another, Admiral of the Channel Guard; while among the vessels built for the Royal Navy were included four galleys.

In administration, seamanship, and strategy the reign of James I is the low-water mark of our period, and though an improvement is visible under Charles I, the Commonwealth found much to reform. Even in these reigns, however, the fleet was not allowed utterly to decay: in mere numbers it was still imposing, and by most foreigners it was accepted at its paper strength. The early Stuarts cannot be accused of indifference to the navy: the real charge against them is that they took too much interest and had too little knowledge; that they meddled in technical details, which they regarded as matters of opinion.

A study of this period is valuable mainly because it affords many examples to be avoided; but there is this further interest, that it throws some light on the preceding period. The Elizabethans learnt their seamanship in the school of experience; its fundamental principles were second nature to them; and, though they doubtless had long discussions of tactics among themselves, they were chary of committing their ideas to paper, lest foreigners should pluck out the heart of their mystery. The age of practice was followed by the age of theory—of diaries, nautical dictionaries, and treatises on tactics and seamanship, which are extremely valuable from our standpoint because they make explicit what the Elizabethans had taken for granted. The following extract, for instance, illustrates a principle which Drake had learnt in his boyhood, and would not have dreamed of putting on paper, but which may easily escape the notice of a modern student who has never sailed in a square-rigged ship.

29. SAILING BEFORE THE WIND

(Sir Kenelm Digby's *Voyage to the Mediterranean*. Camden Society.)

2 Jan. 1629) In my chase I tried all the ways for advantage that I could imagine, and being before the wind I found that I lost least when I followed him with all my sails drawing, though I lengthened my way: and I think I may defend this paradox with good reason, that with some ships, chasing one that goeth before the wind, with another quartering with one tack aboard till you get your chase upon your beam, then making an angle and lying as far on the other side with your other tack aboard

until you have got him again upon the beam (which now will be nearer to him), is better than to chase in a straight line; for you advantage yourself more by the freshness of your way (all sails drawing) than you hinder yourself by lengthening it.

30. Sailing Close-Hauled

This seems a convenient place for two passages which show how close to the wind an English fleet could sail at this time.

(a) Essex to Cecil, July, 1597. (Quoted in Corbett's *Successors of Drake*, p. 174.)

The wind is now W. by S., so as we stand close by the wind and the water is smooth, we make our way good S. at the least.

(b) Mainwaring's *Seaman's Dictionary*.

A cross-sail ship in a sea cannot make her way nearer than 6 points unless there be tide or current which doth set to windward.

31. Ship-building in 1618

This period saw a steady improvement in the design and rig of ships. The two following extracts show that, while the policy of cutting down upper-works was gaining more support, it had to fight its way: Sir William Monson, whose *Naval Tracts* were in MS form in 1624, had served against the Armada, and was regarded as an authority on seamanship.

In the station list of the *Speedwell* it will be noticed that there are no soldiers.

(a) Report of the Special Commission of 1618. (*S.P. Dom. Jas I*, CI.)

(Abstract of suggested Establishment.)

		Tonnage
4	'Ships Royal'	1200–800
14	'Great Ships'	800–600
6	'Middling Ships'	450
2	'Small Ships'	350
4	'Pinnaces'	250–80

Ships, 30. Tons, 17,110.

Reasons for this Proportion and no greater

1. This Navy will contain at least 3,050 tons more than the Navy of Queen Elizabeth when it was greatest, and flourished most.

2. The former Navies had but four Royal Ships, which were held sufficient for the honour of the State, as being more than the most powerful nations by sea had heretofore; and for service

specially on our coast, ships of 650 are held as forcible, and more yare[1] and useful than those of greater burden, and are built, furnished, and kept with a great deal less charge.

8. These 30 ships will require as many mariners and gunners as these kingdoms supply, at all times, now traffic carrieth away so many, and so far.

9. The common building of great and warlike ships, to reinforce the Navy when need shall require, may well contain his Majesty's number and charge within these bounds.

(There follow 'Reasons for this Proportion and no fewer.')

The Manner of Building

The next consideration is the manner of building, which in ships of war is of greatest importance, because therein consisteth both their sailing and force.

The ships that sail best can take or leave (as they say), and use all advantage the winds and seas do afford. And their mould, in the judgment of men of best skill, both dead and alive, should have the length treble to the breadth, and the breadth near in like proportion answerable to the depth, but not to draw above 16 foot water, because deeper ships are seldom good sailers, and ever unsafe for our rivers, and for the shallows, harbours, and all coasts of our or other seas. Besides, they must be somewhat snug built, without double galleries and too lofty upperworks, which overcharge many ships, and make them loom fair, but not work well at sea.

And for strengthening the ships, we subscribe to the new manner of building approved by the late worthy Prince[2], the Lord Admiral, and the Officers of the Navy (as we are informed), in these points:—

1. In making three orlops[3], whereof the lowest being placed 2 foot under water, both strengtheneth the ship, and, though her sides be shot through, keepeth it from bulging[4] by shot, and giveth easy means to find and stop the leaks.

2. In carrying these orlops whole floored throughout, from end to end, without falls or cutting off by the waist, which only to make fair cabins hath decayed many ships.

---

[1] Handy.
[3] At this period a synonym for 'deck.'
[2] Prince Henry.
[4] See footnote on p. 6.

3. In laying the second orlop at such convenient height, that the ports may bear out their whole tier of ordnance in all seas and weathers.

4. In placing the cook-rooms in the forecastle, as other warships do. Because, being in the mid-ship and in hold, the smoke and heat so search every corner and seam, that they make the oakum spew out, and the ships leaky and soon decay. Besides, the best room for stowage of victuals is thereby so taken up, that transporters must be hired for every voyage of any time. And, which is worst, when all the weight must be cast before and abaft, and the ships are left empty and light in the midst, it makes them apt to sway in the back, as the *Garland* and divers others have done[1].

(*b*) Monson on the Build of Ships. (*N.R.S.* xlv, p. 91.)

There are two manner of built ships: the one with a flush deck, fore and aft, snug and low by water; the other lofty and high charged, with a half deck, forecastle, and cobridge heads. The ship with a flush deck I hold good to fight in, if she be a fast ship by the wind and keep herself from boarding[2]. She is roomsome for her men, and yare to run to and again in her; but she is not a ship to board, unless it be a merchant, or another ship that is inferior to her in strength and number of people. For if it happen that she be boarded, and put to her defence, she lieth open to her enemy; for gaining her upper deck you win her, having neither forecastle nor other close-fight to retire unto; and in that case half the defensive part of the ship is the strength of the forecastle. When her deck shall be gained, and her people beaten down into the second deck, the only help is to use stratagems by fire in making trains of divers fashions to blow up the upper deck and men upon it.

As I have said, such a ship that has neither forecastle, cobridge head, nor any other manner of defence but with her men only; that hath no fowlers, which are pieces of greatest importance after a ship is boarded and entered, or lieth board and board;

---

[1] Mainwaring gives six reasons against having the cook-room in the forecastle, urging that it should be placed 'in the hatch-way, upon the first orlop.'

[2] See footnote on p. 6.

for the ordnance stands her in little stead, and are as apt to endanger themselves as their enemy, for in giving fire it may take hold of pitch, tar, oakum or powder, and burn them both for company: but a murderer or fowler being shot out of their own ship, laden with dice shot, will scour the deck of the enemy and not suffer the head of a man to appear. The advantage of a ship with a flush deck, that boards another to windward, is this:— she may with her lee ordnance shoot the other under water, and herself in no hazard; the ship that is boarded to leeward of her is at the other's mercy, and becomes weak in comparison of the other to windward. Whoever enters and takes possession of the upper deck of such a ship, that is plain fore and aft, shall be able to cut down her masts, shrouds, and all things over head; that though he take her not, yet she shall be left a wreck in the sea, and perish.

A high built ship is the better for these reasons—majesty and terror to the enemy, more commodious for the harbouring of men. She will be able to carry more artillery, of greater strength, within-board, and make the better defence. She will overtop a lower and snug ship; her men cannot be so well discerned, for that the waist-cloths will take away the view and sight of them.

And lastly, to speak of a ship with three decks, thus it is:—she is very inconvenient, dangerous, and unserviceable; the number and weight of the ordnance wrings her sides and weakens her. It is seldom seen that you have a calm so many hours together as to keep out her lower tier, and when they are out, and forced to haul them in again, it is with great labour, travail and trouble to the gunners when they should be fighting.

32. A Station List of 1619

Reasons against the Proposition of Lessening the Number of Men aboard the King's Ships at Sea. About 1619. (*S.P. Dom. Jas. I*, CIX, No. 137.)

It is to be considered what number of men are necessarily required to handle the great number of weighty ordnance aboard the King's Ships in a fight, what men to man the top, to handle sails, to answer an enemy with small shot, to watch the powder room, to clear the hold against all chances, or to ply upon a lee shore in a stress of weather. And I appeal to any man that hath been in a fight in any of the King's Ships, **or** hath beat it out the whole winter between lands, whether the proportion formerly allowed be not with the least. For my own part my experience hath taught it me, and I know no man of judgment will deny it.

It is further to be considered that idlers must of necessity be aboard the ship, as Cook, Stewards, Purser, Surgeon, Grummets[1], etc., which fill up the book with names, but in a fight or stress of weather are not useful; for the mistaking of a rope by an unskilful person, either in fight or upon a lee shore, may be the loss of all.

I have added an accompt of every particular employment aboard the King's Ships, with the number required thereunto, and all those in the least proportion that may be, not troubling your Lordship with more than the instance of these two ships, that may give satisfaction for other ships of greater or lesser burthen.

A Note to maintain the Number of Men allowed in his
Majesty's Ships underwritten.
Viz.

The *Speedwell.*

	Men
This Ship hath 36 pieces of Ordnance, for the plying whereof is required Gunners	18
Men to stand by crows, tackles, and portropes	48
Men to ply the small shot	50
Men to conduct, steer, hand the sails, and man the tops	50
Men in the powder room	4
Carpenters	4
Trumpeters	3
Chirurgeon and his Mates	3
Steward and his Mates	4
Cook and Mates	3
Boys	3
Total	190

Besides the Captain and his retinue.
(Similarly the *Phoenix*, 22 guns, required 95 men.)

1 Gromets, boys.

33. Dunkirk Frigates

The following extracts show that the foreigner was ahead of us in appreciating the true nature of the cruiser. At this time, just as a boy was regarded as a little man, and was dressed in exactly the same fashion; so small English war-vessels were built and rigged like big ships. The Dunkirk privateers, however, to whom speed was essential, were building frigates, with a single deck, no forecastle or poop, a length $3\frac{1}{2}$ to 4 times their beam, and probably a modification of the lateen rig used by the Mediterranean corsairs.

Sir John Pennington to the Lords of the Admiralty, Feb. 2, 1635/6.

I conceive it may be advantageous for his Majesty's service to set out the *Petite Mort* of Dieppe, and the *Swan*[1] of Flushing that I sent into Sandwich (which is a Dunkirk built and a rare goer) with the fleet: they may teach his Majesty's ships to go, or at leastwise there may be something observed from them that may be good for the future.

Captain Kettleby to Windebank, March 14, 1636/7.

The *Nicodemus*, his Majesty's frigate[2], is returned from the Western coast, whose captain and company report her to be the most absolute sailer in the world; for she runs from every ship she sees, to use the captain's own phrase, as a greyhound doth from a little dog.

34. Single-ship Tactics

These two reigns saw no fleet actions. The following extract from Boteler's *Sea Dialogues* (Sloan MS. 758) was written *c.* 1630 and describes single-ship tactics.

Admiral. But all this being done[3], and she found an enemy, and a fighting one, what now is next to be done?

Capt. Your ship being aforehand made ready, by the taking down of all wainscot cabins, or at the least stuffing them with beds, seagowns and the like, to serve as bulwarks against shot, half butts and hogsheads of water being also made fast upon the

---

[1] In a letter of January 16th Pennington calls her 'the swiftest sailer in the world,' and says 'they took her from them by an accident.'

[2] Also Dunkirk built.

[3] When a stranger has been properly hailed, as well with trumpets as the voice, and has refused to come under your lee.

decks, with blankets and the like to stuff soaking in them, to quench all accidental fires; the hold of the ship being likewise well cleared by the ship-sides, that so the carpenters may the sooner and surer find the enemy's shot and stop the leaks; all the yards of all the masts, especially of those belonging to the fighting sails, being sufficiently slung; all the ship's company duly quartered, some of them to the master for the managing of the sails, some to assist the gunners in the traversing of the ordnance, others to the corporals to ply their small shot, some to fill powder in the powder-room, others to carry it from them to the gunners in cartridges and bandoliers; the carpenters, some of them being ready in the hold with sheets of lead, plugs, and the like necessaries, others of them betwixt the decks, prepared for the stopping of such leaks as shall be made by any great shot; the chirurgeons in the hold also, with their chests and instruments, to receive and dress all the hurt men; as likewise the minister in the same place, to comfort and exhort them, especially such as are dangerously wounded; every man taking due notice of his station and task, from whence he is not to budge without leave. All these particulars being (as I say) beforehand duly fitted and ordered, and so the fight upon the instant of a beginning, the first care and consideration that is to be taken and executed is to keep to the windwards of the enemy, and this indeed is a point of such importance, as thereby you shall not only eschew the trouble and blindings that will fall out to yourself, by the smoke of your own ordnance and small shot; but you shall also so annoy and hinder the sight of your enemy, as that he shall not be able to make any certain shot at yourself again, nor find the freedom of looking about, nor be able to discover, and so make use of, any disastrous accident that may fall out to your hurt, or his advantage. Nay, some there are that speak so superlatively of this advantage, of keeping the weather-gage in any fight at sea, that they dare positively affirm that it is impossible to receive any great shot from an enemy to leewards of him that can endanger the sinking of the ship; for, say they, by only letting fly the sheets, and so suddenly righting the hull of the ship upon the receipt of any such shot of danger, the hole or piercing of the shot is brought so far above the water, that no peril of taking in any considerable quantity can ensue.

All this being done, and the captain in his station and place, upon the quarter-deck or poop of the ship, waving the enemy amain[1] with his naked sword; his lieutenant in the forecastle, commanding there; and the master upon the half-deck, to look to the management of all the sails upon all occasions and tackings about; the very first of the fight must needs be with the cannon.

Admiral. And how near are you to be to the enemy, when you thus begin unto him with your cannon?

Capt. In a fight, a broadside is but uncertainly, and, to say truth, ineffectually delivered, and withal expresseth fear, whensoever it is given beyond the distance of musket-shot at point-blank; and the volleys of small shot are as idly bestowed, unless it be within the distance of pistol shot, or carbine at the farthest.

Adm. And being within this distance, what is the manner of fight with these fiery weapons, and how is it to be managed?

Capt. First of all, your chase-pieces are to be given, and so coming up nearer with her, and then your whole broadside in order, as your pieces will be brought to bear. This being done, you are to run a good berth ahead of him, if you can possibly; and then to edge up into the wind, and to lay your foresail and main-topsail (which are the fighting sails) on the back-stays; that so, your consorts (if you have any) may have the like opportunity to come up and to do as you have done, and also that the enemy herself may again shoot ahead of yourself, that so a second time you may recharge upon her.

Adm. How else are you to do in this second charge?

Capt. An especial care being taken to keep your loof, to which end you are intentively to observe all your enemy's motions (as to tack your ship whensoever she (*sic*) tacks his, and the like), you are again to edge in with her, and in your way, if you find any number of her men upon the decks, and lying open unto you, you may give her a volley of small shot; and presently upon it (being gotten up side by side with her), you are to bestow your bow-pieces and then your full broadside; and

[1] *Amain* is a term used by Men of War (and not by Merchantmen) when they encounter a ship, for that implies as much to the other as to bid him yield. (Mainwaring.)

then, letting your ship fall off with the wind, your whole chase and weather broadside. The which being done, bring your ship round, that your stern pieces may be given also; all which being performed, and your great guns thus employed, you are with all speed to bring your tacks close aboard again; that so you may be sure to keep your wind.

(Follows a discussion on 'entering.')

35. Stratagems Used at Sea

Monson's Naval Tracts. (*N.R.S.* XLVII, p. 144.)

27. Prospective glasses, if they were not so common, were an excellent stratagem to be used in many cases at sea, and yet it is no hard thing to deceive those that use them. For a merchant ship, that carries not above ten or twelve men, may have the shapes of men made that those twelve may seem to be one hundred afar off. They likewise may have counterfeit pieces made of wood, which the glass cannot discern from iron, to the terror of the assailant. It may as well serve for a man of war to stow his men, save so many as may sail the ship, in hold and embolden the other to come near him.

36. Monson on the Blockade of French Ports

The principle of the following was sound, but could not be carried out in this period: strategy is dependent upon administration.

Monson's Naval Tracts. (*N.R.S.* XLVII, p. 16.)

A Project to prevent the French landing in England, if they become our Enemies.

But our surest course, of all others, will be with some ships to beleaguer their harbours of rendezvous in France a good distance from the shore, for fear of embaying. We must consider that such winds as serve to bring them for England make a secure road upon that coast to ride in. And such winds as are dangerous to keep that shore make it impossible for the French to put out of harbour.

37. Pirates off Dartmouth

During these years the Barbary corsairs and Dunkirk privateers (not to mention English pirates) infested home waters. Charles, unlike James, finally realised that only a fleet could protect our coasts and shipping from them.

(Mayor of Dartmouth to the Privy Council, April 28, 1626. (*S.P. Dom. Ch. I*, xxv, No. 78.)

May it also please your Honours to be advertised that divers Sallee men-of-war are lately come into this channel. They have taken within these ten days last past a bark of Weymouth, one other of this town, and one of Plymouth, being bound all for the Newfoundland, and upon probable grounds it is presumed that they have surprised divers others of this and other ports, in so much that it is humbly desired that your Lordships, out of your tender care of the safety of the Kingdom, would be pleased to take such course as to your wisdoms shall seem fit, that the coast may be guarded, and these infesting enemies may be suppressed; for otherwise it is feared that we shall suffer much by those Barbarians, who have within these twelve months last past bereaved his Majesty of many good and serviceable subjects, and have much impoverished this part of the Kingdom.

WILL. PLUMLEIGHE, Mayor.

38. Dartmouth asks for Fortifications

S.P. Dom. Ch. I, xxxii, 83.

Right Honble.

Our duetie in all humilitie p'mised. Maie it please yor LL^{ps} to be adu'rtised that wee haue received yr L̃tres dated the xix^{th} of this instant moneth of Julie, vppon the xxix^{th} of the same; And doe in the behalfe of ourselves, and the whole Towne acknowlidg that wee cannot expres how much wee are bound vnto y^r Hon^{rs} for y^r adu'tizement of the hostile preparacons of the Spanniard; of wch because wee formerlie feared, wee have allreadie made divers fortificacons to impeach the landing of anie approching Enemie, being thereunto enioyned by the Commissioners heretofore appointed by y^r LL^{ps} for the vewing of the Forts and Castles of this County; but now being therevnto warranted by theis y^r LL^{ps} L̃tres wee purpose to implore the further direccofis and help of the deputy Lieuten^{ts}, and to doe our vttmost endeavors in erecting such other fortificacons as may be behoofull for vs. Maie it please yor Honors to take it into y^r consideracon That when wee have made the fortificacons, wee shall want divers Ordnance to defend them, for that wee have but Nynetene peeces of Ordnance belonging to his Maties Castle and forts here, all which, wth powder and other prouisions belonging vnto them, wee have heretofore bought at our owne charge; Wee therefore are humble sutors vnto y^r Hon^{rs} that youe would be pleased to mediate for vs unto his most excellent Matie, that his Matie would be soe gratious vnto vs, as to conferr vppon vs some more Ordnance for the better strengthning of our Towne, and such fortificacons as shalbe made by vs. But when wee have done the vtmost of our endeauors in this behalfe, yet the situation of our Towne being such as it is, wee feare that wee shall hardlie defend ourselues against the Enemie in respect of the manie easie landing places wch are on both sides wthin five myles distance of vs, And therefore wee haue thought it our duetie to adu^{r}tise y^r LL^{ps}, That there is a place two myles distant from vs to the westward, called Blackpoole, and a great Baie, called Torrbay, three myles from vs to the Eastward, at either of wch places the Enemie may easily land, and marching towards our Towne take the hills, wch are above vs, and beate vs out of the Towne and Forts, when wee shall not be able to impeach them in anie sort; wee therefore humblie referr the fortifying of those places vnto y^r LL^{ps} further direccons and care, for if the Enemy land at either of them wee cannot possebly hold the Towne. And thus craveing pardon for our boldnes, and humbly intreating y^r Hono^{rs} to rest assured that wee will not be defective in anie thing (as farr as our habilities will extend) wch may be expected from good and loyall subiects, and such as will euermore be most observant of y^r LL^{ps} comands wee humblie take our leave. Dartmouth this xxxth of July 1626.

Yo^r LL^{ps} to be commanded

WILL PLUMLEIGHE maior

	ROBT FOLLETT	ROBERT MARTIN
THO: SPURWAIE	JOHN SMYTH	ROGER MATHEW
		ANDREW VOYSEY.

To the Right hon^{ble} the Lords and others of his Maties most hono^{ble} privy Councell.

39. Lindsey's Instructions, 1635

It is well known that Charles I spent the proceeds of the ship-money writs upon the navy. The first Ship-Money Fleet cruised in the Channel from May to October, 1635, under the command of the Earl of Lindsey, who was given the following instructions:

Instructions of Lords of the Admiralty to the Earl of Lindsey, May 2nd, 1635. (*S.P. Dom. Ch. I*, CCLXXXVIII, No. 17.)

The ships appointed to be presently under your Lordship's charge are his Majesty's ships the *Merhonour*, Admiral, the *James*, Vice-Admiral, the *Swiftsure*, Rear-Admiral, the *St George*, *St Andrew*, *Henrietta Maria*, *Vanguard*, *Rainbow*, *Red Lion*, *Reformation*, *Antelope*, *Leopard*, *Swallow*, *Mary Rose*, *Adventure*, his Majesty's pinnaces the *Lion's First*, *Third*, *Eighth*, and *Tenth Whelps*, and of Merchant's Ships the *Sampson*, *Freeman*, *Royal Exchange*, *William and Thomas*, and the *Pleiades*: with these ships and vessels your Lordship is to employ your best industry, diligence and courage principally for guard of the Narrow Seas, and his Majesty's subjects and allies trading through the same, And are from time to time so to dispose of the ships under your charge, that all parts of the Seas, as well from the Start westward as the rest of the Sleeve[1] from the Start to the Downs, and from thence northward, may be secured from men of war, pirates and sea rovers, and all picaroons that interrupt the trade and commerce of his Majesty's dominions.

Your Lordship is to have care to repair and to send some of your fleet to such places in the Narrow Seas where you shall hear or learn any pirates, sea rovers, or picaroons frequent, and to use all possible means to suppress or apprehend them; And that you may the sooner meet with them, you are never to lie still in one place no longer than needs you must, but ever (upon all occasions and as often as wind and weather will permit) to keep abroad at sea yourself, and likewise to send forth all ships and vessels under your Lordship's charge to range and scour the said Seas.

And if you chance to meet in his Majesty's Seas any fleet or ships belonging to any foreign Prince or State, you are to expect that the Admiral or Chief of them (in acknowledgement of his

[1] The English Channel.

Majesty's sovereignty there) shall perform their duty and homage in passing by, and if they refuse to do it and offer to resist, you are to force them thereunto, and to bring them in to answer such their high contempt and presumption according to law.

In this your Lordship's employment you are not to permit or suffer any men of war to fight with each other, or man of war with merchant, or merchant with merchant in the presence of his Majesty's ships in any part of the Narrow Seas, but to do your best to keep peace in those seas for the freer and better maintenance of trade and commerce through the same, for that all men trading or sailing within those his Majesty's Seas do justly take themselves to be *in pace Domini Regis,* and therefore his Majesty in honour and justice is to protect them from injury and violence.

As your Lordship meets with any men of war, merchant, or other ship or vessel belonging to any foreign Prince or State, either at sea, or in any road or other place where you or any of his Majesty's fleet shall happen to come, your Lordship is to send to see whether there be any of his Majesty's subjects aboard them; and if any seamen, gunners, pilots, or mariners, either English, Scots, or Irish, shall be found aboard any of them, you are not only to cause such of his Majesty's subjects to be taken forth and committed and disposed aboard or otherwise, in such sort as they may be forthcoming to answer their contempt to his Majesty's proclamation in that kind, but also friendly to admonish the captains or principal commanders and officers in such foreign ships or vessels that they receive or entertain aboard any of their ships no more of his Majesty's said subjects, that his Majesty may have no cause to resent it at their hands.

If your Lordship shall descry any fleet at sea, that you may probably conjecture hath a purpose to encounter, oppose, or affront you, your Lordship shall first ply to get the wind, and after you the whole fleet in the due order of their squadrons shall do the like, and when you come to join battle, no ship shall presume to assail the enemy's Admiral or Vice-Admiral but only you and your Vice-Admiral, if you be able to reach them, and the other ships are to match themselves as equally as they can, and to succour one another as cause shall require, not wasting their powder at small vessels or victuallers, nor shoot afar off, nor till they come side to side.

40. THE CLAIM TO THE SALUTE

We must not lightly dismiss the English claims to the sovereignty of the British seas because to us they appear absurd and monstrous: in their day they were taken seriously, and were a motive of action.

S.P. Dom. Ch. I, CCCLXI, No. 41.

Right Honble,

May it please your Lordship to understand that on the 2nd of this month off the Lizard we gave chase to 4 sail of Hollanders' great ships homeward bound from the coast of Brazil. They were all to windward of us, the wind westerly; three of them had flags abroad. The Admiral, Vice-Admiral, and one more stretched it ahead of us out of shot; the Rear-Admiral came within reach of the pinnace. Mr Rabnett gave fire to a piece thwart his forefoot[1], and he shot another fair over the pinnace's quarter, and kept up his flag and topsails. The pinnace shot a second and a third at him. At length the Admiral and Vice-Admiral took in their flags, lowered their topsails, and laid their ships by the lee. The pinnace ran up with the Rear-Admiral, who notwithstanding kept all aloft, and called to him to strike for the King of England. He made answer he would when he came to his Admiral, neither did he lower his topsails until he brought up his ship by the lee. When I came up with them (being at least a league astern), I sent for the Admiral, who came on board me, and excused his not striking his flag and bearing up with us, alleging he did not know us at first. For his Rear-Admiral, he told me that if he had done amiss he was to suffer for it, and that he would by no means justify what he had done. The captain of the Rear-Admiral I have taken out of his ship and sent to Plymouth Fort, to be kept there until such time as your Lordship shall please to release him. All that he can say in his own behalf is that he took us to be ships of Dunkirk; but the weather was very clear, we all had our jacks and ensigns abroad, and the pinnace was so near him that he must know her.

Your most faithful servant,

HEN. STRADLING.

Dreadnought, off the Lizard, June 8th, 1637.

[1] 'This word *forefoot* implies no more, but one ship's lying or sailing across another ship's way.' (Mainwaring.)

41. Defects of the Ship-Money Fleets

The following papers throw light upon some of the administrative weaknesses of Charles I's Navy.

(a) 1635. Sir Wm Monson's papers of Propositions, January 12, 1635/6. N.R.S. XLIII, p. 380.)

In the last voyage I have seen more topmasts carried by the board in a reasonable gale of wind than I have known in great storms in the Queen's time when we have kept the seas 4, 5, or 6 months together and never anchored in all that space. And therefore I hold it fit, for the avoiding the like inconvenience, that one of his Majesty's ship-carpenters in ordinary be appointed to go in the fleet to view and direct all things belonging to ships, as masts, yards, and other things within his element.

(b) 1636. Extract of the several particulars attested by Captains and others under their hands, upon their examinations taken on the thirteen Articles presented by the Earl of Northumberland to his Majesty sitting in Council touching the defects and abuses of the Navy[1]. (S.P. Dom. Ch. I, cccxxxviii, No. 39.)

1. Divers of your Majesty's ships are so old and decayed that the repair of them is a great and continual charge, and the ships are able to do little service.

2. The girdling of some of your Majesty's ships and taking away their galleries will add much to their force.

3. The leakiness of so many of his Majesty's ships and illness of their masts must proceed from some negligence.

4. That all his Majesty's ships are furnished with much ill cordage.

5. The making mean men prestmasters doth occasion abuses.

6. Laying in six months' victual is very incommodious.

7. Much of the victuals naught and short in the proportions.

8. The want of a treasurer very inconvenient to all the fleet.

9. The paymaster refuseth to pay men turned over from other ships, if they bring not tickets from the ships where they have first served.

10. The paymaster will pay no tickets but to the parties themselves unto whom the money is due.

[1] Each article is followed, in the original, by particular instances.

11. If the paymaster have it in his power to refuse whom he will, he may draw men to what composition he pleaseth.

12. Great sums are owing to the Chest.

13. That 2*s*. in the pound is usually abated upon all such moneys as are lent to supply the poor men's wants upon any occasion.

42. MERVIN URGES THE MEN'S GRIEVANCES

Sir Henry Mervin to the Lords Commissioners of the Admiralty, September 25th, 1629. (*S.P. Dom. Ch. I*, CXLIX, No. 90.)

I beseech your Lordships for the honour of the state suffer not the service to become a scandal, but be pleased to take speedy course for the redress hereof: for foul winter weather, naked backs, and empty bellies make the common men voice the King's service worse than a galley slavery; and necessitous wants together with famine pleading the cause of their disorders, lays open a way to what they are too prone already to—mutinous disobedience and contempt of all commands, for necessity hath no law.

Sir Henry Mervin to the Earl of Dorset, September 25th, 1629. (*S.P. Dom. Ch. I*, CXLIX, No. 92.)

My Lord,

I have written to the Lords Commissioners the state of six ships here in the Downs, two of which, the *Dreadnought* and *Third Whelp*, have neither meat nor drink; the *Tenth Whelp* hath drank water these three days. The shore affords a soldier relief or hope, the sea neither; now, with what confidence can punishment be inflicted on men that mutiny in these wants? My Lord, be pleased to judge impartially what scandal these neglects must throw upon your Lordship here at home, and how much the honour of the state suffers abroad. The necessity of the times can be no reason that ships neither are supplied nor called home by what time their victualling shall have end. The *Lion, Adventure*, and the *Fourth Whelp* have now each about 20 days' victualling, no proportion to seat withal; and, without speedy care, not sufficient to expect a new supply[1]. I beseech

[1] This passage is obscure, and may be a copyist's error. Mr W. G. Perrin has kindly supplied this note: 'I think he means this: The *Lion, Adventure,*

your Lordship think of us, and let us have present order to go
for Portsmouth, where petty warrant[1] may relieve us in case of
necessity, until such farther order be taken as the Lords shall
think fit; for in the Downs can be no staying; for, if order should
be given for our supply here, we have not victual to subsist
until it can come to us, unless the victualler be already furnished.
These neglects be the cause that mariners fly to the service of
foreign nations to avoid his Majesty's. My Lord, let not your
eye that looks on the public good overlook this mischief; for
without better order his Majesty will lose the honour of his
seas, the love and loyalty of his sailors, and his Royal Navy will
droop. I beseech your Lordship pardon plainness that proceeds
from an honest heart, for the disease admits no palliated physic.

43. VICTUALS

(a) *An Advice of a Seaman*, by Nathaniel Knott, dedicated to the Arch-
bishop of Canterbury, 1634. (*S.P. Dom. Ch. I*, CCLXXIX, No. 106.)

I must call to your minds the great abuse that of late years
hath taken possession of victuallers of his Majesty's Navy, who,
not remembering the liberality and large allowance of his
Majesty, or forgetting it of purpose, cut the sailors short of their
allowance; so that they have not so much, or so good, as they
are paid for: and where they are prevented in the first, they
exceed in the latter. Our eyes have seen the many hogsheads of
beer which in a voyage hath been thrown overboard, and that
not in the end of a voyage (which might have palliated their
falsehoods) but within one month next after they first set sail.
The damages that issue hence are more than at first sight they
seem; for this is the original cause of those diseases which haunt
ours more than the ships of foreign nations.

The brewers have gotten the art to sophisticate beer with
broom instead of hops, and ashes instead of malt, and (to make
it look the more lively) to pickle it with salt water, so that

and the *Fourth Whelp* have 20 days' supply, which is insufficient for them to
seat themselves (*i.e.* stay permanently) in the Downs, & moreover insufficient
for them to remain there while new supplies are forthcoming (expect=wait
for); therefore they must go to Portsmouth forthwith.'

[1] Ships in harbour received three or four days' victuals at a time, upon
the voucher of the clerk of the check.

whilst it is new, it shall seemingly be worthy of praise, but in one month wax worse than stinking water.

There are of this disorder (as of all others) no doubt many favourers, who will be ready to say that the love of the pot maketh me to plead for strong beer. Perhaps such a slanderer scarce deserves of the kingdom a draught of common water to wash his inky mouth; howbeit we will endeavour to give him satisfaction; for, first of all, I do not plead for strong beer, but wholesome. Secondly, I will make it appear that in this consists the ruin or happy success of the voyage; for if either they cast the beer overboard or drink it, the voyage is at an end—the first way through want, the next by diseases that are engendered by unwholesome beer. Little do those monster-bellied brewers think (or if they do, they make less conscience) of the watching, labour and miseries of a poor sailor, in double danger both of the fight and of shipwreck, by day parched with the heat of the sun, by night nipt and whipt with blustering tempests; and when he is wet, cold, and hungry, should not the poor soul have a can of beer to refresh him, but he must say *Mors est in olla* when he drinks it, or a cake of bread, but he must think he is set to a penance when he eats it? The price of good and bad is all one, if care were in the receiver and the deliverer no deceiver.

They that know how hot the Southern countries are in the summer time, and the bare allowance of a sailor, would not wish him a draught of stinking puddle to quench his thirst, or if they should, they were dog-hearted men. Let me but ask you why our men are more subject to the small-pox, to calentures, and to that terror of sailors, the scurvy, than other nations? Look into the Hollanders, who drink water, and thou shalt find them healthy and as fat as Hebe. On the other side, but cast an eye into our English ships, who drink beer, and they look as mortally as a death's head with a bone in's mouth: they swallow the cause in their drink.

As much care as is to be had of this I would have taken for salting of the flesh which they shall eat: the heat of the South seas will search whether it be well salted or no: if not, it soon turns to carrion, and lumps of putrefaction. There is a common proverb, that nothing will poison a sailor. Perhaps they have poisoned many that use it; God grant they may poison no more.

(b) Boteler's *Sea Dialogues.*

Capt. Without doubt, over much, and indeed excessive feeding upon these salt meats at sea cannot but procure much unhealthiness and great infection, and is certainly one main cause that our English are nowadays so subject to calentures, scorbutes[1], and the like contagious sickness, above all other nations; so that it were to be wished that we did more conform ourselves to the Spanish and Italian nations, who lived most upon rice, oatmeal, biscuits, figs, olives, oil, and the like; or at least to our neighbours the Dutch, who content themselves with a far less proportion of flesh and fish than we do, and in stead thereof, do make up their meals with pease, beans, wheat, flour, butter, cheese, and those white meats, as they are called.

Adm. It were well indeed if we could bring ourselves to this provident and wholesome kind of sea-feeding; but the difficulty lieth in that the common seamen with us are so besotted in their beef and pork, that they had rather adventure on all the calentures and scurvies in the world, than to be weaned from their customary diet, or but so much as to lose the least bit of it.

44. GENTLEMEN CAPTAINS

The following is an early complaint against 'gentlemen captains.' In the Tudor period, the admiral in command of a great fleet was a nobleman, but his staff and the captains, whatever their birth, would almost all be experienced seamen. In Stuart times no abuse was more serious than the frequent appointment of inexperienced landsmen to the command of ships.

(a) Advice of a Seaman.

It is apparent that every creature is most able in his own element: how easily is the fiercest beast overcome when he is in the water; on the other side, how quickly are the strongest and most cruel fishes dead when they are on the dry ground! The element of a land Captain is the land; the sea, of a sea Captain. He that will know how much the success of actions hang upon their commanders, let him compare the ships of the King of Spain with those of the Netherlands. In the one he shall find a brave Signior, a Rhodomantados that shall ruffle it out in his silks and cloth of gold, with whom there is none in favour but

---

[1] Scurvies.

a company of marmosets that can frame themselves to his humour. Look into his ship, and it looks like the Augean[1] stables (I believe the English are their imitators); but if you go into a Hollander, you shall see a good plain fellow that hath been tenant to Proteus for term of life, and with him every man esteemed in his place; his ship shall be a very pattern for all nations (it is all that is praiseworthy in them), and for fight every man placed to his quarter, so that there is not the least confusion that can be thought. The event when these commanders meet is, that Don Rogero (the Spaniard) must strip him from his silver sleeves and velvet cassock, and learn to wear Harry Butterbox's open breeches and his thrum cap.

I dare lawfully look back to the times of our fathers, but not compare them. What was the reason that in the reign of that famous Queen (whose memory shall live into eternity) the English were lords of the seas, but that seamen were lords of the ships? Who sees not the other part of this comparison? I will give you an emblem of a late captain, better known to others than to himself, who, being a fresh-water soldier, was sick with the savour of the sea; and his men pumping the ship in their watch, it gave a noisome smell (which notwithstanding is a good sign of a tight ship), whereof this young Neptune in a fume demanding the reason, reply was made that it was the pump. 'Why,' quoth he, 'cast it overboard, for if it stink so, I will have none in my ship!' This was a sweet captain! Or if you would have this compared with another, I can tell you of one who, being at sea in his argosy, a sail was descried. The captain demanded where; answer was made, 'Right in the wind.' The captain, full of bell metal, cried, 'Bear up, for I will speak with him.' The master told him it was impossible to bear up against the wind, whereat, his fury assuaged, he prayed God to send him safe to Salisbury Plains (a place belike from whence he had received some courtesy), 'for there I can ride and never observe the winds.'

(b) Monson. (*N.R.S.* XLIII, p. 435.)

The seamen are much discouraged, of late times, by preferring of young, needy, and inexperienced gentlemen captains over

---

[1] MS. 'Egean.'

them in their own ships; as also by placing lieutenants above the masters in the King's ships, which have never been accustomed by the English till of late years.

45. Sea Punishments

'Gentlemen captains' were unpopular, not only on account of their professional ignorance, and lack of sympathy with the wretched state of the men, but because they were often arbitrary in their punishments.

(a) Boteler's *Sea Dialogues*.

Capt. As for the punishment at the capstan, it is when, a capstan's bar being thrust through the hole of the barrel, the offender's arms are extended to full the length, and so made fast unto the bar crosswise, having sometimes a basket of bullets, or some other the like weight, hanging upon his neck; in which posture he continueth till he be made either to confess some plot or crime, whereof he is pregnantly suspected; or that he hath received such condign suffering as he is suffered to undergo by the censure of the captain.

The punishment of the bilboes is when a delinquent is put in irons, or in a kind of stocks that they use for that purpose, the which are more or less heavy and pinching, as the quality of the offence is proved against the delinquent.

The ducking at the main yard arm is when a malefactor, by having a rope fastened under his arms, and about his middle, and under his breech, is thus hoisted up to the end of the yard, from whence he is again violently let fall into the sea, sometimes twice, sometimes three several times one after another; and if the offence be very foul, he is also drawn under the very keel of the ship, the which they term keel-raking, and whilst he is thus under water, a great gun is given fire unto, right over his head, the which is done as well to astonish him the more with the thunder thereof, which much troubles him, as to give warning unto all others to look out and to beware by his harms.

And these are the common and usual ways of inflicting of punishments upon delinquents at sea, the which also in capital causes, as murders, mutinies, and the like, are so transcended, that where there is otherwhiles a ducking at the main yard end, there is a hanging to death executed in the same place; but this is never done, but by some especial Commission, or at the least by a Martial Court. As for all petty pilferings, and commissions of that kind, these are generally punished with the whip, the offender being to that purpose bound fast to the capstan. And the waggery and idleness of the ship-boys are paid by the boatswain with the rod, and commonly this execution is done upon the Monday mornings, and is so frequently in use, that some mere seamen and sailors do believe in good earnest that they shall never have a fair wind, until the poor boys be duly brought to the chest, that is, whipped every Monday morning.

(b) Monson. (*N.R.S.* XLIII, p. 435.)

The seaman is willing to give or receive punishment deservingly, according to the laws of the sea, and not otherwise in the fury of passion of a dissolute, blasphemous, swearing commander. Punishment is fittest to be executed in cold blood, the next day after the offence is committed and discovered.

46. Reputation of English Merchantmen abroad

When the worst has been said of the early Stuarts, these points must be remembered: (1) That their administration, however bad compared with that of their predecessors and successors, was no worse than that of their foreign rivals, and that their fleets, *e.g.* that of Mansell to the Mediterranean in 1620–1, and the Ship-Money Fleets, were of great diplomatic importance. (2) That in days when merchantmen went armed, the King's ships formed but a part of the naval strength of the kingdom, and were responsible for only a part of its reputation.

(a) Piero Contarini, Venetian Ambassador Extraordinary in England, to the Doge and Senate, March 2nd, 1618. (*Cal. S.P. Ven.* p. 161.)

I have engaged five most capital vessels, and by reason of the readiness of their captains to serve your Serenity and their abhorrence of the name Spaniard, I trust they will do the best possible service. Some Flemish ships were offered me at a much cheaper rate, and also of much heavier tonnage; but the English being held in infinitely greater account by reason of the strength of their build, the quality of their guns, and their crews, which yet more excel all other nations in battle, I did not choose to part with them.

(*b*) Sir Kenelm Digby's *Voyage*, 1628. (Camden Soc. vol. XCVI.)

Whereas all other ships did run from us as fast and as long as they could, I yet never met with any English, were they in never so little or contemptible vessels, but they stayed for us and made ready for fight.

(*c*) Sir Kenelm Digby to Sir John Coke, September 29th, 1635, Paris. (*Hist. MSS. Commn.* 12, II, 95.)

In all which[1] our master will have a power to keep the balance even, if he keep a fleet at sea and his navy in that reputation it now is in; for I assure your Honour that is very great, and although my Lord of Lindsey do no more than sail up and down, yet the very setting of our best fleet out to sea is the greatest service that I believe hath been done the King these many years.

[1] The internal weakness of France.

THE COMMONWEALTH AND PROTECTORATE

THE Interregnum is one of the most important periods in our naval history. The navy was called upon to undertake services of the most various kinds, in different parts of the world: to transport and co-operate with armies, to blockade and bombard hostile ports, to protect commerce, to strengthen the hands of our diplomatists by 'showing the flag,' and to wage a long and stubborn war against a formidable enemy. These duties (which were admirably performed) necessitated a large increase in the size of the navy, which, between the execution of Charles I and the restoration of Charles II, was strengthened by the addition of more than 200 vessels, of which nearly one-half were new-built[1].

Before this period, ships had been roughly divided into 'rates'; the practice now became regular. It should be noted that the grading was made for the convenience of administrators, not of officers afloat: the object was to make the pay of officers proportionate to their responsibility; the different 'ranks' did not represent different types, each of peculiar construction and with peculiar functions; they merged imperceptibly into one another.

47. RATES OF SHIPS

The Navy Commissioners to the Admiralty Committee. January 20th, 1652/3. (*N.R.S.* xxx, p. 396.)

Right Honourable,—We have considered how to distinguish the State's ships into ranks and are of opinion that the respective numbers of men set under each rate, and so upwards to the ranks next before should be settled, and so all officers receive their pay accordingly, viz.:

1st rank	2nd	3rd	4th	5th	6th
Men	Men	Men	Men	Men	Men
400 and upwards	300	200	140	80	40

And for all small vessels under forty men to be without the rates, and to be paid as the service shall deserve, which, if your Lordships approve of, we pray your direction for our government therein.

[1] Of these, seven carried 60 guns or over, and twelve more 50 or over.

48. Battle of the Kentish Knock

Since, before the First Dutch War, no battles had been fought at sea between two efficient fleets of broadside sailing ships, the tactics proper to such actions had not as yet been evolved. In the early battles of the war, the fleets had no real cohesion, as will be seen from the following account of the Battle of the Kentish Knock. (It will be noticed that we had discarded the 'long bowls' tactics used against the Armada.)

A Letter from Gen. Blake's fleet. (*N.R.S.* XVII, p. 282.)

Sir,—On Sept. 25 (Oct. 5), 1652, there was a great meeting of the officers of the fleet with General Blake about engaging with the Hollanders then about Goodwin Sands, and it was resolved, after several meetings, that on Tuesday last[1] we should endeavour to engage with them. And accordingly on Tuesday last we sailed towards them, and the Hollanders stood to us, being well manned, and every ways very well fitted, and about our number, each party being between 50 and 60 sail, and the Hollanders had two Admirals.

First Major Bourne[2] with the *Andrew* led on, and charged the Hollanders stoutly, and got off again without much harm. Captain Badiley with his ship also (for we have one of the Badileys a captain with us, besides Captain Badiley in the Straits), he charged exceeding gallantly; but was in very great danger to have lost his ship, for the Hollanders were so close on both sides of him, charging against him, that one might have flung biscuits out of his frigate into the Dutch ships.

All his sails were so torn and shattered that he could not sail either to or fro, or any more but as the tide drove him, and there were about 60 men killed in that frigate, and she had near 100 shot in her hull, and was in danger of sinking or taking; but, blessed be God, they got her safe to harbour, the fight being not above 6 leagues from the shore.

The water being shallow upon the sands, we were in some danger of sustaining great loss, in so much that the *Sovereign*, and the ship in which General Blake[3] was, with the admiral began to stick, but, blessed be God, were got off again without any great harm thereby.

[1] Sept. 28 (Oct. 8).

[2] Afterwards Commissioner at Harwich, where Monck praised his 'extraordinary care and diligence.'　　[3] A mistake for Penn.

The *Sovereign*—that great ship, a delicate frigate[1] (I think the whole world hath not her like)—did her part; she sailed through and through the Holland fleet, and played hard upon them. And at one time there were about 20 Holland frigates upon her; but, blessed be the Lord, she hath sustained no very great loss, but in some of her tacklings, and some shot in her, which her great bigness is not much prejudiced with.

49. THE FIRST APPEARANCE IN INSTRUCTIONS OF THE LINE AHEAD

After the Battle of Dungeness, Blake was given Deane and Monck as colleagues. All three were scientific soldiers, to whom haphazard fighting was distasteful. The results of their deliberations are seen in the following instructions, which enjoin the line ahead as the squadronal formation at the beginning of an action, and provide for its extension to the whole fleet, at the discretion of the Commander-in-Chief. When once this formation was introduced, everyone could see that it enabled a fleet to develop its maximum fire: it was Columbus's egg over again. One may emphasize the fact that tactics are dependent upon seamanship: without the experience gained by the Commonwealth ships in long cruising together, the adoption of this formation would have been impossible.

In this war the battle-fleet still consisted largely of armed merchantmen. With these the Generals at Sea wished to dispense: they had learnt the immense superiority of a professional over a volunteer army, and they wished to extend the principle to the navy. The new formation made the disappearance of the merchantmen inevitable: not only could they not manœuvre with the necessary precision, but they would be so many weak points in the line, exposing it to the risk of being broken. This consideration soon created a distinction between warships which were powerful enough to fight in the line, and those which were fit only to serve as cruisers; in the following half-century there was a steady increase in the number of guns a ship had to carry in order to qualify for the line of battle.

Instructions by Blake, Deane and Monck for the better ordering of the fleet in sailing. March 29th, 1653. (*N.R.S.* XXXVII, p. 266.)

3. That no one presume to go to windward of the chief of his squadron in sailing at any time unless in chase or fight.

---

[1] This was the famous *Sovereign of the Seas*, built by Phineas Pett in 1637, and called by Mr Oppenheim 'the largest, most ornate, and most useless ship afloat.' Being crank-sided, she was in 1652 cut down to two decks. Mr Gregory Robinson says (*Mariner's Mirror*, VII, 124) that the term 'frigate' 'was, I believe, generally used for all ships, great and small, during the Commonwealth.'

4. That in tacking or sailing at any time everyone keep good order, and not strive for the wind, or place, one of another, whereby prejudice or damage may come to any ship or ships of the fleet, but that every captain, lieutenant, master, master's mate, or pilot of a ship of less rank, give place to one of a greater; and if they be of one rank, then the younger captain to give place to the elder, provided that no captain, lieutenant, master, master's mate, or pilot whatsoever strive or endeavour to take place of another ship, though she be of a lesser rank, so as damage may ensue to either ship, upon pain of cashiering and loss of pay, both in better ship and elder captain, as well as the lesser and younger.

Fighting Instructions, March 29th, 1653. (*N.R.S.* xxix, p. 99 and xxxvii, p. 262.)

2. At sight of the said fleet the vice-admiral, or he that commands in chief in the 2nd place, and his squadron, as also the rear-admiral, or he that commandeth in chief in the 3rd place, and his squadron, are to make what sail they can to come up with the admiral on each wing, the vice-admiral on the right wing, and the rear-admiral on the left wing, leaving a competent distance for the admiral's squadron if the wind will permit and there be sea-room enough.

3. As soon as they shall see the general engage, or make a signal by shooting off two guns and putting a red flag over the fore-topmast-head, that then each squadron shall take the best advantage they can to engage with the enemy next unto them; and in order thereunto all the ships of every squadron shall endeavour to keep in a line with their chief, unless the chief of his squadron shall be either lamed or otherwise disabled (which God forbid!), whereby the said ship that wears the flag should not come in to do the service which is requisite. Then every ship of the said squadron shall endeavour to keep in a line with the admiral, or he that commands in chief next unto him, and nearest the enemy.

6. That if any ship shall be necessitated to bear away from the enemy to stop a leak or mend what else is amiss, which cannot be otherwise repaired, he is to put out a pennant on the mizen-yard-arm or ensign staff, whereby the rest of the ships

may have notice what it is for; and if it should be that the admiral or any flagship should do so, the ships of the fleet or of the respective squadron are to endeavour to keep up in a line as close as they can betwixt him and the enemy, having always one eye to defend him in case the enemy should come to annoy him in that condition.

7. In case the admiral should have the wind of the enemy, and that other ships of the fleet are to windward of the admiral, then upon hoisting up a blue flag at the mizen-yard, or the mizen-topmast, every such ship is then to bear up into his wake or grain[1] upon pain of the severest punishment. In case the admiral be to leeward of the enemy, and his fleet or any part thereof to leeward of him, to the end such ships to leeward may come up into the line with their admiral, if he shall put abroad a flag as before and bear up, none that are to leeward are to bear up, but to keep his or their luff to gain his wake or grain.

9. If we put up a red flag on the mizen shrouds or on the mizen yard-arms, we would have all the flag-ships to come up into the grain and wake of us.

10. If in time of fight God shall deliver any of the enemy's ships into our hands, special care is to be taken to save their men as the present state of our condition will permit in such cases, but that such ships be immediately destroyed by sinking or burning the same, that so our own ships be not disabled or any work interrupted by departing of men or boats from the ships[2].

Given under our hands at Portsmouth, this March 29th, 1653.

ROBERT BLAKE.
RICHARD DEANE.
GEORGE MONCK.

---

[1] 'Grain'=the opposite of 'wake.'

[2] In the previous December, 1652, Parliament, besides raising the pay of officers and men, had passed the following resolution (*N.R.S.* xxx, p. 286): That all captains, seamen, and others that do or shall serve in any of the State's own or merchants' ships employed in their service, shall for time to come in lieu of all prizes have and receive from the State, for every ship or prize they shall lawfully take, the sum of 10s. for every ton the said ship shall measure, and £6. 13s. 4d. for every piece of ordnance, to be shared and divided amongst them proportionally, according to the respective places and offices in the ship in which they served; and for every man-of-war sunk or destroyed by firing or otherwise, to have £10 a gun only.

50. The Battle of the Gabbard

The first of the following extracts proves that the Instructions of March 29th were observed in the next battle, The Gabbard, June 2–4, 1653; the second shows that Monck regarded the line ahead as a starting-point, as a means of beginning an action under favourable conditions, not as an end in itself: to him, as to Cromwell, tactics were the accessory to, not a substitute for, hard fighting.

A Letter from the Hague. (*N.R.S.* XLI, p. 109.)

Upon the Thursday following, the 12th instant[1], the English found the Dutch fleet in the height of Dunkirk, and when they approached them, they stayed upon a tack, having the wind, within twice cannon shot about half an hour, to put themselves in their order they intended to fight in, which was in file at half cannon shot, from whence they battered the Hollanders furiously all that day, the success whereof was the sinking two Holland ships. Towards night Tromp got the wind, but soon lost it again, and never recovered it the two following days during which the fight continued, the Dutch steering with a slow sail towards their own coast. The second day the English still battered them in file, and refusing to board them upon equal terms, kept them at a bay but half cannon distance, until they found some of them disordered and foul one against another, whom they presently boarded with their frigates (appointed to watch that opportunity) and took; and this they continued to do until the Holland fleet approached the Wielings, when they left them (by reason of those sands) upon Saturday night.

51. The Battle of Scheveningen, July 31st, 1653

Cubitt[2] to Blackborne, August 2nd, 1653. (*N.R.S.* XLI, p. 367.)

Sir,—Having attended upòn the Hollander upon his own coast ever since the 3rd of June last, the most part of our fleet coming to Solebay to put ashore our sick men, on the 26th of the last month about twenty-eight sail appeared in sight about the Helder, we riding close by the Texel, by which we conceived Tromp was ready with his fleet at the Wielings, the which at

---

[1] June 2nd, O.S.   [2] Captain of the *Tulip*, 32 guns.

night we weighed, got under sail the 29th about noon, we saw the Holland fleet which came from the Wielings, eighty-four sail as we are informed, which presently gave way, but near Egmont some of ours and theirs interchanged shot. The wind next day blowing West-North-West very hard, we lay one by the other, they nearer the shore than we, not far from Gravesant. That night their Texel fleet and this met and joined; the 31st the weather being seasonably fair, in the morning both standing off to sea, we tacked upon them and went through their whole fleet, leaving part of one side and part on the other side of us; in passing through we lamed them several ships and sunk some; as soon as we had passed them we tacked again upon them and they on us, passed by each other very near; we did very good execution on him, some of their ships which had all their masts gone struck their colours and put out a white handkerchief on a staff and hauled in all their guns; my men were very desirous to go to them, there being two of them very close by us, but the fight being but then begun I would not suffer it. They were after fired by others when the fight was over. As soon as we had passed each other both tacked, the Hollander having still the wind and we keeping close by; we passed each very near one another and did very great execution upon each other. We cut off this bout some of his fleet which could not weather us and therefore forsook him on this board; some of them were sunk and we had the *Oak* fired by one of their branders. We tacked again upon them and they upon us and this bout was most desperately fought by either almost at push of pike. A Flushinger was sunk close by the *Victory*; he, intending to board the *Victory*, had entered three or four of his men with their pole-axes, but the *Victory's* carpenter's axe cut them down on the side of the ship. Our General must needs gall them very much this bout and so did all our ships, being constantly very near especially this last charge, two of their Admirals coming up close to the *Resolution*[1] and had much ado to weather her, at which time the very heavens were obscured by smoke, the air rent with the thundering noise, the sea all in a breach with the shot that fell, the ships even trembling and we hearing everywhere messengers of death flying; eight or ten sail of his ships not being able to

[1] Monck's flagship.

weather us forsook their fleet. We tacked again upon them but they, having had enough of it and their heads looking to fathers-landward, thought it not safe to tack any more but would willingly have gotten to the Meuse or Goree, but we beat them to leeward and stood after them half-way the coast of Holland betwixt the Meuse and Texel; the wind veering out at the South-West and beginning to blow with dirt and rain, several of our ships being disabled in their masts and yards, our General laid his head off and so did all our fleet. The Hollander I think is gone for the Texel.

52. COMMERCE-PROTECTION

At the beginning of the war, the strategy of both sides was dominated by the importance of Dutch commerce, which it was the main object of the English battle-fleet to attack directly, and of the Dutch battle-fleet to shepherd. The following extract shows that the Dutch soon learnt the main principle of commerce-protection.

News from the Hague, March 24th, 1652/3. (*N.R.S.* xxxvii, p. 251.)

The Committee of the States General for sea affairs having advised with Admiral Tromp and other chief officers of the Navy concerning the safe going and returning of such of their merchant ships as are ready to go out from hence, or to return from abroad, the said officers are of opinion that our merchant ships should do best to lie still and not stir outward nor homeward while the English are strong at sea, but expect till our ships first go to encounter the English, and either beat them or drive them into their harbours, which being done our merchantmen may then securely go and come with small convoys.

53. A DUTCH STRATAGEM

The Weekly Intelligencer, November 9th, 1652. (*N.R.S.* xxx, p. 33.)

It is advertised from Holland that the Dutch are setting forth their fleet, which consisteth of one hundred and twenty ships, twenty whereof are fireships, which they do much rely on; Tromp and Evertsen are to command the van consisting of seventy sail, and De With and Ruyter are to follow after with the rear. The principal design of their Admiral is to convoy the merchantmen bound for France, Spain, and Portugal, who are said to be above two hundred sail; and this was designed to have been performed sooner, but the Hollanders were in distress both for men and money. It is said that they will not fight with us if possible they can decline an engagement. Howsoever, their Admiral doth carry with him a council of war, and a fiscal, who are to try and also to execute such captains as shall be found not to do their duties. The Dutch boast much of their fireships as carrying 24 and 30 guns, appearing like men-of-war, but indeed are no such things, having only two or three guns, and all the rest are painted, and so placed as they may best deceive the eye, and be the less suspected when they come to service.

54. THE FLAG

Treaty of Westminster, April 5, 1654.

13. That the ships and vessels of the said United Provinces, as well those of war as others, which shall meet any of the men-of-war of this Commonwealth in the British seas, shall strike their flag and lower the topsail, in such manner as the same hath ever been observed at any times heretofore, under any other form of government.

55. PAY OF OFFICERS IN 1653

In studying the administration of this period, we should remember that, until its last years, it was free from the great weakness of both the early and the later Stuarts—lack of money. The Commonwealth Government, like Henry VIII, lived largely on capital—on the fines paid by 'delinquents'—and devoted more than half the national income to the navy. The money voted for the navy was spent on it, which was not always true in Stuart times. Further, the Commonwealth found the right men for administration, as well as for fighting—men remarkable for industry, ability, honesty, and sympathy with the seamen. 'Never, before or since,' says Mr Oppenheim, 'were the combatant branches of the navy so well supported:...they had every assistance that foresight and earnestness could give.' The strain of the Dutch War naturally revealed some weaknesses which provoked complaints; but the complaints have a different ring from those of Stuart times: they assume that the administrators are anxious to do justice.

H. & H.   5

The following table, reprinted by permission from Mr Oppenheim's *Administration of the Royal Navy*, gives the monthly pay of officers after the increase of 1653. It remained unaltered during the reign of Charles II.

	1st rate			2nd rate			3rd rate			4th rate			5th rate			6th rate		
	£	s.	d.	£	s.	d.	£	s.	d.	£	s.	d.	£	s.	d.	£	s.	d.
Captain	21	0	0	16	16	0	14	0	0	10	0	0	8	8	0	7	0	0
Lieutenant	4	4	0	4	4	0	3	10	0	3	10	0	—			—		
Master	·7	0	0	6	6	0	4	13	8	4	6	2	3	7	6	—¹		
Master's mate or pilot	3	6	0	3	0	0	2	16	2	2	7	10	2	2	0	2	2	0
Midshipman	2	5	0	2	0	0	1	17	6	1	13	9	1	10	0	1	10	0
Boatswain	4	0	0	3	10	0	3	0	0	2	10	0	2	5	0	2	0	0
Boatswain's mate	1	15	0	1	15	0	1	12	0	1	10	0	1	8	0	1	6	0
Quartermaster	1	15	0	1	15	0	1	12	0	1	10	0	1	8	0	1	6	0
Quartermaster's mate	1	10	0	1	10	0	1	8	0	1	8	0	1	6	0	1	5	0
Carpenter	4	0	0	3	10	0	3	0	0	2	10	0	2	5	0	2	0	0
Carpenter's mate	2	0	0	2	0	0	1	16	0	1	14	0	1	12	0	1	10	0
Gunner	4	0	0	3	10	0	3	0	0	2	10	0	2	5	0	2	0	0
Gunner's mate	1	15	0	1	15	0	1	12	0	1	10	0	1	8	0	1	6	0
Surgeon	2	10	0	2	10	0	2	10	0	2	10	0	2	10	0	2	10	0
Corporal	1	15	0	1	12	0	1	10	0	1	10	0	1	8	0	1	5	0
Purser	4	0	0	3	10	0	3	0	0	2	10	0	2	5	0	2	0	0
Master Trumpeter	1	10	0	1	8	0	1	5	0	1	5	0	1	5	0	1	4	0
Cook	1	5	0	1	5	0	1	5	0	1	5	0	1	5	0	1	4	0

¹ 'The captain the master.'

56. Care of Sick and Wounded

The Admiralty Committee to the Navy Commissioners. January 4, 1652/3. (*N.R.S.* xxx, p. 339.)

5. You are to consider what relief is fit to be made to the widows, children, and impotent parents of such as shall be slain in the service.

6. You are to inform yourselves of all hospitals employed for the cure of sick and wounded people, etc.

Proposals of Navy Commissioners (undated). (*N.R.S.* xxxvii, p. 223.)

That three persons of approved ability and godliness (whereof one to be a surgeon) be appointed to attend this service, with a competent salary.

That the Commissioners thus constituted give seasonable and timely direction to the mayors and chief officers of all sea-port towns to make provisions for all sick and wounded men as they shall be set on shore from any of the ships in the State's service, and to employ what surgeons or other means are in those several places attainable, for their relief and cure; and upon notice of a deficiency in any place of such helps as are necessary in that kind, they are to provide either by removing them, or by sending surgeons and medicaments to them, that the recovery and cure of the distressed may not be retarded or prejudiced.

That the Commissioners aforesaid, or any two of them, do seriously consider the condition and damage of all such persons as are or shall be wounded in the service of the Commonwealth, and give them such allowance as they shall judge requisite, not exceeding £10 gratuity to any one person, nor £6. 13s. 4d. yearly pension to any, and in such cases wherein they, or any two of them, do judge a greater allowance ought to be given, they are to certify their opinions, with the grounds, to the Commissioners of the Admiralty, and act further therein, as order from them shall be given.

The said Commissioners, or any two of them, shall likewise duly consider the condition of the widows, children and impotent parents of such as have been, or shall be, slain in the service, and to give such gratuities to them not exceeding £10 as in their judgments be most agreeable to rules of charity, and may demonstrate the State's sense of their suffering conditions, and in extraordinary cases to report as before. In all which a vigilant eye is to be had to the certificates that are brought to evince the truth of the suffering of any, that they come from known creditable persons, and so thereby deceits in abuse of the State's bounty may be prevented.

57. COMPLAINTS OF SEAMEN

Kendall to Admiralty Commissioners, July 13, 1653. (*N.R.S.* XLI, p. 275.)

The complaint is very great amongst the seamen: first, for the withholding of their wages, which they have earned with the hazard of their lives, which causes the wives and children of many of them to suffer much hardship, and disheartens them from the service. Secondly, for the violent pressing and carrying away those poor men whose wages is so stopped without any care taken for their distressed families in their absence. Thirdly, the bad provision is made for them at sea, being necessitated in many ships to feed upon unwholesome and stinking victuals, whereby many of them are become sick and unserviceable, and many are dead. Shall not their blood be required at the hands of those that, for their gain, undertake the victualling, though they be persons greatly in favour, and may have an appearance of honesty and godliness? Certainly the great God of heaven and earth will make inquisition for blood if men do not. It cannot but be fresh in your memories how the arm of the Lord hath from time to time been made manifest in pulling down the mighty from their seats and breaking all unjust powers in pieces.

58. Court-Martial's Approval of a Petition

Calendar of Clarendon State Papers, II, No. 2038. October 17, 1654.

Report of a Council of War, held aboard the *Swiftsure* (present: Vice-Admiral John Lawson, Rear-Admiral Dakins, 17 captains, 5 lieutenants, and a master), to consider a petition presented by the seamen of the fleet for presentation to the Protector; at which it was resolved unanimously that it was lawful for the seamen to present their grievances by way of petition, and, with few dissentients, that the points complained of were real grievances, and that the Vice-Admiral should send the petition and these resolutions to the Protector.

Followed by a copy of the petition, representing the hardship and injustice of impressment, and the sufferings of seamen's families from the long delay in payment of their wages, and praying that sailors may be hired freely, as is done by the Dutch, and payment made every six months at furthest.

59. An English Fleet in the Straits of Gibraltar, 1651

Blake's two expeditions to the Mediterranean were of great diplomatic importance. France and Spain had not made peace with each other at the end of the Thirty Years' War, and were still fighting. In this struggle the English fleet could interfere decisively, either by cutting the communications of Spain with her possessions in Italy (and through them with Austria), or by rendering them secure against the possibility of French attack.

It need hardly be said that in this period there are no complaints of Mediterranean pirates in the Channel. The Dunkirkers continued to give a certain amount of trouble, until their town was taken by the Ironsides.

P. Gibson to W. Penn, son of Sir William Penn; March, 1711–12. (Granville Penn, *Life of Sir William Penn*, II, 612.)

The admiral[1], with six ships of his fleet...sailed to Gibraltar, where we arrived about Michaelmas, 1651; and where we stayed cruising at least three months, by dividing the fleet into two parts: viz. three ships in each division, the admiral and one riding in Old Gibraltar Road, ready to second any division who sailed out in an evening; so as to be in the middle of the Straits, or further towards the coast of Barbary, to look out for ships going into the Straits. And, if any were seen in the morning, the squadron to leeward (who stood not to the coast of Spain before mid-day), or those in Gibraltar Bay, made to them; so as few ships went into the Straits but they were spoken with, if friends, or taken, if enemies.

60. Blake's Mediterranean Fleet, 1654

J. Weale, *Journal of a Voyage to Tunis, Algiers, etc.* (B.M. Sloane MSS. 1431.)

1654.

Monday, Oct. 30. This day I am 24 years of age. About 7 in the morning we come in sight of land, and about 12 the General[2] came to an anchor near Cadiz road. Striking his flag, he saluted the town with about 21 piece of ordnance; they answered him again with, I think, five for one; and also the ships in the road, which were about 30 sail, saluted him two at a time with abundance of guns, so that we thought they would never have done. The general thanked them with five guns, and so it ceased. It is reported in the fleet that the Spaniards are at a stand, and know not what to think of us, whether or not we come for war.

Monday, Nov. 6. The Capt. and myself go aboard the

[1] Sir William Penn, left in command upon Blake's return home.
[2] Blake.

General, and from them go ashore to Gibraltar with us. Item Mr Rudyerd, Mr Witchcot, Mr Rainsborough and several of our own ship's company. The Governor desireth to speak with us, and saluted the Captain very courteously with information that the King, his Master, ordered him to entertain us with the best accommodation of the country. We were conducted to a house which was the King's Custom-house, and there we were entertained with bread and wine, fig, cheese, cake, grapes, raisins of the sun, almonds, and Spanish nut, and a many ceremonies to boot.

Tuesday, Nov. 7. At an anchor in Gibraltar Road. Capt. Stayner of the *Plymouth* frigate cometh in and some others. The General is very angry with them. They immediately go out again to Capt. Hill, Commander of the *Worcester*, and Commander-in-Chief of the squadron.

Wednesday, Nov. 8. At an anchor in Gibraltar road. The *Langport* frigate cometh to us about 2 in the afternoon, and by the General's order goeth out in the evening commander of the squadron, with our frigate, the *Ruby*, and three or four more, the *Langport* meeting with 4 Algiers men-of-war, which had met a Sallee man-of-war who had taken an Englishman, and the Algiers men compelled them to deliver up those captives which they had, and redelivered them to the *Langport*; so that we see plain that we are not only a terror to the French [and] the Spanish, but also the Turks seek to get into our favour.

THE RESTORATION NAVY

THE very mention of the Restoration Navy at once suggests the name of Samuel Pepys, to whose industry and ability it owed much, and to whose diary, letters, and registers we are indebted for our detailed knowledge of the period. We must not, however, forget that Pepys was the servant of masters who kept in touch with every branch of naval administration. The Duke of York's knowledge of naval affairs is well known. Charles II's interest in the navy was wide, if not deep: after the Duke of York's resignation of the office of Lord High Admiral in 1673, all important matters (and many which were trivial) were decided by the king.

This period is interesting from three main standpoints: the experience of the Second and Third Dutch Wars produced important developments in tactics; the place of Holland as our naval rival was taken by France; and all departments of the navy were subjected to a process of standardisation and systematisation. The restored monarchy inherited from the Commonwealth the strongest navy in existence, the value of which was fully realised. It was necessary to organise this force on a permanent basis. The orders and 'Establishments' of this period cover the whole field of naval activity, afloat and ashore. Practice did not always square with theory, partly owing to Charles II's financial weakness, partly owing to the decline in public morality. But it would be as unwise to ignore the theory as to accept it without question: with all their faults, the later Stuarts and their agents left the navy stronger than they found it.

Many of the officers who held commands at the Restoration were excellent seamen but of doubtful loyalty, while few Cavaliers had enough sea experience to take their place. The Duke of York accordingly devised the following method of securing a supply of efficient and reliable officers.

61. THE MIDSHIPMAN

P.R.O. Ad. 2, 1745.

Sir Richard Stayner,—His Royal Highness, being desirous to give encouragement to such young gentlemen as are willing to apply themselves to the learning of Navigation, and fitting themselves to the service of the sea, hath determined that one volunteer shall be entered on every ship now going forth; and for his encouragement, that he shall have the pay of a midshipman[1],

[1] The earliest mention of midshipmen is in 1643. In January, 1653, the Admiralty Committee ordered 20 seamen to be rated midshipmen in each first-rate, and so in proportion down to 4 in each sixth-rate, their pay ranging from £2. 5s. a month in a first-rate to £1. 10s. in a sixth-rate. (The pay of an able seaman was £1. 4s.) From December 14, 1655, no one was to be so rated unless able to undertake an officer's duties.

and one midshipman less be borne on the ship. In prosecution of this resolution, I am to recommend to you the bearer, Mr Tho. Darcy, and to desire you that you would receive him according to the intentions of His Royal Highness, as I have acquainted you, and that you would show him such kindness as you shall judge fit for a gentleman, both in the accommodating him in your ship, and in farthering his improvement.

I am

Your affectionate friend,
W. COVENTRY.

May 7, 1661.

62. THE LIEUTENANT

Establishment of December 18, 1677. (*Pepysian MSS.* 2867, p. 241.)

And our further will and pleasure is, that the qualifications without which no person shall from henceforward be accounted capable of the employment of lieutenant in any of our ships be as followeth:

1. To have spent so much time actually at sea in one or more voyages in our service as (after abatement made for all intervals of voyages) shall together amount to 3 entire years at least, and to have served in the quality, and have performed the duty, of an ordinary midshipman in some one of our ships for the space of one year of the three, receiving midshipman's pay for the same.

Provided that the aforesaid serving us as an ordinary midshipman for the space of one of the said three years shall not be interpreted to extend to any person who hath at this day served us at sea for more than two years in the quality of a volunteer by warrant from ourself or our High Admiral, and shall abide the examination, and answer in every respect what is in this our Establishment required from him, saving in that of his having actually performed the duty of an ordinary midshipman.

2. Nor to be under 20 years of age at the time of his first admission to the said office.

3. To produce good certificates under the hand of the several commanders under whom he hath served, testifying the several

voyages he hath been employed in, with his sobriety, diligence, obedience to order, application to the study and practice of the Art of Navigation expressed therein, and his strict performance of the duty of an ordinary midshipman for one year, saving in the case above excepted.

4. To produce a like certificate, under the hand of one at least of the Principal Officers and Commanders of our Navy, who hath served us as a Commander, as also of two other Commanders, one whereof to have been a Flag-Officer, and the other a Commander of one of our ships of the first or second rate, or in case no Flag-Officer shall by their distance from town be at that time to be resorted to, some other like Commander of a first or second rate ship, jointly signifying their being (upon a solemn examination of the said person on that behalf had at the Office of our Navy) fully satisfied in his ability to judge of and perform the duty of an able seaman and midshipman, and his having attained to a sufficient degree of knowledge in the Theory of Navigation capacitating him thereto.

63. A RE-EXAMINATION

Pepys to Navy Officers, March 26, 1678.

My Lords and Gentlemen,

Whereas the bearer, Mr McDonnel, relying upon the improvements he has made of his knowledge in the theory and practice of Navigation since his being examined therein, has made a second application to his Majesty that he may be admitted to a re-examination according to the establishment lately made by his Majesty bearing date the 18th of December last, touching the qualifications of persons pretending to the office of lieutenant in his Majesty's ships; these are, &c. (in the usual words).

While the above letter shows that not all candidates passed the examination for the rank of lieutenant, there is abundant evidence that Charles frequently gave commissions to undeserving applicants. The loose habits and neglect of duty of the 'gentlemen captains' had the worst possible effects upon discipline. The following extracts are typical of many to be found in Pepys's diary and letter-books.

64. 'Gentlemen Captains' Again

(*a*) *Diary*, October 20, 1666.

Commissioner Middleton[1] says that the fleet was in such a condition as to discipline, as if the Devil had commanded it; so much wickedness of all sorts. Enquiring how it come to pass that so many ships had miscarried this year, he enquired: and the pilots do say, that they dare not do nor go but as the Captains will have them; and, if they offer to do otherwise, the Captains swear they will run them through. He says that he heard Captain Digby, my Lord of Bristol's son, a young fellow that never was but one year, if that, in the fleet, say that he did hope he should not see a tarpaulin have the command of a ship within these twelve months.

(*b*) Pepys to Capt. Killigrew, December 22, 1673. (Pepysian Library, No. 2849, p. 433.)

I have received your letter of the 20th instant, and as to that part of it which concerns the character you give of Mr Clinton, I should very willingly have found it to have mentioned the other qualifications of a good sea officer besides that of valour, his Majesty being enough satisfied that that without sobriety and seamanship is lost, and too often proves rather fatal to the service than truly useful.

(*c*) S. Pepys to Capt. Rooth, January 24, 1673/4. (Pepysian Library, No. 2850, p. 61.)

I am much importuned by some persons of quality at court for the obtaining some employment for one Capt. Clinton, a gentleman of an honourable family, kinsman to Capt. Killigrew, and a reformado[2] (as I take it) at this time with him in the *Monck*. For the rendering which the more justificable for me to give one to, I did some time since write to Capt. Killigrew for a character of this gentleman, who in answer tells me that he apprehends him fit for a sea officer, by reason he hath been with him a whole year at sea and in three engagements, where he saith he behaved himself like a gentleman and an under-

[1] Colonel Thos. Middleton, Commissioner at Portsmouth, Surveyor in 1667.

[2] An officer with rank but no command.

standing man, a character which I confess wants a good deal of that which must lead me to think a man fit to make a sea officer of: I mean downright diligence, sobriety, and seamanship, without which no man can serve his Majesty as he ought, or at least will ever be so thought by me to do. In case, therefore, while you remain in the Downs you can have an opportunity of informing yourself truly and thoroughly in the good or bad qualifications of this gentleman, I entreat you to make use of it and give me an impartial account of what you shall learn concerning him; for as no man living can be more inclined than myself to favour a gentleman that is a true seaman, so neither is there any man more sensible than (after many years' observation) I am, of the ruinous consequences of an over-hasty admitting persons to the office and charge of seamen upon the bare consideration of their being gentlemen.

I remain

Your very affectionate friend & humble servant,

S. PEPYS.

(*d*) Pepys to Sir John Holmes, April 18, 1679.

You are greatly in the right in what you observe and wish touching that distinction so much laboured to be kept up by some between Gentlemen and Tarpaulin Commanders, and the liberty taken by the first of thinking themselves above the necessity of obeying orders and conforming themselves to the rules and discipline of the navy, in reliance upon the protection secured to them therein through the quality of their friends at court. And as long as I have the fortune of remaining in the place I am, I will continue to do my part towards the rectifying of it, let the consequence to my particular be the worst they and their friends can make it.

65. ARMAMENTS IN 1677

The following is one of the tables from the 'solemn, universal, and unalterable adjustment of the gunning and manning of the whole fleet' adopted on November 3, 1677. The ships given are the largest and smallest of each rate. (In the great building programme of this year—one first-rate of 1500 tons and 100 guns, 9 second-rates of 1300 tons each and 90 guns, and 20 third-rates of 1000 tons each and 70 guns—the armament of each rate was homogeneous.) (*N.R.S.* XXVI, p. 235.)

Rates	Names	Numbers, Natures, and Weights					
		Lower Deck			Middle Deck		
		Number	Nature	Weight in tons	Number	Nature	Weight
1st	*Royal Sovereign* {	26 24	Cannon of 7	78 72	28 26	24- p'ders	51 47¼
	St Michael {	Not given ...	...	...	...	...	...
2nd	*Royal Katherine* {	26 24	Demi- cannon	58¼ 53¾	26 24	Whole culv.	41¼ 37¾
	Rainbow {	22 20	,, ,,	46 41¾	22 20	Demi- culv.	37¼ 30
3rd	*Edgar* {	26 24	,, ,,	63 58	...	...	...
	Dunkirk {	24 22	24- p'ders	46½ 42½	...	...	...
4th	*Leopard* {	24 22	,, ,,	50 45¾	...	...	...
	Nonsuch {	20 18	Demi- culv.	25¾ 23	...	...	...
5th	*Sapphire* {	18 16		28 23¾	...	...	...
	Rose {	16 14		20 17½	...	...	...
6th	*Lark* {	... ...	... ...		... ...	... ...	
	Young Spragge {	... ...	... ...		... ...	... ...	

of the Guns carried on each Deck

Upper Deck			Quarter-Deck and Forecastle			Poop			Total		
Number	Nature	Weight	Number	Nature	Weight	Number	Nature	Weight in cwts.	Number	Weight	—
28	Demi-	38	14	Light	9.4	4	3-	16	100	177	War at home
26	culv.	35¼	10	saker	9.19	4	p'ders	16	90	162¼	Peace, and war abroad
...	...		...	...		...	...		90		
...	...		...	...		...	...		80		
24	Saker	26¾	8	„	5	...	...		84	131¼	War
20	„	22¼	6	„	3¾	...	...		74	117½	Peace
14	„	18	6	„	3	...	...		64	101¼	W.
10	„	16	4	„	3	...	...		54	90¾	P.
26	12-	43	16	„	9.14	4		16	72	116½	W.
24	p'ders	39½	12	„	6.17	2		8	62	104¾	P.
24	Demi-	28½	10	„	5.12	2		8	60	81	W.
20	culv.	23¾	10	„	5	...	...		52	71¼	P.
22	Saker	23	8	„	4	...	...		54	77	W.
18	„	18¾	6		3	...	...		46	67½	P.
18	„	12¼	4		1½	...	...		42	39½	W.
14	„	9½	4		1½	...	...		36	34	P.
10	Light	8½	4	Minion	1½	...	...		32	38	W.
8	saker	6¾	4	„	1½	...	...		28	32	P.
8		4¾	4		1¼	...	...		28	28½	W.
8		4¾	4		1¼	...	...		26	26	P.
16	Saker	13¼	2		¾	...	...		18	14	W.
16	„	13¼	...	...		...	...		16	13¼	P.
10		5¼	...	...		...	...		10	5¼	W.
10		4	...	...		...	...		10	4	P.

66. Distribution of Ships in time of Peace

The corollary of the disappearance of merchantmen from the war-fleet and of the establishment of a permanent fighting navy was the protection of the former by the latter, in peace as well as in war. (The Commonwealth Navy had convoyed merchantmen as far as the Mediterranean.)

A Proposal for reducing the Charge of the Navy to £200,000 per Annum[1]. (Sir William Coventry, 1667; quoted by Granville Penn, II, p. 528.)

The other part of the navy to be considered is the charge of setting ships to sea for ordinary uses in times of peace. To which, if £100,000 more[2] be allotted, his Majesty may, during the winter, maintain at sea ten ships, of the rates following:

Of the 3rd rate	1, bearing 200 men
4th rate	2	250
5th rate	4	320
6th rate	3	105
		875

For the summer, his Majesty may maintain twenty-four ships, of the rates following:

Of the 2nd rate	1, bearing 280 men
3rd rate	2	400
4th rate	5	625
5th rate	9	720
5th rate	7	245
		2270

With the winter fleet, his Majesty may keep at

Tangier and the Mediterranean	1 or 2
Jamaica	1 or 2
Ireland	2
Narrow seas	4

If it shall be thought fit, one or two may be deducted from the summer fleet, and the winter guard increased.

[1] Approved by the King in Council, March 16, 1668/9.
[2] In addition to the charges in harbour.

With the summer fleet, his Majesty may keep at

Jamaica	2
Tangier and the Mediterranean	6
Ireland	3
Greenland	1
Iceland and Westmondy	2
Newfoundland	2
Land's End	2
Downs, herring fishing, and all accidental occasions	5
For Norway trade	1

67. LEAD SHEATHING

Pepys to Sir John Narbrough, at Leghorn, June 14, 1675. (Letter-book IV, p. 132, Pepysian Library.)

I have not omitted to inform his Majesty touching your observation touching Lead Sheathing, and the extraordinary damage which you seem to have taken notice of to arise to the ironwork from that manner of sheathing. Which observation though his Majesty well approves of, as that which may lead us to some further inquiries on the subject, yet he doth not seem to incline to your philosophy upon it, by which you do impute that excess of rust in the iron to its being covered with lead and nailed with copper nails, it not appearing to him how lead and nails should have any such effect upon the iron. However (as I told you) it doth administer matter both to you there and the Officers of the Navy here for having more particular regard for the future to the condition of the ironwork of ships so sheathed, which shall hereafter fall within their and your view, and in the meantime hath led his Majesty to the making this use of that other part of your note, which relates to the seas washing away by degrees the very substance of the lead, to direct the Officers of the Navy to consider whether it may not be reasonable to increase something the thickness of our lead sheathing, in order to its better resisting the force and fretting virtue of the sea.

68. Learning from Foreigners

At the Restoration the French navy consisted of twenty or thirty vessels all told; by 1677, thanks to the zeal of Colbert, it numbered 270. In that year Parliament voted £600,000 for building 30 ships of the first three rates. Henceforth, throughout the eighteenth century, English naval architects were markedly inferior to those of France.

Sir Anthony Deane's 'Observations touching the Improvement of the English Navy from Foreigners.' (*Naval Minutes*, p. 268. Pepys Lib.)

In the years '72 and '73 the French brought a squadron of about 35 ships to the Spithead at Portsmouth which were to join with us against the Dutch. There were several excellent ships with 2½ decks that carried from 60 to 74 guns, more especially one called the *Superbe*, which his Majesty and Royal Highness went on board of. This ship was greatly commended both by the French and English that went on board her. She was 40 foot broad, carried 74 guns and 6 months' provisions, and but 2½ decks; our frigates, being narrower, could not store so much provisions nor carry their guns so far from the water. Which Sir A. D. observing measured the ship and gave his Majesty an account thereof, who was pleased to command A. D. to build the *Harwich* as near as he could of the *Superbe's* dimension; which was done according with such general satisfaction as to be the pattern for the 2nd and 3rd Rates built by the late Act of Parliament, which is generally agreed to be without exception, and the highest improvement that is known to this day.

As to our 3-deck-ships, the French and Dutch build them upwards of 44 foot broad; but we build none of our deck ships of the 3 Rate above 41 broad, and several under; by which means the *Henry*, the *Katherine*, etc., were useless until they were girdled. And to prevent the like for the future, his Majesty has directed those nine three-deck-ships of the 2nd Rate built and abuilding to be near 45 foot broad, which is another improvement we had not till the year '73, the builders of England before that time having not well considered it that breadth only will make a stiff ship.

69. THE RESULTS OF NEGLECT

In 1679 the excitement caused by the Popish Plot led to the virtual banishment of the Duke of York (who had continued to advise the king in private even after the Test Act), to the imprisonment of Pepys, and to the appointment of new and inexperienced Admiralty Commissioners. 'No king,' wrote Pepys, 'ever did so unaccountable a thing to oblige his people by, as to dissolve a Commission of the Admiralty then in his own hand, who best understands the business of the sea of any prince the world ever had, and things never better done, and put it into hands which he knew were wholly ignorant thereof, sporting himself with their ignorance.' This is not the jaundiced verdict of a disappointed placeman: by this time Pepys was absorbed in the navy, the ruin of which hurt him more than his own dismissal. The 30 new ships were allowed to rot: Pepys demolished the excuse that their construction and materials were faulty, and exposed the real causes.

Pepys, *Memoirs of the Royal Navy* (1690).

The present effects of which last papers and the observations next preceding amounting to nothing less than a plain detection of the vanity of those suggestions touching the root of this calamity, nought remained whereon the same could with any appearance of consequence be charged, save the plain omission of the necessary and ordinary cautions used for the preserving of new-built ships. Divers of them appearing not to have been once graved[1] nor brought into dock, since they were launched. Others, that had been docked, sent out again in a condition needing to be brought in a second time. Their holds not cleaned nor aired, but (for want of gratings and opening their hatches and scuttles) suffered to heat and moulder, till I have with my own hands gathered toadstools growing in the most considerable of them, as big as my fists. Some not once heeled or breamed[2] since their building, but exposed in hot weather to the sun, broiling in their buttocks and elsewhere, for want of cooling with water (according to the practice of our own, as well as all foreign nations), and that exposure yet magnified by their want of ballast for bringing them deep enough into the water. Port-ropes also wanting

[1] Equivalent to 'breaming'; *vide* n. 2.
[2] Breaming is when a ship is brought aground or on the careen to be trimmed, that is, to be made clean; they burn off the old weeds or stuff which hath gathered filth which they usually do either with reeds, broom, old ropes or the like. (Mainwaring.)

wherewith to open the ports, for airing them in dry weather, and scuppers upon their gun-decks in wet, to prevent the sinking of rain through their shrunken seams into their holds and among their timbers. Planks not opened upon the first discovery of their decays, nor pieces put in where defective; but instead thereof, repaired only with caps of board and canvas. Which ought also to have been done upon the ordinary estimate of the navy, that provides for everything needful to the preservation of ships in harbour, but more especially for the graving one-third of the whole every year; whereas some, even of the old ships, appear not to have been so looked after, in five or six.

From which, and other like omissions, it could not but fall out (as indeed it did) that some of these unfortunate ships were already become rotten, while others built of the very same stuff, at the same place, by the same hand, and within the very same time for merchant service, succeeded well and continued so.

70. Administrative Difficulties in the Second Dutch War

S.P. Dom. Ch. II, clii, No. 45.

Portsmouth,
29th March, 1666.

Sir,

I have received both yours of the 27th instant. In answer to that relating to the *Mars,* I am of my former opinion, that without much cost in boxing out her stern to amend her steerage she cannot be fit for any service; for that all the men that came in her generally saith she is not to be governed at sea, and several other captains tell me they were fearful to be near her at any time; so that I judge that work is fit and of necessity to [be] done if she go any voyage.

Then she is so tender sided, that the men that came in her were afraid she would have drowned them before they could recover this place, and truth is any man that seeth her must judge her to be a tender ship, especially having so great a weight of ordnance in her as she hath; yet I am apt to believe for the New England trade, with only 24 or 26 guns of a reasonable weight, the ship, being boxed out in her stern, may be a very serviceable ship for many years, for with masts they may keep in her what ballast they please to make her stiff. I shall speedily appoint an appraisement to be made of her and send it to you.

I am now in your other of the 27th instant, in answer to which Mr Tippets will bring a draught of the dock with him when he cometh to London, and I doubt not but he will give you such satisfaction in everything relating to the dock that you will forthwith order the doing it with all expedition, for that I verily believe the King will save the whole charge of it in one year after finished in men's labour, besides by how much better the work will be done, I need not trouble you with to tell you, and there is no doubt that, had we a dock sufficient for 2^d and 3^d rate ships, besides that we have, the King's ships which have been fitted from hence this winter had been at sea two months since with the same men that we have had, and prevented much other damage which is done afloat and not to be prevented; and this I presume I can in reason make appear, that no part of England that I know is more proper for docks than this place, for third rate ships downward, yet we had the *Swiftsure* in this winter; for springs we need not fear. As to Capt. Teate's despatch from hence, surely we shall have all things on board in 20 days, and in that time I believe she may be ready to sail.

I am glad I am not mistaken in the not having the masts made, for that workmen are very scarce with us, several having died this winter, and indeed not the worst of our workmen. I take notice of the size of the masts ordered to be sent, which shall be done accordingly.

I am not only sorry but ashamed to see such men as are sent from Devonshire; an affidavit of two of them I send to Sir William Coventry, by which you may perceive how the King is served by them that are employed to impress men; for not one seaman of 10 of them that cometh to this place.

Capt. Teate brought 66 people with him. I confess, albeit several of them are pitiful people, yet they are much better than them that come in the *Golden Lion* from Dartmouth. There is, notwithstanding, but 3 of them discharged, one of which had the falling sickness, a lame arm, and no seaman; another had the dead palsy on one side and had not any use of his right arm; the third as bad as any of the other unwell comers, a pitiful person, and all so extreme lousy that it was a sad sight to see them; but all that are sound and well is continued; yet some of them are put sick on shore.

I did in my former give you an account that Mr Mayor was at London when this business was prosecuted, and that his deputy was here, and did tell you that the men were cleared without bail, neither had I the least notice of it until we came to pay the rope-makers. I saw the man that bought the ropes come for his wages. I confess I wondered at it, and demanded of him how he came out of jail. He told me he was quitted. I demanded who quitted him. He told me the Mayor which was then in absence of Capt. Johnson, old Mr Cobberly. I told him if Mr Mayor had quitted him out of prison, I would put him out of the King's service and out of his wages; so he went away without his wages. I suppose the King oweth 8 or 9 months' wages, which will help for the goods he bought. This is all I know; however, it's believed the bail that is now taken is since the trouble that hath been about it. As to Capt. Johnson, since I showed your letter he hath absented himself very little, and I am apt to believe will be very careful for the future; for he tells me he will wholly give up the business of the town unless it be upon some extraordinary occasion, when of necessity he must be there; and I believe you will not for the future have any occasion of dislike of him.

The placing the store in place mentioned cannot give any interruption to the spinners, and it shall be carried out with all diligence as soon as bricks and lime can be got to carry it out. I shall order a survey of the boats and send it to you speedily.

As to the sawyers, they are half sick, and I fear some of them will die. They are thoroughly humbled, and petition upon petition, and I could almost petition for them too, albeit I am very angry with the men showing them so much kindness as to procure order from you to pay them their money here, which was a great kindness to them in regard it was by bill; and promising them that I would pay them myself if you sent not money down, all would not do; yet, since mercy is better than sacrifice, if they do so any more, I dare almost undertake to be punished for them; however, do therein as God shall direct you. Their wives and poor children are to be pitied. However you order them, send none down; for Mr Tippets tells me this country affords' sufficient, but I have not heart to press them, not having any press warrant.

The Capt. of the *Essex* come to town last night. It cannot be convenient for the King's service that them that have the charge of it to be absent: they leave business with the Lieut., and it may be he is either a fool or knave, and so the business is carried on accordingly. I would wish this error were amended: it may be done with ease.

I am offered 600 load of timber—100 and odd load of stranders and knees, the rest most of it compass timber. It's said to be the best parcel that is fallen in this country, but the price is 48s. per load to take his pay in course according to the act. I have appointed him that hath it to be with me Thursday next, and then to hear his answer. I beg your speedy order about it, and about the hemp I last advised of.

The *Delft* is arrived from Jersey. The Captain tells me she is very foul: it's about 5 months since he was cleansed here; his victuals is spent and long boat lost: few ships goeth out but lose their boats. I never saw or heard of so little care as now is found generally of almost all the officers in general: they act as if it were their duty to destroy rather than to preserve. Pray advise whether the *Delft* shall come in to clean or not.

(In margin: Leave her; refer him to Sir W. Coventry.)
Endorsed: Portsmth, 29th March (1666).

Comr. MIDLETON.

71. THE DUKE OF YORK'S ADDITIONAL INSTRUCTIONS, April 10 or 18, 1665

The following instructions (71–74) should be read in the light of the battles after which they were issued. For a full discussion of their importance, reference should be made to Sir Julian Corbett's 'Fighting Instructions' (*N.R.S.* XXIX, pp. 110–172), where he makes clear the conflict between two tactical schools—that represented by the Duke of York and Penn, 'which inclined to formality, and by pedantic insistence on well-meant principles tended inevitably to confuse the means with the end,' and that of Monck and Rupert, 'which was inclined anarchically to submit all rules to the solvent of hard fighting, and to take tactical risks and unfetter individual initiative to almost any extent rather than miss a chance of overpowering the enemy by a sudden well-timed blow.'

N.R.S. xxix, p. 126.

Additional Instructions for Fighting

1. In all cases of fight with the enemy the commanders of his majesty's ships are to endeavour to keep the fleet in one line, and as much as may be to preserve the order of battle which shall have been directed before the time of fight.

2. If the enemy stay to fight us, we having the wind, the headmost squadron of his majesty's fleet shall steer for the headmost of the enemy's ships.

3. If the enemy have the wind of us and come to fight us, the commanders of his majesty's fleet shall endeavour to put themselves in one line close upon a wind.

4. In the time of fight in reasonable weather, the commanders of his majesty's fleet shall endeavour to keep about the distance of half a cable's length one from the other, but so as that according to the discretion of the commanders they vary that distance according as the weather shall be, and the occasion of succouring our own or assaulting the enemy's ships shall require.

6. None of the ships of his majesty's fleet shall pursue any small number of ships of the enemy before the main body of the enemy's fleet shall be disabled or shall run.

8. In case it shall please God that any of his majesty's ships be lamed in fight, not being in probability of sinking nor encompassed by the enemy, the following ships shall not stay under pretence of securing them, but shall follow their leaders and endeavour to do what service they can upon the enemy, leaving the securing of the lame ships to the sternmost of our ships, being assured that nothing but beating the body of the enemy's fleet can effectually secure the lame ships. This article is to be observed notwithstanding any seeming contradiction in the fourth or fifth articles of the instructions formerly given.

Duke of York's Supplementary Order, April 27, 1665.

1. When the admiral would have all the ships to fall into the order of 'Battailia' prescribed, the union flag shall be put

into the mizen peak of the admiral ship; at sight whereof the admirals of the other squadrons are to answer it by doing the like.

2. When the admiral would have the other squadrons to make more sail, though he himself shorten sail, a white ensign shall be put on the ensign staff of the admiral ship.

72. PRINCE RUPERT'S ADDITIONAL INSTRUCTIONS, 1666

N.R.S. xxix, p. 129.

1. In case of an engagement the commander of every ship is to have a special regard to the common good, and if any flagship shall, by any accident whatsoever, stay behind or be likely to lose company, or be out of his place, then all and every ship or ships belonging to such flag is to make all the way possible to keep up with the admiral of the fleet and to endeavour the utmost that may be the destruction of the enemy, which is always to be made the chiefest care.

This instruction is strictly to be observed, notwithstanding the seventeenth article in the Fighting Instructions formerly given out[1].

2. When the admiral of the fleet makes a weft[2] with his flag, the rest of the flag officers are to do the like, and then all the best sailing ships are to make what way they can to engage the enemy, that so the rear of our fleet may the better come up; and so soon as the enemy makes a stand then they are to endeavour to fall into the best order they can.

73. FINAL FORM OF THE DUKE OF YORK'S ORDERS, 1673

N.R.S. xxix, p. 152.

3. In case the enemy have the wind of the admiral and fleet, and they have sea-room enough, then they are to keep the wind as close as they can lie, until such time as they see an opportunity

---

[1] *I.e.* Article 1 of the Additional Instructions on p. 85.

[2] 'A flag stopped together at the head and middle portion and slightly rolled up lengthwise.'

by gaining their wakes to divide the enemy's fleet; and if the van of his majesty's fleet find that they have the wake of any considerable part of them, they are to tack and stand in, and strive to divide the enemy's body; and that squadron that shall pass first, being got to windward, is to bear down on those ships to leeward of them; and the middle squadron is to keep her wind, and to observe the motion of the enemy's van, which the last squadron is to second; and both of these squadrons are to do their utmost to assist or relieve the first squadron that divided the enemy's fleet.

(The *Admiralty MS.* has this *Observation*: 'Unless you can outstretch their headmost ships there is hazard in breaking through the enemy's line, and it commonly brings such disorders in the line of battle that it may be rather omitted unless an enemy press you near a lee shore. For if, according to this instruction, when you have got the wind you are to press the enemy, then those ships which are on each side of them shall receive more than equal damages from each other's shot if near, and in case the enemy but observed the seventh instruction— that is, to tack with equal numbers with you—then is your fleet divided and not the enemy's.')

7. In case his majesty's fleet have the wind of the enemy, and that the enemy stand towards them, and they towards the enemy, then the van of his majesty's fleet shall keep the wind; and when they are come within a convenient distance from the enemy's rear, they shall stay until their whole line is come up within the same distance from the enemy's van; and then their whole line is to tack (every ship in his own place), and to bear down upon them so nigh as they can (without endangering their loss of wind); and to stand along with them, the same tacks aboard, still keeping the enemy to leeward, and not suffering them to tack in their van; and in case the enemy tack in the rear first, he who is in the rear of his majesty's is to tack first, with as many ships, divisions, or squadrons as are those of the enemy's; and if all the enemy's ships tack, their whole line is to follow, standing along with the same tacks aboard as the enemy doth.

74. Lord Dartmouth's Instructions, Oct. 1688

N.R.S. xxix, p. 170.

5. If the admiral should have the wind of the enemy, when other ships of the fleet are in the wind of the admiral, then upon hoisting up a blue flag at the mizen yard or mizen topmast, every such ship is to bear up into his wake or grain upon pain of severe punishment. In this case, whether the line hath been broke or disordered by the shifting of the wind, or otherwise, each ship or division are not unreasonably to strive for their proper places in the first line of battle given, but they are to form a line, the best that may be, with the admiral, and with all the expedition that can be, not regarding what place or division they fall into or between.

6. In case his majesty's fleet have the wind of the enemy, and that the enemy stands towards them and they towards the enemy, then the van of his majesty's fleet shall keep the wind, and when they are come at a convenient distance from the enemy's rear they shall stay until their own whole line is come up within the same distance from the enemy's van; and then the whole line is to tack, every ship in his own place, and to bear down upon them so nigh as they can without endangering the loss of the wind—(Note that they are not to bear down all at once, but to observe the working of the admiral and to bring to as often as he thinks fit, the better to bring his fleet to fight in good order; and at last only to lask away[1] when they come near within shot towards the enemy as much as may be, and not bringing their heads to bear against the enemy's broadsides)— and to stand along with them the same tacks on board, still keeping the enemy to leeward, and not suffering them to tack in their van.

---

[1] *I.e.* to come down aslant, with a quartering wind. Neglect of this precaution caused much loss in the eighteenth century.

WILLIAM III AND ANNE

OF the many illustrations of strategic problems furnished by this period, the best known is the Beachy Head campaign, the starting-point for all discussions of 'a fleet in being.' The phrase was coined by Torrington on this occasion; the idea, if not new, had never been so clearly expressed.

75. TORRINGTON EXPLAINS HIS STRATEGY

The Earl of Torrington to the Earl of Nottingham[1], June 26, 1690 (Quoted in *The Earl of Torrington's Speech to the House of Commons, In November*, 1690, published 1710.)

My Lord,

Every day since my last we have been in sight of the French fleet. Tuesday we were strengthened with Admiral Evertsen, two Dutch, and two English men-of-war, in all five. Wednesday morning with the day we got under sail with 55 men-of-war and 20 fireships, the wind easterly, with intention to attack the French; but the morning proved so hazy that we were forced to anchor again. The wind came about to the south-west, and in half an hour it cleared up again. Then we saw the French fleet in a line under sail about three leagues from us to the windward. We got immediately under sail, and stood upon a line to the southward, the Blue having the van. The wind favouring us a little, I saw a probability of weathering two-thirds of the French fleet, and made a sign for the fleet to tack, which they accordingly did, and stood directly with them. The French tacked and stood from us, and went a point or two from the wind till night; both fleets then anchored. It is unaccountable why the French shunned us; for though they had many ships to leeward and scattered, they had enough in a body to have given us more than sufficient work. I do acknowledge my first intention of attacking them a rashness that will admit of no better excuse, than that, though I did believe them stronger than we are, I did not believe it to so great a degree. I find by their manner of working that, notwithstanding their strength, they act with some caution, and seem to be willing to

[1] Secretary of State, and member of the Council of Nine which advised Mary during William's absence in Ireland.

add to the advantage of force that of wind too. Their great strength and caution have put soberer thoughts into my head, and have made me very heartily give God thanks they declined the battle yesterday. And indeed I shall not think myself very unhappy if I can get rid of them without fighting, unless it may be upon equaller terms than for the present I can see any prospect of. I find I am not the only man of that opinion, for a Council of War I called this morning unanimously agreed we are by all manner of means to shun fighting with them, especially if they have the wind of us, and retire, if we cannot avoid it otherwise, even to the Gunfleet, the only place we can with any manner of probability make our party good with them in the condition we are in. We have now had a pretty good view of their fleet, which consists of near, if not quite, 80 men-of-war fit to lie in a line, and 30 fireships, a strength that puts me besides the hopes of success if we should fight, and really may not only endanger the losing of the fleet, but at least the quiet of our country too; for if we are beaten, they, being absolute masters of the sea, will be at great liberty of doing many things they dare not attempt whilst we observe them, and are in a possibility of joining Vice-Admiral Killigrew and our ships to the westward[1]. If I find a possibility, I will get by them to the westward to join those ships; if not, I mean to follow the result of the Council of War. In the meantime, I wish there might be speedy orders given to fit out with speed whatever ships of war are in the River of Chatham, and that the ships to the westward proceed to Portsmouth, and from thence, if the French come before the River, they may join us over the Flats. This is the best advice I can give at present; but had I been believed in winter, the kingdom had not received this insult. Your Lordship now knows the opinion of the Flag Officers of both Dutch and English fleets, which I desire you will lay before her Majesty, and to assure her that, if she has other considerations, whenever she pleases to signify her pleasure, her commands shall be punctually obeyed, the consequence be what it will.

Off the Isle of Wight,
June 26, 1690.

[1] Killigrew was coming from the Mediterranean with 16 ships of the line; Sir Cloudesley Shovel had 6 in Irish waters.

76. Mary orders Torrington to fight

Egerton MSS. 2621, f. 91.

Marie R.

Right Trusty & Right Well-Beloved Cousin & Counsellor, We greet you well. We have heard your Letter dated June 26th to our Secretary of State, & do not doubt of your Skill & Conduct in this important Conjuncture, to take all Opportunities of Advantage against the Enemy: But we apprehend the Consequences of your retiring to the Gunfleet to be so fatal, that We choose rather that you should upon any advantage of the Wind give battle to the Enemy, than retreat farther than is necessary to get an advantage upon the Enemy. But in case you find it necessary to go to the Westward of the French Fleet, in order to the better joining with you our Ships from Plymouth, or any others coming from the Westward, We leave it to your discretion, so as you by no means ever lose sight of the French Fleet, whereby they may have Opportunities of making attempts upon the Shore, or in the Rivers of Medway or Thames, or get away without fighting. And so We bid you heartily farewell. Given at our Court at Whitehall, this 29th Day of June, 1690. In the Second Year of Our Reign.

By Her Majesty's Command.

To Our Right Trusty & Right Well-Beloved Cousin & Counsellor, Arthur Earl of Torrington, &c.

77. Torrington's Defence of his Tactics at Beachy Head

Speech, p. 29.

It is true,* the French made no great Advantage of their Victory, though they put us to a great Charge in keeping up the Militia; but had I fought otherwise, our Fleet had been totally lost, & the Kingdom had lain open to an Invasion. What then would have become of us in the Absence of his Majesty, & most of the Land-Forces? As it was, most Men were in fear that the French would invade; but I was always of another

Opinion, which several Members of this Honourable House can witness: for I always said, that whilst we had a Fleet in being, they would not dare to make an Attempt.

In my Letter of the 29th of June, the matter is stated pretty plain: whilst we observe the French, they can make no Attempt either on Sea or Shore, but with great disadvantage; and if we are beaten, all is exposed to their Mercy.

And notwithstanding the Reports, that the *Sovereign*[1] was not engaged, there is not a Third of the Ships in the Fleet, of Dutch & English, that have lost so many men by the Enemy's shot.

I now beg leave to answer such Objections, as I hear have been made.

First, That it is wondered I made a Gap in our Line.

I did it because our Line was shorter than the Enemy's; & because in the posture the Enemy lay, I thought it less dangerous to have an Interval near the centre, than leaving either the Van or Rear uncovered, & by it giving the Enemy an immediate Opportunity to weather us.

This I may be bold to say, That I have had time enough & cause enough to think of it; & that upon my word were the Battle to be fought over again, I do not know how to mend it, under the same Circumstances.

78. RUSSELL'S FIGHTING INSTRUCTIONS, 1691

The following instructions, issued in 1691 by Russell, were most probably the work of Torrington.

N.R.S. xxix, p. 188.

I. When the admiral would have the fleet draw into a line of battle, one ship ahead of another (according to the method given to each captain), he will hoist a union flag at the mizen peak, and fire a gun; and every flagship in the fleet is to make the same signal.

II. When the admiral would have the fleet draw into a line of battle, one ship abreast of another (according to the method given to each captain), he will hoist a union flag and a pennant at the mizen-peak, and fire a gun; and every flagship in the fleet is to do the same.

[1] Torrington's flag-ship.

III. When the admiral would have the admiral of the white and his whole squadron to tack, and endeavour to gain the wind of the enemy, he will spread a white flag under the flag at the main topmast-head, and fire a gun, which is to be answered by the flagships in the fleet; and when he would have the admiral of the blue do the same, he will spread a blue flag on that place.

IV. When the admiral would have the vice-admiral of the red, and his division, tack and endeavour to gain the wind of the enemy, he will spread a red flag from the cap at the fore topmast-head downward on the backstay. If he would have the vice-admiral of the white do the same, a white flag; if the vice-admiral of the blue, a blue flag at the same place.

V. When the admiral would have the rear-admiral of the red and his division tack and endeavour to gain the wind of the enemy, he will hoist a red flag at the flagstaff at the mizen topmast-head; if the rear-admiral of the white, a white flag; if the rear-admiral of the blue, a blue flag at the same place, and under the flag a pennant of the same colour.

VI. If the admiral be to leeward of the fleet, or any part of the fleet, and he would have them bear down into his wake or grain, he will hoist a blue flag at the mizen peak.

VII. If the admiral be to leeward of the enemy, and his fleet, or any part of them, to leeward of him, that he may bring those ships into a line, he will bear up with a blue flag at the mizen peak under the union flag, which is the signal for the line of battle; and then those ships to leeward are to use their utmost endeavour to get into his wake or grain, according to their stations in the line of battle.

VIII. If the fleet be sailing before the wind, and the admiral would have the vice-admiral and the ships of the starboard quarter to clap by the wind, and come to the starboard tack, then he will hoist upon the mizen topmast-head a red flag. And in case he would have the rear-admiral and the ships of the larboard quarter to come to their larboard tack, then he will hoist up a blue flag at the same place.

IX. When the admiral would have the van of the fleet to tack first, he will put abroad the union flag at the flagstaff on the fore topmast-head, and fire a gun, if the red flag be not abroad; but if the red flag be abroad, then the fore topsails shall be lowered a little, and the union flag shall be spread from the cap of the fore topmast downwards, and every flagship in the fleet is to do the same.

X. When the admiral would have the rear-admiral of the fleet tack first, he will hoist the union flag on the flagstaff at the mizen topmast-head, and fire a gun, which is to be answered by every flagship in the fleet.

XI. When the admiral would have all the flagships in the fleet come into his wake or grain, he will hoist a red flag at the mizen peak, and fire a gun; and the flagships in the fleet are to make the same signal.

XII. When the admiral would have the admiral of the white and his squadron make more sail, though himself shorten sail, he will hoist a white flag on the ensign staff; if the admiral of the blue, or he that commands in the third post, a blue flag at the same place; and every flagship in the fleet is to make the same signal.

XIII. As soon as the admiral shall hoist a red flag on the flagstaff at the fore topmast-head, every ship in the fleet is to use their utmost endeavour to engage the enemy, in the order the admiral has prescribed unto them.

XIV. When the admiral hoisteth a white flag at the mizen peak, then all the small frigates of his squadron that are not in the line of battle are to come under his stern.

XV. If the fleet is sailing by a wind in a line of battle, and the admiral would have them brace their headsails to the mast, he will hoist a yellow flag on the flagstaff at the mizen topmast-head, and fire a gun, which the flagships in the fleet are to answer. Then the ships in the rear are to brace to first.

XVI. The fleet lying in a line of battle, with their headsails to the mast, and if the admiral would have them fill and stand on, he will hoist a yellow flag on the flagstaff at the fore top-mast-head, and fire a gun, which the flagships in the fleet are to answer. Then the ships in the van are to fill first, and to stand on. If it happen, when this signal is to be made, that the red flag is abroad on the flagstaff at the fore topmast-head, the admiral will spread the yellow flag under the red.

XVII. If the admiral see the enemy's fleet standing towards him, and he has the wind of them, the van of the fleet is [to] make sail till they come the length of the enemy's rear, and our rear abreast of the enemy's van; then he that is in the rear of our fleet is to tack first, and every ship one after another, as fast as they can, throughout the line, that they may engage on the same tack with the enemy. But in case the enemy's fleet should tack in their rear, our fleet is to do the same with an equal number of ships; and whilst they are in fight with the enemy, to keep within half a cable's length one of another, or if the weather be bad, according to the direction of the commanders.

When the admiral would have the ship that leads the van of the fleet (or the headmost ship in the fleet) when they are in a line of battle, hoist, lower, set or haul up any of his sails, the admiral will spread a yellow flag under that at the main topmast-head, and fire a gun, which the flagships that have flags at the main topmast-head are to answer; and those flagships that have not, are to hoist the yellow flag on the flagstaff at the main topmast-head, and fire a gun. Then the admiral will hoist, lower, set or haul up the sail he would have the ship that leads the van do.

XVIII. If the admiral and his fleet have the wind of the enemy, and they have stretched themselves in a line of battle, the van of the admiral's fleet is to steer with the van of the enemy's and there to engage them.

XIX. Every commander is to take care that his guns are not fired till he is sure he can reach the enemy upon a point-blank; and by no means to suffer his guns to be fired over by any of our own ships.

XX. None of the ships in the fleet shall pursue any small number of the enemy's ships till the main body be disabled or run.

XXI. If any of the ships in the fleet are in distress, and make the signal, which is a weft with the jack or ensign, the next ship to them is strictly required to relieve them.

XXII. If the admiral, or any flagship, should be in distress, and make the usual signal, the ships in the fleet are to endeavour to get up as close into a line, between him and the enemy, as they can; having always an eye to defend him, if the enemy should come to annoy him in that condition.

XXIII. In case any ship in the fleet should be forced to go out of the line to repair damages she has received in battle, the next ships are to close up the line.

The first three figures illustrate Article IV of the Fighting Instructions, the fourth is from the Duke of York's Instructions for Fireships, 1672.

The four figures on this plate illustrate Articles XIII, XXVII and XXX
of the Fighting Instructions.

XXIV. If any flagship be disabled, the flag may go on board any ship of his own squadron or division.

XXV. If the enemy be put to the run, and the admiral thinks it convenient the whole fleet shall follow them, he will make all the sail he can himself after the enemy, and fire two guns out of his fore-chase; then every ship in the fleet is to use his best endeavour to come up with the enemy and lay them on board.

XXVI. If the admiral would have any particular flagship, and his squadron, or division, give chase to the enemy, he will make the same signal that is appointed for that flagship's tacking with his squadron or division, and weathering the enemy.

XXVII. When the admiral would have them give over chase, he will hoist a white flag at the fore topmast-head and fire a gun.

XXVIII. In case any ship in the line of battle should be disabled in her masts, rigging or hull, the ship that leads ahead of her shall take her a-tow and the division she is in shall make good the line with her. But the commander of the ship so disabled is not on any pretence whatever to leave his station till he has acquainted his flag or the next flag officer with the condition of his ship, and received his directions therein. And in case any commander shall be wanting in his duty, his flag or the next flag officer to him is immediately to send for the said commander from his ship and appoint another in his room.

XXIX. If the admiral would have any flag in his division or squadron cut or slip in the daytime, he will make the same signals that are appointed for those flagships, and their division or squadron, to tack and weather the enemy, as is expressed in the third, fourth, fifth, and sixth articles before going.

XXX. When the admiral would have the red squadron draw into a line of battle, abreast of one another, he will put abroad a flag striped red and white on the flagstaff at the main topmast-head, with a pennant under it, and fire a gun. If he would have the white squadron or those that have the second post in the fleet, to do the like, the signal shall be a flag striped red, white, and blue, with a pennant under it, at the aforesaid place. And if he would have the blue squadron to do the like he will put on the said place a Genoese ensign, together with a pennant.

But when he would have either of the said squadrons to draw into a line of battle, ahead of one another, he will make the aforesaid signals, without a pennant; which signals are to be answered by the flagships only of the said squadrons, and to be kept out till I take in mine. And if the admiral would have any vice-admiral of the fleet and his division draw into a line of battle as aforesaid, he will make the same signals at the fore topmast-head that he makes for that squadron at the main topmast-head. And for any rear-admiral in the fleet and his division, the same signals at the mizen topmast-head; which signals are to be answered by the vice- or rear-admiral.

In 1703 Rooke issued the above Instructions, with a few verbal alterations and the following additions:
(i) A provision in Art. XVII for the whole fleet to tack together, if the admiral thought fit.
(ii) A signal for forming line ahead with a large wind (Art. XXXI).
(iii) Art. XXXII: When the fleet is in the line of battle, the signals that are made by the admiral for any squadron or particular division are to be repeated by all the flags that are between the admiral and that squadron or division to whom the signal is made.
In this form they became the *Permanent Fighting Instructions* of the eighteenth century.

79. THE THEORY OF THE LINE

It is characteristic of the naval genius of the two peoples that, while the English originated the line ahead and developed it step by step, as experience dictated, it was a Frenchman who first wrote a reasoned and systematic treatise upon the subject. It is easier for a modern reader to understand the tactics of the period from Père Hoste's[1] book than from the sets of English fighting instructions, because he gives the reasons which they take for granted: the French Jesuit was logical; the English admirals were original.

L'Art des Armées Navales, 1697.

Part I, § 5 (The Order of Battle).

Remark 1. Before explaining more fully the order of battle, the advantages of the fleet to windward must be considered, and also those of the fleet to leeward.

[1] Paul Hoste, 1652–1700, Professor of Mathematics at the Royal College of Marine, Toulon. He accompanied d'Estrées and Tourville in their campaigns. One of his illustrations is reproduced on p. 106; the others have been reduced to diagrammatic form.

I. The fleet to windward can approach the enemy, when and as near as it pleases, as has been shown in the battle of the Texel. Thus, the fleet which is to windward can choose the time and the distance which suit it best.

II. If the fleet to windward be more numerous, it can send a detachment to attack the rear of the enemy, which will cause inevitable confusion. A more numerous fleet to leeward has not the same advantage, as its rear cannot attack the enemy to windward.

III. If several ships of the fleet to leeward are disabled, either in the van or rear, or even in the centre, the fleet to windward can more easily send fireships down on them, and more easily send detachments to attack any vessels attempting to escape. Thus, when several ships of the fleet A B are disabled, the fleet C D will send ships and fireships to destroy them, and will endeavour to cut off the van or rear of the enemy, and the wind will give such advantages for executing that object as will make it difficult for the fleet A B to defend itself.

IV. The weather position has the further advantage of being free from the inconveniences caused by the smoke in a ship to leeward.

1. The wind blows back the smoke of the guns, stifling the gunners, and interrupting their sight of the enemy. 2. The same smoke prevents the sailors from working the ship, and it is often mixed with sparks which burn the sails and the rigging, and cause a thousand accidents.

Remark 2.

It cannot be denied that a fleet to leeward possesses very great advantages; in fact, some have held the leeward to be at least as good as the weather position. But I think that on careful examination one will not agree with this view, but will find the advantage of the wind most desirable, whether one's fleet be stronger or weaker than the enemy. I admit that there are exceptional cases when the leeward position is preferable, for instance, when the wind is violent, or the sea high, or in an action between few or single ships; but when two large fleets are fighting under favourable weather conditions, the one to windward has a great advantage over the other. Still, the fleet to leeward has the following advantages:

I. The fleet to leeward engages on its weather side, and consequently its ships can use their lower batteries, without any fear that a gust of wind will make the water enter their ports. This is undoubtedly a very great advantage, especially in a fresh wind. One can hardly exaggerate the confusion among the best disciplined crew, when gusts make the vessel heel over from time to time, forcing them to close the ports against the waves.

II. A fleet to leeward can more easily cover its disabled ships. For if vessels of the fleet to leeward happen to be disabled, they have only to drop to leeward to withdraw from the fight and repair their damages without being exposed to the enemy's fire. This could not be done so easily by disabled ships belonging to the fleet to windward.

III. The fleet to leeward can more easily break off the action in case of need; for it has only to bear up in the order to be described later; while the fleet to windward cannot retire from the action except by breaking through the enemy, which is very dangerous.

Remark.

I quite realise that a fleet which bears up is running great risk if the enemy is in a state to pursue. But there are circumstances which may enable it to do so with impunity, e.g. the approach of night, a rising wind or sea, when the enemy is embarrassed with a convoy, etc.

Chapter VI, More Particular Explanation of the Order
of Battle.

II. Fleets should be ranged on one of the close-hauled lines for several reasons. 1. The fleet E F (Fig. 1), which is to windward (and sailing 8 points from the wind) would lose its advantage if it did not form a close-hauled line; for the fleet H G to leeward could gain the wind, or cut it. 2. The fleet to windward, E F, would allow the enemy, H G, to approach as much as it liked, and consequently to determine the range and the time of the battle. True, the fleet E F could haul to the wind, but this would entail two inconveniences; for the fleet E F would seem to flee if it sailed close to the wind without being ranged on a wind, and it would find it very difficult to preserve its line, for the ships would be in quarter line.

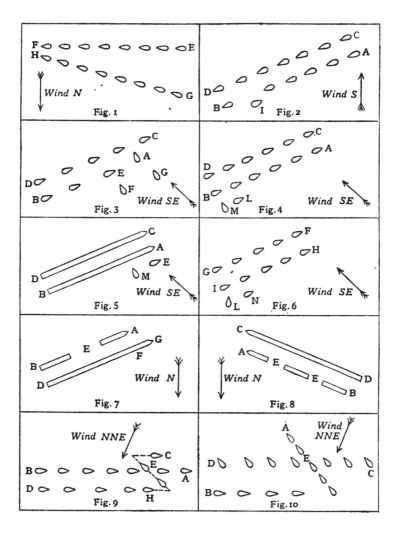

Fig. 1
Wind N

Fig. 2
Wind S

Fig. 3
Wind SE

Fig. 4
Wind SE

Fig. 5
Wind SE

Fig. 6
Wind SE

Fig. 7
Wind N

Fig. 8
Wind N

Fig. 9
Wind NNE

Fig. 10
Wind NNE

III. Another reason for placing the weathermost fleet on a wind is that the disabled ships may bè the more easily enabled to draw out of action; for if the ship I, in the fleet A B (Fig. 2), be disabled, she can keep away four points on the starboard tack, without falling to leeward on the enemy, who is in a close-hauled line on the port tack. Thus, provided she does not drift more to leeward than a ship would do under storm-sails, she will pass without difficulty to windward of her own fleet, and receive all necessary aid. This would not be the case if the fleet A B were in line 8 points from the wind.

Part V, Section VII. To Double upon the Enemy.

The more numerous fleet will endeavour to engage the enemy in such a way as to leave its rearmost ships astern, which will thereupon turn on the enemy to double upon him, and to place him between two fires.

Remark 1. If the more numerous fleet has the weather-gage, it can more easily double upon the enemy rear and place it between two fires; but if the more numerous fleet is to leeward, it should none the less leave its rear astern, because the wind may change during the action; besides, the fleet to leeward can gradually bear up as it fights, to allow its rear to hug the wind and double upon the enemy.

Remark 2. I know that many accomplished persons hold that the van of the enemy should be doubled upon; since, if the enemy van is once in disorder, it falls aboard of the rest of the fleet, and infallibly throws it into confusion. For if the leading ship, A, of the fleet A B (Fig. 3) finds itself dismasted, it falls aboard of the ships astern, which in turn fall aboard of the ships astern of them, and soon all the ships, no longer able to advance, foul each other and form a confused tangle. This will seem probable, if we do not reflect that the fleet A B is ranged on a line, with intervals which give room to the ship A to pass to windward of the ship E, which can facilitate this by bearing up a little, with no fear of confusion. The leading ship A could extricate itself still more easily if the fleet A B were to leeward; whence I conclude that it is no great advantage for the fleet C D to have doubled upon the van of A B, since the ships of the fleet A B which are crippled can withdraw without the ships G, F, being able to pursue them, unless they wish to be exposed to the whole fire of the enemy fleet, and to run the probable risk of destruction. If, on the other hand, the ships L, M, of the fleet C D (Fig. 4), have doubled upon the rear, B, and the ship B happens to be disabled, it cannot avoid becoming the prey of the ships L, M, which will fall upon it, or will force it aboard the rear, D.

Remark 3. Similarly, if the ships E, M, of the fleet C D (Fig. 5), had doubled upon the van, A, they would have run a serious risk of being destroyed; for if the ship E is crippled, how can it rejoin its own fleet? Will it not be easy for the enemy to find countless ways of destroying it? If, on the contrary, the ships L, N, of the fleet F G (Fig. 6), have doubled upon the rear, I, of the enemy, and the vessel L is crippled, it will remain astern without being attacked by the rear, I, which will be fully occupied with the ships G, N. (Example, La Hogue, 1692.)

Section VIII. To avoid being doubled.

To avoid being doubled it is essential to prevent the enemy from having ships astern of us, to which end one can adopt several methods when one is much inferior in number:

1. If one is to windward, one can ignore some of the enemy van, making one's van, A, engage their second division, F. In this manner their first division, F G (Fig. 7), will be almost useless, and if it wishes to carry a press of sail to tack on us, it will lose much time, and risk being separated by the calm which usually occurs in actions of this sort because of the loud reports of the guns. Again, one can leave a great gap, E, in the middle of the fleet, provided one takes the precautions necessary to prevent our van from being cut off. In this manner, however inferior one may be in number, one can prevent the enemy from having ships astern of one.

Example.

There are those who commend Admiral Herbert's method of drawing up his fleet, when he bore down on the French in the battle of Bevesier[1], 1690. Being inferior in number, he had resolved to make his main effort against our rear. He accordingly ordered the Dutch, who formed the van, to attack our second

[1] Beachy Head.

division; then he opened his fleet in the centre, leaving a large gap abreast of our centre; after which he opposed his English[1], in very close order, to our rear, and lay off slightly with his own division, so as to prevent the French from taking advantage of the gap he had left, to double on the Dutch. In effect this rendered our leading division almost useless, since it was forced to make a very long board to tack on the enemy's van; and, the wind having dropped, it had difficulty in coming into action in time to share the glory. On the other hand, the English, in extremely close order, had at first some advantage over our rear, which an accident caused to give way; but the vessels astern, inspired by the example of the Comte d'Estrées, Vice-Admiral of France, who commanded the rear division, made such a gallant resistance to the great number of English attacking them, that the latter, unable any longer to withstand the fire of the French, hugged the wind, and were towed by their boats to windward of the victors.

2. If the inferior fleet is to leeward, it can leave more of a gap in the centre, and less in the van; but it must have a small detachment of warships and fireships, to prevent the enemy from profiting by the gaps to divide the fleet.

3. Others prefer laying it down as a general rule, that the flag-officers of the inferior fleet should engage the flag-officers of the enemy; for by this means several enemy vessels will remain useless in the intervals, E (Fig. 8), and the enemy will not be able to double upon you.

Remark.

This method, however, has its drawbacks, for the leading and rear ships of each division are exposed to the fire of two ships, and it does not avoid the danger that the rear division may be doubled upon by the enemy rear. To obviate these drawbacks, one can put the biggest ships at the head and rear of each division, and one can ensure that the rear division does not leave enemy ships astern of it.

4. Others prefer that the three squadrons of the weaker fleet should each engage one of the enemy squadrons, taking care that each squadron lays abreast of the enemy in such a way as to

---

[1] *I.e.* his rear.

leave several enemy ships ahead of it, rather than any at all astern.

5. Finally, there are those who hold that the inferior fleet should leave between its ships intervals great enough to allow its line to equal that of the enemy; but this last course is undoubtedly the least good, for it enables the enemy to employ his whole force against the inferior fleet. I admit, however, that this method may be preferred to the others in certain circumstances, as when the enemy ships are considerably less powerful than those of the less numerous fleet.

Section X. To pass through the Enemy's Fleet.

1. One finds, in the accounts of the battles in the Channel between the English and the Dutch, that their fleets often passed through one another, i.e. the fleet C H D (Fig. 9), which was to leeward, having sailed a little ahead, tacked in succession and cut through the fleet A B at the point E, and having tacked a second time at the point C, gained the wind of the enemy. But the latter tacked in turn, and cut through the fleet which had just gained the wind. In this manner the two fleets passed through one another several times, which exposed them to be cut off, taken, and to have several ships destroyed on both sides.

Remark.

This manœuvre is as bold as it is delicate, and demands the highest professional skill for it to succeed.

2. To me it appears easy for the fleet C D to prevent the fleet A B from cutting through it. 1. When the fleet A B tacks in succession, the fleet C D can tack together, which will prevent the leading ship, A, from ever reaching the enemy to cut through. 2. If the fleet C D is unwilling to tack together at first, for fear of seeming to flee, it can allow the van, A, of the fleet A B (Fig. 10), to pass through to the point E, and then, tacking together, it will put the enemy ships, E, between two fires, and, having speedily crushed them, it will easily cut off the leading ship, A, and the other enemy ships which have already broken through.

3. I do not see, then, that we need greatly fear the enemy who aims at passing through us; and I do not even think that

one ought to perform this manœuvre except under one of the three following conditions: 1. If one is driven to it, to avoid a greater evil. 2. If the enemy fleet, leaving a great gap in the middle of his squadrons, renders a part of our fleet useless. 3. If several ships, F, G, of the fleet C D are disabled; for then one can make the ships E, H tack together, and then the rest, H B, of the fleet A B in succession, to try to cut off the rear, G D. (See Plate opposite.)

4. One is sometimes obliged to pass through the enemy fleet to succour our ships that the enemy has cut off, in which case some risks must be run. But one must observe several precautions: 1. One must close up one's fleet as much as possible. 2. One should carry a press of sail, without troubling to fight when passing through the enemy. 3. The ships that have passed through should tack as soon as possible, to prevent the enemy from standing on the same tack as the fleet which passes through them.

On looking back upon the half century of tactical development which began with the First Dutch War, we see continuous growth. Experience gave rise to theory, and theory was tested by experience. The existence of two schools—one conservative, formal, and laying most stress upon defence; the other progressive, and eager for attack—prevented excessive haste on the one hand, and stagnation on the other. At the end of the century the resources of the defence were stronger than those of the attack: the pendulum was at the top of the backward swing. There it stopped. The battle of Malaga (1704) was the last fleet action for 40 years[1]. During the long peace, tactics became stereotyped. That is why the Permanent Fighting Instructions proved harmful: their framers had regarded them as one aspect of truth, as a temporary resting-place; a later generation, having no experience of other codes, was too prone to regard them as infallible and unalterable, as an end in themselves: not realising that unchangeableness may connote absence of life.

80. Big or Small Ships?

Opinions differed not only as to the conduct of fleets in action, but also as to the types of ships of which they were composed.

Evelyn's *Diary*, March 7, 1690.

I dined with Mr Pepys, late Secretary to the Admiralty, where was that excellent shipwright and seaman (for so he had been, and also a Commissioner of the Navy), Sir Anthony Deane. Amongst other discourse, and deploring the sad condition

[1] The one-sided action off Cape Passaro may be ignored.

PLATE FROM HOSTE'S *L'ART DES ARMÉES NAVALES*

of our navy, as now governed by inexperienced men since this Revolution, he mentioned what exceeding advantage we of this nation had by being the first who built frigates[1], the first of which ever built was that vessel which was afterwards called the *Constant Warwick*, and was the work of Pett of Chatham, for a trial of making a vessel that would sail swiftly; it was built with low decks, the guns lying near the water, and was so light and swift of sailing, that in a short time he told us she had, ere the Dutch war was ended, taken as much money from privateers as would have laden her; and that more such being built, did in a year or two scour the Channel from those of Dunkirk and others which had exceedingly infested it. He added that it would be the best and only infallible expedient to be masters of the sea, and able to destroy the greatest navy of any enemy if, instead of building huge great ships and second and third rates, they would leave off building such high decks, which were for nothing but to gratify gentlemen-commanders, who must have all their effeminate accommodations, and for pomp; that it would be the ruin of our fleets, if such persons were continued in command, they neither having experience nor being capable of learning, because they would not submit to the fatigue and inconvenience which those who were bred seamen would undergo, in those so otherwise useful swift frigates. These being to encounter the greatest ships would be able to protect, set on, and bring off, those who should manage the fire-ships; and the Prince who should first store himself with numbers of such fire-ships would, through the help and countenance of such frigates, be able to ruin the greatest force of such vast ships as could be sent to sea, by the dexterity of working those light, swift ships to guard the fire-ships. He concluded there would shortly be no other method of sea-fight; and that great ships and men-of-war, however stored with guns and men, must submit to those who should encounter them with far less number. He represented to us the dreadful effect of these fire-ships; that he continually observed in our late maritime war with the Dutch that, when an enemy's fire-ship approached, the most valiant commander and common sailors were in such consternation, that though then, of all times, there was most need of the guns, bombs, etc., to keep the

[1] See p. 39.

mischief off, they grew pale and astonished, as if of a quite other mean soul, that they slunk about, forsook their guns and work as if in despair, every one looking about to see which way they might get out of their ship, though sure to be drowned if they did so. This he said was likely to prove hereafter the method of sea-fight, likely to be the misfortune of England if they continued to put gentlemen-commanders over experienced seamen, on account of their ignorance, effeminacy, and insolence.

81. Superiority of French Naval Architects

Though the following is not contemporary, being published in 1802, it emphasises an important point.

Charnock, *History of Marine Architecture*, III, 16.

The loss which the enemy sustained on this occasion[1] was confined entirely to ships which had once been in the possession of, and had been built by, the English themselves; of these the *Salisbury*, 50 guns, was taken; the *Blackwall*, of the same force, with the *Deal Castle* and *Squirrel*, of 24 guns each, either foundered at sea, or were wrecked on the coast of Holland. These accounts furnish self-evident examples either of a superiority in skill, with respect to the French, or a strange predilection for particular and absurd principles, which strongly influenced the minds of British marine architects at that period. The advantage in point of sailing appears beyond controversy to have been in favour of the French ships, the *Salisbury* falling alone a victim, as the rest in all probability would have done, notwithstanding Forbin's ability and address, had not his ships, to use the seamen's phrase, considerably fore-reached those of the British.

It is no less worthy of remark that very few ships captured by the enemy from the British have ever continued long the property of their new possessors. If it has so happened that one of them, being in company with others of French construction, has ever fallen in with any English squadron, that ship, almost without exception, has been among those captured, and most frequently the first which has fallen. Exclusive of the *Salisbury* already noticed, the *Pembroke*, retaken in the same war, the

[1] Forbin's expedition of 1708.

Warwick, the *Ardent*, and the *Alexander*, besides a number of other vessels of inferior rate, in times much more modern, are additional proofs of the same principle. On the other hand, the recapture of any ship, frigate, or vessel of inferior rate, from the British, which was originally French, is a circumstance extremely uncommon.

The first of the following extracts from Halifax's *Rough Draught of a New Model at Sea* (published 1694, but probably written earlier) is a striking appreciation of sea-power; the hope expressed in the second was on the verge of fulfilment: 'After the Revolution,' says Sir Clements R. Markham, 'the admirals were professional seamen, with a few exceptions, and the captains had invariably been brought up to the sea as a profession.'

82. THE IMPORTANCE OF SEA-POWER

I will make no other introduction to the following discourse, than that as the importance of our being strong at sea was ever very great, so in our present circumstances it is grown to be much greater; because, as formerly our force of shipping contributed greatly to our trade and safety, so now it is become indispensably necessary to our very being.

It may be said now to England, Martha, Martha, thou art busy about many things, but one thing is necessary. To the question, What shall we do to be saved in this world? there is no other answer but this, Look to your moat.

The first article of an Englishman's political creed must be, that he believeth in the sea, &c. without that there needeth no general council to pronounce him incapable of salvation here.

We are in an island, confined to it by God Almighty, not as a penalty but a grace, and one of the greatest that can be given to mankind. Happy confinement, that hath made us free, rich, and quiet; a fair portion in this world, and very well worth the preserving; a figure that ever hath been envied, and could never be imitated by our neighbours. Our situation hath made greatness abroad by land conquests unnatural things to us. It is true, we have made excursions, and glorious ones too, which make our names great in history, but they did not last.

83. The Ideal Naval Officer

After arguing that 'A Commonwealth is not fit for us, because we are not fit for a Commonwealth,' and that 'We are no more a People, nor England can no longer keep its name, from the moment that our Liberties are extinguished,' Halifax proceeds:

It appeareth then that a bounded monarchy is that kind of government which will most probably prevail and continue in England; from whence it must follow that every considerable part ought to be so composed, as the better to conduce to the preserving the harmony of the whole constitution. The Navy is of so great importance, that it would be disparaged by calling it less than the life and soul of government.

Therefore to apply the argument to the subject we are upon; in case the officers be all tarpaulins, it would be in reality too great a tendency to a commonwealth; such a part of the constitution being democratically disposed may be suspected to endeavour to bring it into that shape. In short, if the maritime force, which is the only thing that can defend us, should be wholly directed by the lower sort of men, with an entire exclusion of the nobility and gentry, it will not be easy to answer the arguments supported by so great a probability, that such a scheme would not only lean toward a democracy, but directly lead us into it.

Let us now examine the contrary proposition, viz. that all officers should be gentlemen.

Here the objection lieth so fair, of its introducing an arbitrary government, that it is as little to be answered in that respect, as the former is in the other. Gentlemen, in a general definition, will be suspected to lie more than other men under the temptations of being made instruments of unlimited power.

The two former exclusive propositions being necessarily to be excluded in the question, there remaineth no other expedient than that there must be a mixture in the Navy of gentlemen and tarpaulins, as there is in the constitution of the government, of power and liberty. It is possible the men of Wapping may think they are injured, by giving them any partners in the dominion of the sea. But I shall in a good measure reconcile myself to them by what follows; viz. the gentlemen shall not be capable of bearing office at sea, except they be tarpaulins too; that is to say, except they are so trained up by a continued habit of living at sea, that they may have a right to be admitted free denizens of Wapping. When a gentleman is preferred at sea, the tarpaulin is very apt to impute it to friend or favour: but if that gentleman hath before his preferment passed through all the steps which lead to it, so that he smelleth as much of pitch and tar, as those that were swaddled in sail-cloth; his having an escutcheon will be so far from doing him harm, that it will set him upon the advantage ground: it will draw a real respect to his quality when so supported, and give him an influence and authority infinitely superior to that which the mere seaman can ever pretend to.

When a gentleman hath learned how to obey, he will grow very much fitter to command; his own memory will advise him not to inflict too rigorous punishments. To expect that quality alone should waft men up into places and employments, is as unreasonable, as to think that a ship, because it is carved and gilded, should be fit to go to sea without sails or tackling.

84. Explanation of Rooke's Instructions, 1704

The following 'explanation' of Rooke's Instructions of March 24, 1704 (which are not themselves of particular interest), and his Secret Instructions of March 29 illustrate Marlborough's genius as a strategist. In his plan of campaign for 1704, the main blows were to be struck by himself and Eugene on the upper Danube, and by the Duke of Savoy and the Anglo-Dutch fleet against Toulon. These documents illustrate the tremendous value of our Mediterranean fleet in welding together the different members of the coalition, in distracting the enemy by feints, and in concentrating in secret for the attack on the real objective.

S.P. Dom. Entry Book 208, p. 123.

Whitehall, 24 March, 1703–4.

Sir,

     I am commanded to explain to you the intentions of the Queen in the enclosed order.

You will see in the order itself one reason which induces her Majesty to wish the Fleet in the Mediterranean, lest if you should stay for certain intelligence that Nice was attacked, you might come too late to relieve it; and though, upon the certainty of it, your former orders direct you to sail thither, yet, while it is uncertain, her Majesty leaves to the Council of War to determine the operations of the Fleet, though she thinks it can nowhere be so useful as in the Mediterranean; and therefore you should press the English and Dutch officers to comply with you in the execution of her Majesty's opinion; for 'tis certain that the French are daily sending recruits by sea to their army in Italy, which nothing can prevent but our Fleet; and if the French increase their army, and the Emperor be not able to reinforce his by recruits, of which there is little appearance, the French will be too strong both for the Imperialists and Savoyards, and such a superiority may be fatal to the affairs in Italy, and in consequence to the Kings of Spain[1] and Portugal, who for that reason are as much concerned as her Majesty and the States General can be to support the Duke of Savoy, and prevent that superiority of the French in those parts, who will thereby be at leisure, when our Fleet is returned, to pour all that army into Spain, to the entire ruin of both those Kings.

And though Nice should not be attempted, and though all the French recruits were already got into Italy, yet if the Emperor should be able to send recruits to his armies in Italy, yet those which are for the army in Piedmont can not join it otherwise than by sea, and they can not pass by sea neither, but under the protection of our Fleet.

And whatever alarm can be given on the coast of Spain which is not inclined to the House of Austria, or whatever support can be given to those Spaniards which are disposed to that interest, 'tis more practicable on the coast of Spain which lies within the Straits, than on any part on this side of the Straits' mouth, Catalonia being most disposed to a revolt, [inhabited by] the best men, and capable of giving the most formidable diversion to the arms of France and the Duke of Anjou.

I am, etc.,

C. Hedges.

Sir Geo. Rooke.

---

[1] *I.e.* The Archduke Charles, the allied claimant.

85. ROOKE'S ADDITIONAL INSTRUCTIONS

Additional Instructions for Our Right Trusty and Well-Beloved Councillor, Sir George Rooke, Knight, Our Vice-Admiral of England, and Admiral of Our Fleet. Given at Our Court at St James's, the 29th day of March 1704, in the Third Year of Our Reign.

S.P. Dom. Entry Book 208, p. 131.

Whereas there are some services of the greatest importance which we have thought fit to commit to your care and conduct, and wherein we can not hope for any success without all possible secrecy, we do therefore signify to you our intentions therein by these private instructions, and would have you, notwithstanding what is contained in our former instructions, apply yourself in the first place to the execution of these services.

You are already acquainted by the Earl of Nottingham, pursuant to our command, with our intentions to attempt Toulon, and with the Duke of Savoy's readiness to concur therein, and with the orders we have sent to our Envoy Extraordinary in that Court to concert the proper methods of executing this design. We need therefore only add, that you will receive upon your arrival in the Mediterranean, or sooner, an account from our said Envoy of what shall have been concerted and resolved by him with the said Duke; or otherwise you may send to Nice, or Villa Franca, some light frigates for advice from our said Envoy, and upon notice from him that the Duke of Savoy continues in the resolution to concur with you in this design, and assist you with his troops in putting it in execution, you are therein to co-operate with the Fleet under your command, preferably to any other services mentioned in any former instructions.

In order hereunto you will receive from our Secretary of State a plan or description of that port, and if you should have an opportunity to get any further or later description of it, you must be sure to do it in such manner as may not give the least umbrage or jealousy of this design, whereof you must not take the least notice to the Ministers of Portugal, or to any other person whatsoever, till you shall think it altogether safe and necessary to consult about the execution of it at a Council of War.

You must therefore spend no more time in alarming the coast of Spain pursuant to our other instructions than what may be necessary to cover this design without losing the opportunity of effecting it, or meeting the Duke of Savoy's forces at the time and place appointed, if they should march by land.

This being the first and principal thing, we leave it to you to execute what follows in these instructions in such manner, and at such time, as you shall judge consistent with it, giving still this attempt on Toulon the preference, excepting the relief of Nice, if that should be attempted by the French, as you were directed by our instructions dated March 14th, and excepting the following of the Toulon squadron, in case they pass the Straits, which in respect of our own safety, and the safety of our Dominions, must be your principal care.

Having performed these services, or as much thereof as is practicable, you are to proceed to Palermo in Sicily, and there make and observe the signals herewith sent you, and if you find it feasible, you are to concur with them in the attempt there, assisting them by our ships and bomb-vessels, and with such of our Marines as are necessary, and by all such other ways as you shall judge proper for reducing that place to the subjection of King Charles III.

If you succeed in this attempt, and you find it practicable to take Messina, you are in that, and all other things, to do your utmost to assist them in freeing themselves from the slavery of France and the present Spanish Government, and to reduce that island to the Dominion of King Charles III.

You are then to proceed to Naples, and to the coast of that Kingdom, and upon the signals given you, you in like manner are to assist the people to shake off the French and Spanish power in favour of the said King.

And if any part of the Emperor's army shall be in that Kingdom, you are, as far as is practicable, to co-operate with the officer commanding those troops in reducing Naples, or any other port of that Kingdom, and in order to it you are in all respects to do your utmost to support and assist the Emperor's army, or any others that declare for King Charles III.

You are to enquire particularly whether there be any possibility of destroying the salt and salt-works at Peguais, and if in your return from the aforementioned services you have time, and shall judge it practicable, you are to land such, and so many, of our Marines as may be sufficient for this service, taking with them such of the French as will join in it, and may conduct our troops to the performance of this service.

If upon your arrival in the Mediterranean you shall have intelligence that there are any troops of the Emperor's on the coast of Tuscany, or Genoa, that want a transportation for joining the forces of the Duke of Savoy, you are in that case to give them all the assistance you can with the ships and transports under your command, in order to their joining, it being a service of very great importance.

A. R.

THE PEACE PERIOD AND NEED
FOR REFORM

OUT of the long period of warfare (1688–1713), which ended with the Peace of Utrecht, Great Britain emerged as the supreme maritime power.

During the succeeding period of peace which coincided roughly with the administration of Sir Robert Walpole, when a French alliance was maintained, the efficiency of the Navy was allowed to decline, partly no doubt from the lack of serious foreign competition, but mainly for want of clean-handed and disinterested governmental control. A period of 'dry-rot' set in affecting all departments of the service.

The extent of the mischief is measured by the failures of the War of Jenkins's Ear and by the conspicuous blunders committed during the earlier years of the War of Austrian Succession.

The need for drastic reforms is illustrated by the extracts which follow. They serve to show that then, as always, there were senior officers in the service who were fully alive to the dangers of administrative corruption and sluggish adherence to strategical and tactical formulas.

The triumphs of the Seven Years' War (1756–63) would have been impossible without the professional zeal of Vernon and Anson.

86. MANNING A SQUADRON

The problem of securing adequate supplies of able seamen was present throughout the eighteenth century, and was never satisfactorily solved. The extract here printed affords a classical example of the haphazard methods adopted for manning a squadron.

Anson's Voyage round the World, 1740–4, by Richard Walter, M.A., Chaplain of the *Centurion*, p. 5.

At last, on the 28th of June 1740, the Duke of Newcastle, Principal Secretary of State, delivered to him his Majesty's instructions, dated January 31, 1739, with an additional instruction from the Lords Justices, dated June 19, 1740. On the receipt of these, Mr Anson immediately repaired to Spithead, with a resolution to sail with the first fair wind, flattering himself that all his delays were now at an end. For though he knew by the musters that his squadron wanted three hundred seamen of their complement (a deficiency which, with all his assiduity, he had not been able to get supplied), yet, as Sir Charles Wager informed him that an order from the Board of Admiralty was dispatched to Sir John Norris to spare him the numbers which he wanted, he doubted not of his complying therewith. But on his arrival at Portsmouth he found himself greatly mistaken, and disappointed in this persuasion; for on his application, Sir John Norris told him he could spare him none, for he wanted men for his own fleet. This occasioned an inevitable and a very considerable delay; for it was the end of July before this deficiency was by any means supplied, and all that was then done was extremely short of his necessities and expectation. For Admiral Balchen, who succeeded to the command at Spithead after Sir John Norris had sailed to the westward, instead of 300 able sailors, which Mr Anson wanted of his complement, ordered on board the squadron 170 men only, of which 32 were from the hospital and sick quarters, 37 from the *Salisbury*, with three officers of Colonel Lowther's regiment, and 98 marines, and these were all that were ever granted to make up the fore-mentioned deficiency.

But the Commodore's mortification did not end here. It has been already observed, that it was at first intended that Colonel Bland's regiment, and three independent companies of a hundred men each, should embark as land-forces on board the squadron. But this disposition was now changed, and all the land-forces that were to be allowed were 500 invalids to be collected from the out-pensioners of Chelsea college. As these out-pensioners consist of soldiers who, from their age, wounds, or other infirmities, are incapable of service in marching regiments, Mr Anson was greatly chagrined at having such a decrepit detachment allotted him; for he was fully persuaded that the greatest part of them would perish long before they arrived at the scene of action, since the delays he had already encountered necessarily confined his passage round Cape Horn to the most rigorous season of the year. Sir Charles Wager, too, joined in opinion with the Commodore, that invalids were no ways proper for this service, and solicited strenuously to have them exchanged; but he was told that persons who were supposed to be better judges of soldiers than he or Mr Anson, thought them the properest men that could be employed on this occasion. And upon this determination they were ordered on board the squadron on the 5th of August. But instead of 500, there came on board no more than 259; for all those who had limbs and strength to walk out of Portsmouth deserted, leaving behind them only such as were literally invalids, most of them being sixty years of age, and some of them upwards of seventy. Indeed it is difficult to conceive a more moving scene than the embarkation of these unhappy veterans: they were themselves extremely averse to the service they were engaged in, and fully apprised of all the disasters they were afterwards exposed to, the apprehensions of which were strongly marked by the concern that appeared in their countenances, which was mixed with no small degree of indignation, to be thus hurried from their repose into a fatiguing employ, to which neither the strength of their bodies, nor the vigour of their minds, were any ways proportioned, and where, without seeing the face of an enemy, or in the least promoting the success of the enterprise they were engaged in, they would in all probability uselessly perish by lingering and painful diseases; and this, too, after they had spent the activity and strength of their youth in their country's service.

87. CHARNOCK ON FRENCH AND SPANISH SHIPS

The supremacy of Great Britain on the seas was in great degree due to superior strategy, seamanship and staying powers. The credit belongs to the men and not to the material. Throughout the eighteenth century our shipbuilding was inferior to that of the French and Spaniards. Our best ships were modelled upon captured vessels[1].

It will be remembered that Lord Anson did invaluable work in providing a rational classification of ships, but our inferiority in actual construction persisted until the Napoleonic Wars. The letter from Sir Charles Knowles[2] affords a clear view of the many defects which Lord Anson strove to remedy.

The passages from Charnock's *History of Marine Architecture* bear additional testimony to the superiority of French and Spanish design.

John Charnock, *History of Marine Architecture*, III, 172 (published 1802).

The practice of France and Spain was only partially imitated by Great Britain. The former country in particular had, for a long time, ceased to construct any three-decked ships, and the cause was very easy to be discovered. They were considered as peculiarly fitted only to the attack of batteries or fortresses;

[1] Sir J. Jervis in a note to Lord Spencer, written in 1797, refers to the *Carnatic* as 'the standard for seventy-fours' (172 ft. gun-deck, 48 ft. beam; 1720 tons). She was a copy of the French *Courageux*.

[2] Sir Charles Knowles, 1697–1777, Rear-Admiral 1747, Governor of Jamaica 1752, Vice-Admiral 1755, Admiral 1760.

attempts which the French nation has been uniformly averse to, so far as they were connected with the operations of their navy. The peculiar excellence of a naval officer was supposed to consist in the ability of making such an arrangement as should enable him, whether in a single ship, or as commander of an extensive fleet, to commence and finish the encounter with his enemy by a distant and scientific cannonade, in which the peculiar abilities of the gunner could be rendered more efficient than the intrepid, fearless temper of the seamen, who seemed to disregard, at least, those of Britain, every measure but that of almost personal contention with their foe. On this principle, the marine architects of France first bent their attention to the formation of such vessels as should, though in the most tempestuous weather, be less agitated by the sea than those of their opponents, and should be able, in defiance of any swell which would totally prevent such a measure in ships of inferior dimensions, to direct their shot, even from the lower tier of guns, in annoyance of the enemy. To this established system are to be attributed the superior dimensions and bulk which the French vessels for several years maintained over those of other countries.

The ships of France and Spain, in their several rates, far exceeded those of every country in Europe, and the marine architects, especially of France, were bold enough to suppose their ships carrying 80 guns, two-deckers, but of dimensions very little, if in any degree, inferior to a British first rate, were capable of contending, under the circumstances before related, with a ship of that class. Notwithstanding certain stubborn facts proved the futility and vanity of this idea, there existed, in reality, certain peculiar excellences which reason admitted the propriety of, and were therefore not to be controverted, or even disputed. The example consequently spread, though slowly, and it is a bare act of justice to the fame of the French ship-builders, that to their studious exertions and experiments is primarily owing the energetical improvement made in modern times on the form, dimensions, and general contour of vessels, be the purpose to which it was intended they should be applied whatever it might.

88. The Defects of the British Battle-ship

B.M. *Anson Corres.*, vol. II, 119.

Superbe

Antigua 6th Jan.

1744/5

My Lord,

The desire I have constantly had from my youth to serve my country has always kept me attentive to the duty of my station, hoping some of my observations might at one time or other prove useful: in that confidence I have presumed to give my opinion of the questions I see the late Admiralty asked Mr Vernon.

The many great complaints that have been made of late years about the badness of our ships of war, both in regard to their figure as to sailing, and to their incapacity for lodging their men, as well as to the badness of materials, and the manner in which they have been built, are not without just foundation; but as my design is not to point out faults altogether, but propose amendments, I hope what I shall offer will have the honour to meet your Lordship's approbation.

The several classes of our ships are certainly very proper, but the different sizes of ships of the same class are by no argument to be supported, for not only confusion but loss of time and great expense are generated by such a method; for example, if six or eight ships of 40, 50, or 60 guns are ordered to be equipped with all possible expedition, the General Establishment from the Navy Board, for masts, yards, sails and rigging are one and the same for all the ships of each class (if it's altered it's very lately); so that one of the new ships fitting or one of the old, have been obliged to take promiscuously such stores as were at hand, whether they were suited to the size of the ship or not, and forced to alter them at sea (if the nature of the service would not admit of its being done in the Dockyards before sailing): such proceedings are certainly detrimental and without doubt hinder dispatch as well as create an extraordinary expense in the annual estimate of the Navy. The same, my Lord, may be alleged with regard to some Ordnance Stores; the ports of these ships of different sizes though of the same rank, are frequently of different heights from the decks, by which means the gun-carriages of one ship won't serve for another; and yet I have known a ship wait to have those altered, which was a considerable expense besides the loss of time in fitting for the sea, and so of several other sorts of stores.

It is therefore most humbly offered to your Lordship's consideration the establishing one general and unalterable dimensions for a ship of each rank, which should be as near as possible the size of those of our enemies (the French and Spaniards), and that the scantlings of their timbers and beams, number of ports alow and aloft, nature of guns, and number of men should also be near the same, and then a Captain who commanded one of them could have no excuse if he did not take a ship of the enemy's of the same class; it having been of late pleaded as an excuse (on meeting with some of the enemy's ships) that they have been bigger ships than ours, carried the ports higher out of the water, had more men and heavier metal. For my own part, My Lord (though our Histories furnish us with great maritime exploits of our forefathers), I have never seen or heard since my knowledge of things that one of our ships alone singly opposed to one of the enemy's of equal force has taken her, and I have been in almost every action and skirmish since the year 1718, and yet we are daily boasting of the prowess of our Fleet. I don't mention this to take away from the honour and courage of many of our Captains, who will always behave well, be they in what ships soever, and claim the regard of your Lordship and their country, but I propose to obviate all objections and excuses that can be made by any set of men whatsoever. And in order to express myself further on the head of ship-building, though I would propose all the ships of each Rate to be of one fixed dimensions, as to their lengths and breadths, I would not have the builders confined as to the figures of their bodies, because that would be cramping or rather destroying their Art, and might prevent the building many prime sailing ships; on the contrary each builder should try his art till an unexceptionable ship of each class was built, and then that ship to remain as a model.

The number of our capital ships is also an immense expense to keep up, and no enemy (nay all Europe together) has not one sixth part of the number to oppose them; if therefore there were but two ships of 100 guns and four of 90 to be established, and a number of ships of 74, 64, & 56 guns to be built (in proportion) in their rooms, it would be both an advantage and a great saving, for those capital ships take a number of men, and when they are ranged in line of battle, it is great chance if they are opposed by more than a 60 or 70 gun ship of the enemy, so that a ship of that rank would answer equally as well, as then there would be a saving of two or three hundred men (or more) out of each such ship, which would more than man a proportionate number of ships of an inferior class.

As I am certain the largeness of the scantling of beam and timbers will never hinder a ship's sailing, I think there can be no objection against their carrying heavier metal: it is the reconciling the figure of the body to the fluid it is to pass through that will determine the sailing, and not the slightness of the vessel, as a proof of which I beg leave to instance the late fleets in the Mediterranean, both French and Spanish, which seemed to be mere logs of wood or solid bodies of timber, compared to our ships, and yet most of them, if not all, outsailed our Fleet.

Another thing I beg leave to observe to your Lordship is that the enemy's ships of each class have always a port or two in a tier more than ours, which as they carry heavier metal, consequently gives them so many larger guns on the upper and lower Decks more than ours. Whereas our ships are generally crowded with a heap of small guns—6-pounders on the Forecastle and Quarter-Deck, especially the 60 and 70; the 70's have no less than 18, and experience had shewn us that a 6-pounder will not go through some of the enemy's ship's sides. Nay, in many places not a 12 p^d; so that one of their ships of 52 guns is near as good as one of ours of 70, and their 64 and 74 gun ships have seldom or ever more than 4 guns of a side on the Quarter-Deck, and those 9-pounders, and two on the Forecastle, which last are generally large, as on the contrary ours are always small, though the principal use of them is to disable a mast or yard, when a ship can't so readily come up alongside; and how necessary it is to have large guns there, I submit to your Lordship's judgment, as well as to have heavier metals alow and more ports in a tier, as our ships will then certainly be more fit for battering either the enemy's ships or forts.

The Spanish and French ships of war that have come within my remarks are as follows:

(Here follow specifications of eight ships, of which the following are examples.)

Ships' Names	No. of Guns		No. of ports on the Lower Deck on a side	Nature of Guns	No. of ports on the Upper Deck on a side	Nature of Guns	No. of ports on the Quarter Deck on a side	Nature of Guns	No. Do. on the Fore-castle on a side	Nature of Guns
	Guns	Men								
St Philip's {	74	850	16	32-pdrs	15	18-pdrs	4	9-pdrs	2	18-pdrs
	74	750								
Fleuron, a French ship	64	550	14	24-pdrs	14	12-pdrs	3	9-pdrs	1	9 (brass)

I shall now give your Lordship a sketch of some of our own ships to oppose them.

(Here follow specifications of eight English ships, of which the following are examples.)

Ships' Names	Guns	Men	Lower Deck — Ports	Guns	Nature of Guns	Upper Deck ports	Nature of Guns	Quarter Deck — Ports	Guns	Nature of Guns	Forecastle	Nature of Guns
Prince Frederick	70	480	13	12	24-pdrs	13	12-pdrs		7	6-pdrs	2	6-pdrs
Superbe	60	400	13	13	24-pdrs	13	9-pdrs	6	4	6-pdrs	1	6-pdrs

by which your Lordship sees the difference, and how our ships are crowded with a number of small guns, and how vastly inferior in number of men. The alterations I would propose (as it may not be practicable to come at the exact dimensions of the enemy's ships at present) are as follows:

	Guns	Men	Lower Deck ports	Nature of Guns	Upper Deck ports	Nature of Guns	Quarter Deck ports	Nature of Guns	Forecastle	Nature of Guns
A ship of	74	640	15	32-pdrs	15	18-pdrs	5	9-pdrs	2	18-pdrs
	64	550	14	32-pdrs	14	12-pdrs	3	9-pdrs	1	12-pdrs

And I flatter myself few objections can be raised to this scheme but which I readily can answer, and believe every Officer in the Navy who has the honour of His Majesty's arms, the good of his Country, and his own reputation at heart, would be glad to see our ships on such an Establishment; for permit me to assure you, My Lord, the knowledge every Officer has of the great disproportion that is at present between our 60 and 70 gun ships and the enemy's fills him with concern, as he cannot acquire that glory and advantage over them his spirit and zeal animates him to, and the unthinking populace are too free to censure without examining into the reason of things, and imagine it strange an English ship of war of 70 guns cannot take a French or Spanish ship of the same force, whereas it is pretty apparent our 70 gun ships are little superior to their ships of 52 guns. But in carrying this scheme into execution care should be taken not to make the ships of too great a draught of water, or by amending one fault a greater will be committed, for the present docks will not be capable to receive the ships which would create an immense expense to alter; therefore the ships must be so much the longer, which will in every respect make them better seaboats, and give space for more guns in a tier as I propose.

As to the reason of our ships not being so durable as the enemy's, or as they were in former times, much might be said thereon, but one principal reason I shall offer at present (which indeed is rather a fault) is that the timber as it is purchased and brought into the yards is laid in heaps, and not regularly expended according to its ages and the time of its being cut down, so that I have seen green timber (which has lain uppermost) used soon after it has come into the yards, and the old timber which has lain undermost (and been seasoned and fit to use) lay till it has rotted, or been so bad that it has decayed soon after it has been converted to use. There are innumerable other faults I could point to your Lordship in the disposition of apartments, store-rooms and powder-rooms in our ships which requires amending, but I fear I have trespassed on your patience already, shall therefore most humbly submit what I have said to Your Lordship's considera- tion and better judgment, and am with the greatest respect,

My Lord,
Your Lordship's most obedient and most devoted
Humble Servant,
CHAS. KNOWLES.

89. Eighteenth Century Victuals

Admiralty records afford convincing evidence of continued neglect and corruption on the part of those responsible for the Victualling of the Navy. To the habitual neglect of the food and, therefore, of the health of the seamen the naval mutinies were largely due. (See *infra*, Documents illustrating Mutinies (*a*), p. 195.)

Admiralty 'In Letters' prove with sad completeness how often an Admiral's hands were tied and a fleet's movements hampered by insufficient and rotten supplies[1]. Many contemporary pamphlets bear witness to the victualling scandals.

William Thompson, *An Appeal to the Public...to prevent the Navy of England being supplied with pernicious Provisions...*(1761).

As a few more Circumstances to prove how indispensably necessary it is that a Parliamentary enquiry should be made into that part of the public money which is appropriated for the victualling of the Navy, I shall therefore introduce the following, viz.

That Mariners in the King's Ships have frequently put their 24 hours' allowance of salt provisions into their tobacco-boxes.

That seamen in the King's Ships have made buttons for their Jackets and Trowses with the Cheese they were served with, having preferred it, by reason of its tough and durable quality, to buttons made of common metal; and that Carpenters in the Navy-Service have made Trucks to their Ships' flagstaffs with whole Cheeses, which have stood the weather equally with any timber.

That the Flour in the King's Ships has been devoured by weevils, and become so intolerably musty, and cemented into such hard rocks, that the men have been obliged to use instruments, with all their feeble power, to break and pulverise it before they could make use of it, as though, in a comparative degree, they had been stubbing to pieces the ruins of an old fortification.

That their bread has been so full of large black-headed maggots and that they have so nauseated the thoughts of it, as to be obliged to shut their eyes to confine that sense from being offended before they could bring their minds into a resolution of consuming it.

[1] *E.g.* Lord Hawke: 'The beer brewed at Plymouth is so bad....Our daily employment is condemning of it.'

That their beer has stunk as abominably as the foul stagnant water which is pumped out of many cellars in London at midnight hour; and that they were under a necessity of shutting their eyes, and stopping their breath by holding of their noses before they could conquer their aversion, so as to prevail upon themselves in their extreme necessities to drink it.

That the same provisions have been issued from His Majesty's Victualling Office which have been rejected by the Officers of the ships they were sent to, and afterwards returned to the said Office and issued again three times to different ships belonging to His Majesty before they could be passed off, because they were so extremely bad!

That the pork, which the Fleet under the command of the late Admiral Boscawen was served with, was so rotten, that when boiled it wasted away to mere rags and crumbs, so that it could be eaten with a spoon, and that when the liquor it had been boiled in was drawn off, it flowed out of the cock of the ship's boiler like curds and whey: it was also so nauseous that it made the men sick who did eat of it; and therefore resolving to fast rather than eat any more of it, they have thrown it privately out of their ship's port-holes to prevent being discovered by the Officers of their ship.

90. The Western Squadron

The paramount importance of a strong Western Squadron as the bed-rock of all our strategy, had always been clear to the true seaman: its reassertion was necessary in the years immediately succeeding Walpole's administration.

From Admiral Vernon's pamphlet, *Some Seasonable Advice from an Honest Sailor*, 1746.

It was always my opinion that a strong squadron kept at sea to the Westward, and a squadron of smaller ships in the North Seas, were the only secure Guardians to these His Majesty's Kingdoms against Invasions.

But I can never be of opinion, nor don't think any Seaman can, that the three-decked ships should be employed to form the squadron in the North Seas, or that any larger than a 70-gun ship should ever be employed in that service, though I think a sixty-gun ship would be big enough, and indeed these large ships appear to me useless for such Services, as we have no Harbours to shelter them in to the Northward, till we come to Edinburgh Frith or Cromarty, and not drift enough for them in such narrow seas, whereas we have Plymouth and Portsmouth for shelter to the Westward, and many fine harbours in Ireland, and an open sea for such large bodies to have sufficient sea-room to drive in

91. Vernon and Additional Fighting Instructions

The tactics of eighteenth century naval battles are unintelligible without some acquaintance with the Fighting Instructions (see *supra*, p. 93). As issued in 1703 by Sir George Rooke they were used with only slight modifications until the close of the American War of Independence.

The Fighting Instructions have received more than their fair share of abuse, being often cited as the sole cause of the many indecisive battles of the eighteenth century. Yet while unenterprising commanders could and did find excuses for half-hearted action in the existence of a formal code, there is ample evidence that resourceful and resolute leaders never allowed themselves, by too rigid observance of the means, to lose sight of the end in view—the destruction of the enemy's fleet.

That the Fighting Instructions of 1703 were insufficient in themselves to secure decisive victories is shown by the series of Additional Fighting Instructions issued first by thoughtful officers like Vernon and Anson, and continued by Hawke, Boscawen, Rodney and Hood. After 1760 these supplements to the old Fighting Instructions were embodied in logical order and remained in force until the new Signal Book revolutionised the whole system of tactics.

The following passages point to Vernon as the 'Father' of Additional Instructions, *circa* 1740.

The introduction of the 'Quarter-line' formation was almost certainly due to Anson, who may have used it in 1747. In 1758 he writes of exercising the Channel Fleet in tactics 'which are in a great part new.'

Extracts from one of the 'Mathews and Lestock' pamphlets, entitled *A Narrative of the Proceedings of His Majesty's fleet in the Mediterranean,* 1741–4. Quoted in *N.R.S.* xxix, p. 206.

Men in the highest stations at sea will not deny but what our sailing and fighting instructions might be amended, and many added to them, which by every day's experience are found to be absolutely necessary. Though this truth is universally acknowledged and the necessity of the royal navy very urgent, yet since the institution of these signals nothing has been added to them excepting the chasing signals, excellent in their kind, by the

Right Honourable Sir J[ohn] N[orris]. Not but that every admiral has authority to make any additions or give such signals to the captains under his command as he shall judge proper, which are only expeditional. Upon many emergencies our signals at this juncture [*i.e.* in the action before Toulon] proved to be very barren. There was no such signal in the book, expressing an order when the admiral would have the ships to come to a closer engagement than when they begun. After what has been observed, it is unnecessary now to repeat the great necessity and occasion there was for it; and boats in many cases, besides their delay and hindrance, could not always perform that duty.

Mr V[ernon], that provident, great admiral, who never suffered any useful precaution to escape him, concerted some signals for so good a purpose, wisely foreseeing their use and necessity, giving them to the captains of the squadron under his command. And lest his vigilance should be some time or other surprised by an enemy, or the exigencies of his master's service should require him to attack or repulse by night, he appointed signals for the line of battle, engaging, chasing, leaving off chase, with many others altogether new, excellent, and serviceable, which show his judgment, abilities, and zeal. The author takes the liberty to print them for the improvement of his brethren, who, if they take the pains to peruse them, will receive benefit and instruction.

92. The First Additional Instruction

Circa 1740. Mathews–Lestock pamphlets. (*N.R.S.* XXIX, p. 214.)

An Additional Instruction to be added to the Fighting Instructions

In case of meeting any squadron of the enemy's ships, whose number may be less than those of the squadron of his majesty's ships under my command, and that I would have any of the smaller ships quit the line, I will in such case make the signal for speaking with the captain of that ship I would have quit the line; and at the same time I will put a flag, striped yellow and white, at the flagstaff at the main topmast-head, upon which the said ship or ships are to quit the line, and the next ships are to close the line, for having our ships of greatest force to form a line just equal to the enemy's. And as, upon the squadrons engaging, it is not to be expected that the ships withdrawn out of the line can see or distinguish signals at such a juncture, it is therefore strictly enjoined and required of such captain or captains, who shall have their signal or signals made to withdraw out of the line, to demean themselves as a *corps de réserve* to the main squadron, and to place themselves in the best situation for giving relief to any ship of the squadron that may be disabled or hardest pressed by the enemy, having in the first place regard to the ship I shall have my flag on board, as where the honour of his majesty's flag is principally concerned. And as it is morally impossible to fix any general rule to occurrences that must be regulated from the weather and the enemy's disposition, this is left to the respective captain's judgment that shall be ordered out of the line to govern himself by as becomes an officer of prudence, and as he will answer the contrary at his peril.

Memorandum. That whereas all signals for the respective captains of the squadron are at some one of the mast-heads, and as when we are in line of battle or in other situations it may be difficult for the ships to distinguish their signal, in such case you are to take notice that your signal will be made by fixing the pennant higher upon the topgallant shrouds, so as it may be most conspicuous to be seen by the respective ship it is made for.

A second Additional Instruction to the Fighting Instructions

If, at any time after our ships being engaged with any squadron of the enemy's ships, the admiral shall judge it proper to come to a closer engagement with the enemy than at the distance we first began to engage, the admiral will hoist a union flag at the main topmast-head and fire a gun on the opposite side to which he is engaged with the enemy, when every ship is to obey the signal, taking the distance from the centre; and if the admiral would have any particular ship do so he will make the same signal with the signal for the captain of that ship.

And in case of being to leeward of the enemy, the admiral

will at the same time he makes this signal hoist the yellow flag at the fore topmast-head for filling and making sail to windward.

And during the time of engagement, every ship is to appoint a proper person to keep an eye upon the admiral and to observe signals.

93. LINE OF BEARING

MS. Signal Book 1756, United Service Institution. (*N.R.S.* XXIX, p. 216.)

Lord Anson's Additional Fighting Instruction, to be inserted after Article the 4th in the Additional Fighting Instructions by Day.

Whereas it may often be necessary for ships in line of battle to regulate themselves by bearing on some particular point of the compass from each other, without having any regard to their bearing abreast or ahead of one another;

You are therefore hereby required and directed to strictly observe the following instructions:

When the signal is made for the squadron to draw into a line of battle at any particular distance, and I would have them keep north and south of each other, I will hoist a red flag with a white cross in the mizen topmast shrouds to show the quarter of the compass, and for the intermediate points I will hoist on the flagstaff at the mizen topmast-head, when they are to bear

N by E	and S by W, one common pennant
N N E	„ S S W, two common pennants
N E by N	„ S W by S, three common pennants
N E	„ S W, a Dutch jack.

And I will hoist under the Dutch jack when I would have them bear

N E by E	and S W by W, one common pennant
E N E	„ W S W, two common pennants
E by N	„ W by S, three common pennants

and fire a gun with each signal.

When I would have them bear from each other on any of the points on the N W and S E quarters I will hoist a blue and white flag on the mizen topmast shrouds, to show the quarter

of the compass, and distinguish the intermediate points they are
to form on from the N and S in the same manner as in the
N E and S W quarter.   ED. HAWKE.

94. NAVAL EDUCATION

Those familiar with naval biography cannot fail to note the diverse modes
by which great sea-commanders made their entry into the service. Leaving
aside careers like that of Blake, who began his naval service at the age of
fifty, and of Benbow, who had long experience in the merchant service
before he became a commissioned officer in the Navy, we find that most of
the distinguished admirals of the eighteenth century began their careers as
volunteers, going to sea usually as 'captain's servants.' Rooke, Anson,
Hawke and Boscawen entered in this manner at the age of fifteen. Young
officers were borne on the ships' books frequently at the early age of seven
or eight; Cochrane indeed was entered in this way at the age of five. There
was, in effect, no qualifying examination nor regulation as to age. Promotion
to the rank of midshipman depended entirely upon the will of the captain:
the school for young seamen was the sea.

For those privileged to possess interest in high quarters special nominations
were procurable from the Admiralty. Such nominees were entered as King's
Letter Boys or Volunteers per Order. As such, Rodney went to sea in 1732 at
the age of thirteen.

These casual modes of entry obtained for the greater part of the eighteenth
century; that they were not considered entirely satisfactory by the Admiralty
is proved by the institution in 1729 of the Royal Naval Academy at Portsmouth, which was actually opened in 1733 and continued to exist till 1806.
Although reconstituted as a College in 1807 the Portsmouth establishment,
as a training school for young officers, survived only till 1837.

The nature of the training received at this academy is shown by the
Regulations, some of which are here printed. The establishment may fairly
be called the precursor if not the ancestor of the Royal Naval College, Dartmouth.

Despite the formal establishment of this definite course of training as
outlined in the regulations here printed, the Academy produced but few
officers who became greatly distinguished. The traditional method of entry
still continued: Jervis, for instance, was rated as able seaman at the age of
thirteen.

Admiralty Office; Nov. 1, 1773.

Rules and Orders relating to the Royal Academy established in
His Majesty's Dock-yard at Portsmouth, for educating
Young Gentlemen to the Sea-Service.

1. No-one shall be admitted into the Academy, but the sons
of noblemen or gentlemen, who shall not be under twelve years

of age, nor above fifteen, at the time of their admission, except 15 young gentlemen, the sons of commissioned officers of His Majesty's Fleet, who are to be educated at the public expense, and may, by His Majesty's Order in Council, dated the 8th October 1773, be admitted at the age of eleven years, but not above fourteen.

2. No scholar shall be admitted into the Academy until he has been examined by the Head-Master in presence of the Governor, who are to judge whether he has made such a progress in his education as may, in their opinion, qualify him to enter upon the plan of education appointed for the Academy, and until he produces a certificate of his morals and good behaviour from the master or person under whom he was last taught.

3. The Lord High Admiral, or Lord Commissioners of the Admiralty for the time being, shall appoint the masters, ushers, and scholars, and may at any time dismiss such as they shall judge deserve it.

4. The Commissioner of His Majesty's Navy for the time being at the dock-yard at Portsmouth shall be Governor of the Academy, and the masters, ushers, and scholars shall be obedient to, and observe, his directions.

7. The scholars are to lodge in separate chambers, and are to board with the master, who is to be paid by each of those who are admitted into the Academy upon the original establishment, the sum of £25 a year and no more, and who is to be paid the like allowance, by bills signed by the Navy Board upon the Treasurer of H.M.'s Navy, for each of the 15 sons of sea officers before mentioned: in consideration of which, he is to keep them a decent and proper table, and to find them in washing, fire, candles, towels, table- and bed-linen, and the necessary utensils of the house.

11. Every scholar is to be provided yearly, at his own expense, with a new suit of blue clothes against His Majesty's birthday, conformable to a pattern suit lodged with the Master, except the sons of sea officers, who are to be allowed, by the Navy Board, £5 a year each, to provide the same.

12. The Master is to take care that all the scholars go neat and decent in their apparel, and that they shew due respect to

the Commission Officers of the Navy, and to the Officers of the Yard, whenever they meet with them.

13. It being intended that the scholars be instructed in Writing, Arithmetic, Drawing, Navigation, Gunnery, Fortification, and other useful parts of the Mathematics; and also in the French language, Dancing, Fencing, and the exercise of the firelock; and a Master, together with a competent number of qualified teachers and ushers appointed for that purpose, the said Master is to settle a Plan for a regular and orderly course in their several studies, and from time to time to vary it as he shall find necessary, which he is to lay before the Lords Commissioners of the Admiralty for their consent and approbation.

14. The hours of teaching shall be the same as are appointed for the shipwrights' working, excepting that the scholars shall be allowed half an hour for breakfast, and an hour and a half for dinner; and no times of intermission or holidays are to be allowed, except such as are observed in the Dockyard, and except Saturday in the afternoon.

15. On Sundays and other days of Public Worship the scholars are constantly to go to Church, accompanied by the Master and teachers.

16. The scholars are to be punished for their faults, during the first year of their being in the Academy, by the rod, by imposition of tasks, or by confinement, at the discretion of the Head-Master; and for more heinous offences by expulsion by order of the Lord High Admiral, or Lords Commissioners of the Admiralty for the time being.

26. Upon application from the parents or guardians of any of the scholars to the Commissioner, he may give them leave, either at Christmas or Whitsuntide, to be absent for three weeks to visit their friends.

27. The Master is to certify the names of such of the scholars as have been a year in the Academy to the Commissioner, after which time they are to be excused from going to school two afternoons in the week, and the Commissioner shall direct one of the Masters Attendants to carry them, one of the said afternoons, into the Rigging-House, and to show them the manner of preparing and fitting the rigging of ships; as also into the store-houses and sail-lofts; and likewise to take them afloat when

any works are doing that are fit for their knowledge, and even to employ them in such works as are proper for them.

29. The Commissioner may likewise appoint any ship or vessel in ordinary, of the smallest rate, to be placed as near the dock-yard as may be, and order the scholars to rig and unrig her frequently, under the inspection of one of the Masters Attendants or Boatswain of the Yard. He may also cause two guns to be placed in her, with their furniture and some powder and shot, and order one of the most experienced gunners of the ships in ordinary to exercise and instruct them in the use of cannon.

30. No scholar is to remain in the Academy above three years, nor less than two years, except the sons of sea officers under the above description, who shall not remain less than three, but may be permitted to continue five years therein, unless they shall sooner have gone through the Plan of Learning and their parents or guardians shall desire to have them sent to sea, or unless they shall have attained the age of 17, beyond which age they are not to remain in the Academy, but shall be sent to sea.

34. The scholars in H.M.'s ships shall be kept to the duty of seamen, but have the privilege of walking on the Quarter-Deck, and shall be allotted a proper place to lie in, without setting up any cabins for them, and they shall be rated on the ships' books with the title of *Volunteers by Order*, and receive Able Seamen's pay.

35. The Captain shall oblige the Volunteers to keep journals, and to draw the appearances of headlands, coasts, bays, and such-like; and the Master, Boatswain, and Schoolmaster shall instruct them in all parts of learning that may qualify them for the duty of Able Seamen and Midshipmen.

36. After two years' service at sea, the Captain of the ship shall rate them Midshipmen Ordinary or Midshipmen, if they are qualified for it.

41. Volunteers educated in the Academy and sent from thence by order of the Lord High Admiral or Commissioners of the Admiralty, to serve in H.M.'s ships, shall be qualified, in point of time, for Lieutenants, after so many years' service at sea as, together with the time specified in the certificate given

them upon their leaving the Academy, shall complete the term of 6 years, provided they have served 2 years thereof as Mates, Midshipmen, or Midshipmen Ordinary in H.M.'s ships, and are not under 20 years of age; but they shall pass the usual examination of their abilities, before they can be preferred.

95. A Cadet 'Passes Out' from Royal Academy, Portsmouth

P.R.O. Admiralty, Secretary, 'Out Letters,' 1759, pp. 62–4.

Whereas Mr Nathaniel Peacock has been educated in the Royal Academy at Portsmouth, and is well qualified to serve His Majesty at sea, you are hereby required and directed to receive him on board His Majesty's ship under your command, and enter him as one of her Complement.

You are to take care that he applies himself to the duty of a seaman; and he is to have the privilege of walking the Quarter-Deck; you are to allot him a proper place to lie in, without setting up any cabin, and you are to rate him Volunteer by Order, which will entitle him to Able Seaman's pay. You are to oblige him to keep a Journal, and to draw the appearance of headlands, coasts, bays, sands, rocks, & such like; and you are to take care that the Master, Boatswain, and Schoolmaster do instruct him in all parts of learning that may qualify him to do the duty of able Seaman and Midshipman.

After two years serving at sea, you are to rate him Midshipman Ordinary, or Midshipman, if he shall be qualified for it.

When your ship shall be at Spithead or in Portsmouth Harbour, you are to direct him to attend the Mathematical Master, in order to his examining his Journals, and representing to us how he has improved himself.

And, at the end of the service in the ship under your command, you are to give him such a certificate of his Sobriety, Diligence, and Skill in the profession of a Seaman, as he shall deserve; as also, of the length of time he has served with you, either as a Volunteer by Order, or a Midshipman.

Given, etc.

96. Wolfe's Tribute to the Fleet

The middle period of the eighteenth century—that covered by the Wars of Jenkins's Ear, the Austrian Succession and Seven Years' Wars—saw many combined expeditions, where fleet and army were in co-operation. These expeditions were too often marked by failure: Vernon could not work with Wentworth; Hawke and Mordaunt were at daggers drawn.

As a set off to these melancholy examples, and in proof that combined operations could and did end in triumphant success, the testimony of Wolfe to the part played by the sister-service is very valuable.

It is not always remembered that without Boscawen, Saunders and the pilots of the fleet, Wolfe could never have reached Quebec to immortalise his name on the Heights of Abraham.

Hist. MSS. Comm., *App. to 9th Report*: Stopford-Sackville MSS. p. 76. Louisburg. Wolfe to Lord G. Sackville, 1758.

The Admiral and the General have carried on public service with great harmony, industry and union. Mr Boscawen has given all and even more than we could ask of him. He has furnished arms and ammunition, pioneers, sappers, miners, gunners, carpenters, boats, and is, I must confess, no bad *fantassin* himself, and an excellent back-hand at a siege. Sir Charles Hardy too in particular, and all the Officers of the Navy in general, have given us their utmost assistance and with the greatest cheerfulness imaginable. I have been often in pain for Sir Charles's squadron at an anchor off the harbour's mouth. They rid out some very hard gales of wind rather than leave an opening for the French to escape.

The Ministry of England do not seem to see that to possess the isle of Aix with 5 or 6 battalions and a Fleet is one or other of the most brilliant and most useful strokes that this nation can possibly strike. It stops up at once the harbours of Rochefort and Rochelle, obstructs and ruins the whole trade of the Bay of Biscay, inevitably brings on a sea-fight which we ought by all means to aim at, and is the finest diversion that can possibly be made with a small force. If you will honour me with the command of 4000 upon that island, and give me a good quantity of artillery, fascines and sand-bags, I will establish myself in such a manner as to make it no easy matter to drive me out, and I am very sure the French would exchange Minorca or anything else to get it back again.

97. NAVIGATION OF THE ST LAWRENCE

Capt. John Knox, *Historical Journal of the Campaigns in North America, 1757–60*, I, 290. London, 1769.

June 25, 1759.

At 3 p.m. a French pilot was put on board of each transport, and the man who fell to the *Goodwill's* lot gasconaded at a most extravagant rate, and gave us to understand it was much against his inclination that he was become an English pilot. The poor fellow assumed great latitude in his conversation, said he made no doubt that some of the fleet would return to England, but they should have a dismal tale to carry with them; for Canada should be the grave of the whole army, and he expected, in a short time, to see the walls of Quebec ornamented with English scalps. Had it not been in obedience to the Admiral, who gave orders that he should not be ill used, he would certainly have been thrown overboard. At 4 p.m. we passed the Traverse, which is reputed a place of the greatest difficulty and danger between the entrance of St Lawrence and Quebec: it lies between Cape Tourmente (a remarkably high, black-looking promontory) and the east end of Orleans on the starboard side, and Isle de Madame on the larboard. Off Orleans we met some of our ships of war at anchor. As soon as the pilot came on board today, he gave his directions for the working of the ship, but the Master would not permit him to speak; he fixed his Mate at the helm, charged him not [to] take orders from any person except himself, and, going forward with his trumpet to the forecastle, gave the necessary instructions. All that could be said by the Commanding Officer, and the other gentlemen on board, was to no purpose; the pilot declared we should be lost, for that no French ship ever presumed to pass there without a pilot. 'Ay, ay, my dear,' replied our son of Neptune, 'but d——me, I'll convince you that an Englishman shall go where a Frenchman dare not show his nose.' The *Richmond* frigate being close astern of us, the Commanding Officer called out to the Captain, and told him our case; he inquired who the Master was, and was answered from the forecastle by the man himself, who told him he was old Killick, and that was enough. I went forward with this experienced mariner, who pointed out the channel to me as we passed, showing me, by the ripple and colour of the water, where there was any danger; and distinguishing the places where there were ledges of rock (to me invisible) from banks of sand, mud, or gravel. He gave his orders with great unconcern, joked with the sounding-boats who lay off on each side, with different-coloured flags for our guidance; and, when any of them called to him, and pointed to the deepest water, he answered, 'Ay, ay, my dear, chalk it down—a d——d dangerous navigation, eh? If you don't make a sputter about it, you'll get no credit for it in England, etc.' After we had cleared this remarkable place, where the channel forms a complete zig-zag, the Master called to his Mate to give the helm to somebody else, saying, 'D—— me if there are not a thousand places in the Thames fifty times more hazardous than this; I am ashamed that Englishmen should make such a rout about it.' The Frenchman asked me if the Captain had not been here before. I assured him in the negative, upon which he viewed him with great attention, lifting, at the same time, his hands and eyes to heaven with astonishment and fervency.

98. The Capture of Quebec

A portion of Saunders's modest dispatch announcing the capture of Quebec is a tribute to the harmony existing between the land and sea service:

I am sorry to acquaint you that General Wolfe was killed in the action, and General Monckton shot thro' the body, but he is now supposed to be out of danger; I am beginning to send on shore the stores they will want, and provisions for 5000 men, of which I can furnish them with a sufficient quantity.

The night of their landing, Admiral Holmes with the ships and troops was about three leagues above the intended landing place; General Wolfe with about half his troops set off in the boats, and dropped down with the tide, and were, by that means, less liable to be discovered by the sentinels posted all along the coast. The ships followed them about ¾ of an hour afterwards and got to the landing place just at the time that had been concerted to cover their landing; and, considering the darkness of the night and the rapidity of the current, this was a very critical operation, and very properly and successfully conducted.

When General Wolfe and the troops with him had landed, the difficulty of gaining the top of the hill is scarce credible: it was very steep in its ascent, and high, had no path where two could go abreast, but they were obliged to pull themselves up by the stumps and boughs of trees that covered the declivity.

I have the pleasure also of acquainting their lordships that during this tedious campaign, there has continued a perfect good understanding between the Army and Navy: I have received great assistance from Admirals Durell and Holmes, and from all the captains; indeed everybody has exerted themselves in the execution of their duty; even the transports have willingly assisted me with boats and people on landing the troops and many other services.

Stirling Castle off Quebec, 21 Septr, 1759.

99. HAWKE AND THE BLOCKADE OF BREST, 1759

The strategy which secured for Great Britain that supremacy at sea upon which depended her national existence and the winning and maintaining of her colonial empire may be fairly summarised in the dual aspects of Blockade and Battle.

Wherever and whenever the seeking out and destruction of the enemy's fleets was held to be a cardinal principle, and acted upon as such, our greatest triumphs at sea were won. If, as so often happened, the enemy were unwilling to hazard all in a general engagement, then it was imperative to keep his fleets marked down (and immobilised) by a system of *Blockade*. The method of watching the enemy's movements with a fleet operating from our own home ports proved too 'open' for complete security; and it could not prevent reinforcements from leaving Brest for America and the Indies.

As Commander-in-Chief in 1759, Hawke was the originator of the famous *close blockade*. His scheme was again employed in greater detail and completeness by St Vincent and Cornwallis to defeat the invasion schemes of Napoleon.

It will be noted that stormy weather compelled the withdrawal of the big ships to Torbay. Little more than half of the month that preceded the Battle of Quiberon Bay could be spent in close-watching Brest.

The passages which follow illustrate some of the difficulties encountered in this close blockade. The reproduction of Hawke's Quiberon Despatch is its own justification.

P.R.O. Admiralty, 'In Letters.'

Sir,   *Ramillies* in Torbay, 6th June, 1759.

For several days preceding my last, by express of the 4th inst., we had had very fresh gales with a great sea. Yesterday it increased so much at S.W. with a thick fog, as to make several of the ships complain, more particularly the new ships. As in this weather it was impossible for the enemy to stir, and our own ships stood in need of a day or two, to get themselves to rights, in the evening I bore away for this place. I shall use the utmost dispatch in getting them ready for sea, which I hope will be by the time, or before, I can receive an answer to this. In that case I shall sail again with any moderate wind; as from the last accounts of the enemy, it appears to me to be of the greatest consequence that we should be on our station again before they can get a fair wind to bring them out.

I have left the *Rochester*, *Melampé*, *Minerva* and *Prince Edward* cutter off Brest.

I am,
Sir,
Your most obedient, humble servant,
EDWARD HAWKE.

John Clevland, Esqr.

Ramillies, at Sea, 12th June, 1759.

8 a.m. The Start N.E. ¾N., distant 19 leagues.

Sir,
The cutter joined me from Capt. Duff, who looked into Brest Road the 7th instant, and then saw eighteen two-decked ships. I shall send from time to time to Plymouth for what may be wanting in the squadron, and, except I shall be drove off by winds and weather, keep them constantly in view, so as either to prevent their coming out, or doing my utmost, in case they should, to take or destroy them.

The sea is not quite down, so that I cannot send you a more particular state of the squadron at present.

I am,
Sir,
Your most obedient, humble servant,
ED. HAWKE.

John Clevland, Esqr.

Hawke's Quiberon Despatch. (Montagu Burrows, *Life of Hawke*, p. 394.)

Royal George, off Penris Point.
November 24th, 1759.

Sir,

In my letter of the 17th by express, I desired you would acquaint their Lordships with my having received intelligence of 18 sail of the line and three frigates of the Brest squadron being discovered about 24 leagues to the north-west of Belle-isle, steering to the eastward. All the prisoners, however, agree that on the day we chased them, their squadron consisted, according to the accompanying list, of four ships of 80, six of 74, three of 70, eight of 64, one frigate of 36, one of 34, and one of 16 guns, with a small vessel to look out. They sailed from Brest the 14th instant, the same day I sailed from Torbay. Concluding that their first rendez-vous would be Quiberon, the instant I received the intelligence I directed my course thither with a pressed sail. At first the wind blowing hard at S.b.E. and S. drove us considerably to the westward. But on the 18th and 19th, though variable, it proved more favourable. In the mean-time having been joined by the *Maidstone* and *Coventry* frigates, I directed their commanders to keep ahead of the squadron, one on the starboard and the other on the larboard bow.

At half past 8 o'clock on the morning of the 20th, Belleisle, by our reckoning, bearing E.b.N. ¼N. about 13 leagues, the *Maidstone* made the signal for seeing a fleet. I immediately spread abroad the signal for the line abreast, in order to draw all the ships of the squadron up with me. I had before sent the *Magnanime* ahead to make the land. At ¾ past 9 she made the signal for seeing an enemy. Observing, on my discovering them, that they made off, I threw out the signal for the seven ships nearest them to chase, and draw into a line of battle ahead of me, and endeavour to stop them till the rest of the squadron should come up, who were also to form as they chased, that no time might be lost in the pursuit. That morning they were in chase of the *Rochester, Chatham, Portland, Falkland, Minerva, Vengeance*, and *Venus*, all which joined me about 11 o'clock, and in the evening the *Sapphire* from Quiberon Bay. All the day we had very fresh gales at N.W. and W.N.W., with heavy squalls.

Monsieur Conflans kept going off under such sail as all his squadron could carry, and at the same time keep together; while we crowded after him with every sail our ships could bear. At ½ past 2 p.m. the fire beginning ahead, I made the signal for engaging. We were then to the southward of Belleisle, and the French Admiral headmost soon after led round the Cardinals, while his rear was in action. About 4 o'clock the *Formidable* struck, and a little after, the *Thésée* and *Superbe* were sunk. About 5, the *Héros* struck, and came to an anchor, but it blowing hard, no boat could be sent on board her. Night was now come, and being on a part of the coast among islands and shoals of which we were totally ignorant, without a pilot, as was the greatest part of the squadron, and blowing hard on a lee shore, I made the signal to anchor, and came-to in 15 fathom water, the Island of Dumet bearing E.b.N. between 2 and 3 miles, the Cardinals W. ½S., and the steeples of Crozie [Croisic] S.E., as we found next morning.

In the night we heard many guns of distress fired, but, blowing hard, want of knowledge of the coast, and whether they were fired by a friend or an enemy, prevented all means of relief.

By daybreak of the 21st we discovered one of our ships (the *Resolution*) dismasted, ashore on the Four. The French *Héros* also, and the *Soleil Royal*, which under cover of the night had anchored among us, cut and run ashore to the westward of Crozie. On the latter's moving I made the *Essex's* signal to slip and pursue her; but she unfortunately got upon the Four, and both she and the *Resolution* are irrecoverably lost, notwithstanding that we sent them all the assistance that the weather would permit. About fourscore of the *Resolution's* company, in spite of the strongest remonstrances of their Captain, made rafts, and with several French prisoners belonging to the *Formidable*, put off, and I am afraid drove out to sea. All the *Essex's* are safe, with as many of the stores as possible, except one Lieutenant and a boat's crew, who were drove on the French shore, and have not since been heard of. The remains of both ships are set on fire. We found the *Dorsetshire*, *Revenge*, and *Defiance*, in the night of the 20th, put out to sea, as I hope the *Swiftsure* did, for she is still missing. The *Dorsetshire* and *Defiance* returned the next day, and the latter saw the *Revenge* without. Thus what loss we have sustained has been owing to the weather, not the enemy, seven or eight of whose line of battle ships got to sea, I believe, the night of the action.

As soon as it was broad daylight, in the morning of the 21st, I discovered seven or eight of the enemy's line of battle ships at anchor between Point Penris and the river Vilaine, on which I made the signal to weigh in order to work up and attack them. But it blowed so hard from the N.W. that, instead of daring to cast the squadron loose, I was obliged to strike topgallant masts. Most of those ships appeared to be aground at low water. But on the flood, by lightening them, and the advantage of the wind under the land, all except two got that night into the river Vilaine.

The weather being moderate on the 22nd, I sent the *Portland*, *Chatham*, and *Vengeance*, to destroy the *Soleil Royal* and *Héros*. The French, on the approach of our ships, set the first on fire; and soon after, the latter met the same fate from our people. In the meantime I got under way, and worked up within Penris Point, as well for the sake of its being a safer road as to destroy, if possible, the two ships of the enemy which still lay without the river Vilaine. But before the ships I sent ahead for that purpose could get near them, being quite light, and with the tide of flood, they got in.

All the 23rd we were occupied in reconnoitring the entrance of that river, which is very narrow, and only 12 foot water on the bar at low water. We discovered 7 if not 8 line of battle ships, about half a mile within, quite light, and two large frigates moored across to defend the mouth of the river. Only the frigates appeared to have guns in. By evening I had twelve long boats fitted as fireships ready to attempt burning them under cover of the *Sapphire* and *Coventry*. But the weather being bad, and the wind contrary, obliged me to defer it till at least the latter should be favourable. If they can by any means be destroyed it shall be done.

In attacking a flying enemy, it was impossible in the space of a short winter's day that all our ships should be able to get into action, or all those of the enemy brought to it. The Commanders and companies of such as did come up with the rear of the

French on the 20th behaved with the greatest intrepidity, and gave the strongest proofs of a true British spirit. In the same manner I am satisfied would those have acquitted themselves, whom bad-going ships, or the distance they were at in the morning, prevented from getting up.

Our loss by the enemy is not considerable. For in the ships which are now with me, I find only one Lieutenant and fifty seamen and marines killed, and about two hundred and twenty wounded.

When I consider the season of the year, the hard gales on the day of action, a flying enemy, the shortness of the day, and the coast they were on, I can boldly affirm that all that could possibly be done has been done. As to the loss we have sustained, let it be placed to the account of the necessity I was under of running all risks to break this strong force of the enemy. Had we had but two hours more daylight, the whole had been totally destroyed or taken; for we were almost up with their van when night overtook us.

Yesterday came in here the *Pallas, Fortune* sloop, and the *Proserpine* fireship. On the 16th I had dispatched the *Fortune* to Quiberon with directions to Captain Duff to keep strictly on his guard. In her way thither she fell in with the *Hebe*, a French frigate of 40 guns, under jury masts, and fought her several hours. During the engagement Lieutenant Stuart, 2nd of the *Ramillies*, whom I had appointed to command her, was unfortunately killed. The surviving officers, on consulting together, resolved to leave her, as she proved too strong for them. I have detached Captain Young to Quiberon Bay, with five ships, and am making up a flying squadron to scour the coast to the southward, as far as the Isle of Aix; and, if practicable, to attempt any of the enemy's ships that may be there.

I am, etc.,

EDWARD HAWKE.

John Clevland, Esqr.

WAR OF AMERICAN INDEPENDENCE,
1778–1783

WHILE the Seven Years' War showed an administrator of supreme genius working in unison with his naval and military 'seconds,' compelling efficiency out of an imperfect system and making the most of the weapons at his command, in the War of American Independence a slack and corrupt government entirely failed not only to cover up defects (much less to remedy them) but to exact loyal service from the many able commanders at its disposal. Granted that the difficulties and dangers of this latter war were immeasurably greater, it is hard to believe that the storms encountered by North and Sandwich would not have been weathered more successfully by Pitt and Anson. In the designing of plans for the conduct of the war, ministers appeared to have learned nothing and forgotten everything. Lord Chatham at any rate was under no delusion, since he found it necessary in time of peace to reiterate the sound and indispensable principles of naval strategy.

Although marked by almost unrelieved failure in its military aspects, the War of American Independence is of vital interest and importance in any study of naval development.

100. THE PRINCIPLES OF NAVAL STRATEGY

Speech by the Earl of Chatham, November 22, 1770, in the Debate on the Duke of Richmond's Motion respecting the Seizure of Falkland's Islands. (*Parliamentary History.*)

The first great and acknowledged object of national defence in the country, is to maintain such a superior naval force at home, that even the united fleets of France and Spain may never be masters of the Channel. If that should ever happen, what is there to hinder their landing in Ireland, or even upon our own coast? They have often made the attempt; in King William's time it succeeded. King James embarked on board a French fleet and landed with a French army in Ireland. In the meantime the French were masters of the Channel, and continued so until their fleet was destroyed by Admiral Russell.

The second naval object with an English minister should be to maintain at all times a powerful western squadron. In the profoundest peace it should be respectable; in war it should be

formidable. Without it, the colonies, the commerce, the navigation of Great Britain lie at the mercy of the House of Bourbon.
While I had the honour of acting with Lord Anson, that able
officer never ceased to inculcate upon the minds of his Majesty's
servants the necessity of constantly maintaining a strong western
squadron; and I must vouch for him, that while he was at the
head of the marine, it was never neglected.

The third object indispensable, as I conceive, in the distribution of our navy, is to maintain such a force in the Bay of
Gibraltar as may be sufficient to cover that garrison, to watch
the motions of the Spaniards, and to keep open the communication with Minorca.

How will your Lordships be astonished when I inform you
in what manner they have provided for these great, these
essential objects? As to the first, we cannot send out eleven
ships of the line so manned and equipped that any officer of
rank and credit in the service shall accept of the command and
stake his reputation on it. We have one ship-of-the-line at
Jamaica, one at the Leeward Islands, and one at Gibraltar; yet
at this very moment, for aught the ministry know, both Jamaica
and Gibraltar may be attacked; and if they are attacked (which
God forbid) they must fall. Nothing can prevent it but the
appearance of a superior squadron.

We could not this day send out eleven ships-of-the-line
properly equipped, and tomorrow the enemy may be masters of
the Channel. If the enemy were to land in full force, either on
this coast or in Ireland, where is your army? What is your
defence?

When America, the West Indies, Gibraltar, and Minorca
are taken care of, consider, my Lords, what part of this army
will remain to defend Ireland and Great Britain.

They who talk of confining a great war to naval operations
only, speak without knowledge or experience. We can no more
command the disposition than the events of a war. Wherever
we are attacked, there we must defend.

101 and 102. DIVISIONS

For permission to print the following note and extract we are indebted to Commander J. H. Owen, R.N.

Middleton's order book in the *Ardent* in 1775 and Howe's standing orders in North America in 1776, together with remarks made by Kempenfelt three years later still, suggest that it was then a new idea for a ship's company to be organised in divisions commanded by the lieutenants and midshipmen. But Admiral Smith's orders—given below—are twenty years older.

By Thomas Smith Esquire Vice Admiral of the White Squadron of his Majesty's Fleet and Commander in Chief of his Majesty's Ships & Vessels employed & to be employed in the Downs.

FOR the more effectual keeping clean the men belonging to his Majesty's Ship under your command which must greatly conduce to their health——YOU are hereby required and directed to observe the following Instructions.

DIVIDE the midshipmen and those acting as such into as many parties as you have lieutenants.

Put one of those parties under the direction of each of the lieutenants.

Divide the rest of your ship's company (carpenter's crew, gunner's crew, quarter masters, other inferior petty officers, boats' crews, and boys, excepted) into as many parties as you have lieutenants, and put one of those parties under charge of each lieutenant.

Each lieutenant to take an account of the clothing and bedding of each man in his party, and report the same to you, keeping an account of the same himself.

Each lieutenant to subdivide his party of men into as many smaller parties as there are midshipmen allotted to him, giving an inventory to each midshipman of the clothes and bedding belonging to each man whom he has put into the said midshipman's party.

Each midshipman to muster the clothes and bedding of each man under his direction twice a week, and take care that the men are always kept tight and shifted as often as mustered; and if at any time any of their clothes and bedding are missing, it is to be reported to the lieutenant whose direction they are under, who is to report it to you, that you may punish the person whose clothes are missing in such a manner as is agreeable to the custom of the Navy.

The master of the ship is to see that his mates and yeomen take care of their respective crews in the same manner.

The coxswains of each boat to do the same by their respective crews.

The captain's steward to do the same with respect to the captain's servants.

The master and his mates, carpenter, gunner, and their mates and yeomen, the coxswains and captain's steward, all to report the condition of their parties to you or the commanding officer.

And that the men's hammacoes may be constantly kept clean and the men not exposed to lie in them before they are effectually dry, you are to order your boatswain to keep such a number of hammacoes always slung as are equal to a twentieth part of your ship's company, to be delivered to the men whose hammacoes are to be washed, which are to be taken back when their own hammacoes are sufficiently dry and delivered to others for the same purpose.

LET each midshipman's party consist as near as possible of proportional numbers of able seamen, ordinary, and landmen, to the intent that if men are wanted to be detached on any service from the ship, the detachments may be made by one or more parties; by which means the men who are not seamen will sooner become so, and all will be kept in better order by being immediately under the eye and direction of the officer they are accustomed to; and for the same reason let the parties be divided, both for half watch and third watch, as near as possible.

And for the more expeditious training of all the men in general to the use of the great guns and small arms, you are to cause the commander of each party to learn the exercise of the same as soon as possible, and that so effectually that they themselves may be able to exercise the men of their parties therein.

And you are likewise at all times to take every opportunity of teaching your landmen to loose, furl, and reef, the sails, and exercise your people at great guns and small arms, or do anything else that may make them serviceable without waiting any signal or motion from the flag.

The commander of each party to be always present with his men on this and all occasions at training them.

And that the people may be instructed in heaving the lead and steering, you are when at anchor to cause all who are not acquainted with heaving the lead to be employed by turns in the chains for the learning the same; and when at sea and the weather moderate, you are always to have an ordinary seaman or landman at your lee helm; and to encourage them to learn this as well as other parts of a seaman's duty, you are to inform them that they cannot be rated able till they are acquainted with those things.

AND for the more effectual preserving his Majesty's Ship under your command from any accident by fire——YOU are hereby required and directed to take into your possession the keys of the storerooms belonging to the boatswain, gunner, and carpenter, and never permit any of the said officers or their yeomen to go into the same without a midshipman, who is to have the keys delivered to him when stores are wanting, and who is to return the same to the officer of the watch or day officer after the stores wanting are taken out.

And you are to lay the strongest injunctions on every officer and man belonging to your ship not to draw off any spirituous liquors of any kind below the upper deck of your ship, strictly charging the petty officers of each party to acquaint you if at any time they find any person whatsoever acting contrary thereto. And the key of the brandy room or any place where spirituous liquors are lodged is to be kept by the first lieutenant and delivered to the mate of the watch at serving time, who is to see the brandy got up and the people served and the remainder put down, after which he is to return the key to the lieutenant.

You are to give directions that no person whatsoever shall burn any candles but in broad low candlesticks, either of brass, copper, iron, or tin; and you are to cause your purser to procure a sufficient number of broad iron candlesticks, with a long pointed piece of iron for fixing to the parts of the ship while the hold is stowing and to the "Bills" [? bitts] and other necessary places to give light while the ship is unmooring.

And you are to cause a midshipman of the watch with two men to go the rounds every hour both day and night between the decks, and in the cockpit, cable tiers, and all over the holds of the ship, as well to see that no lights be lighted from the setting of the watch to its discharge, as to see that all lights which are necessary to be lighted at other times may be secure; and if he finds any candles stuck to the sides or burning in hoop sticks or in any other way than in the above-mentioned candlesticks, he is to report it to the commanding officer that the person so using them may be punished for the same.

And you are to take care that your fire engine be kept in such a part of the quarter deck where it is least liable to be damaged, and that it may always be kept slung in such a manner as will make it most easy to move from one part of the ship to the other; and you are to cause the said engine to be played once a week with its pipes and all its leather hoses, as will make the men expert in the management of it in its different uses as to know if any part of it be out of order; and you are to cause all the leather hoses to be kept well "laquard" and always at hand, either under the awning if you have one or under the half deck if you have not.

And you are to direct that the midshipmen of the watch who go the rounds do see all men they find far gone in drink put into their hammacoes; and if they are riotous and will not continue in them, they are to be confined in the gunroom and their names reported to you or the commanding officer that they may be punished when sober for their offences.

And you are to inform the midshipmen that in the execution of the above order they are not to interrupt the men in mirth and good fellowship while they keep within the bounds of moderation: the intention of it being to prevent excessive drinking, which is not only a crime of itself but often draws men into others which when sober they would most abhor.

> Given under my hand on board his Majesty's Ship Oxford in the Downs this 13th Novr., 1755.

To
Captain James Galbraith
  of his Majesty's Ship
    Swiftsure.

103. THE LOSS OF THE *ROYAL GEORGE*

The finding of the Court-Martial was carefully suppressed by the Admiralty, so that it was made possible for credulous persons to believe in the mythical 'land-breeze' that 'shook the shrouds' as the cause of the disaster. The full minutes are to be found in the Public Record Office.

At a Court-Martial assembled and held on Board His Majesty's Ship *Warspite* in Portsmouth Harbour on Monday, the 9th Day of September, 1782.

Present:

The Hon. Samuel Barrington, Vice-Admiral of the White Squadron and second officer in the command of His Majesty's ships and vessels at Portsmouth and Spithead—President.

Jno. Evans, Esq., Vice-Admiral of the Blue.	Mark Milbank, Esq., Vice-Admiral of the Blue.
Alexr. Hood, Esq., Rear-Admiral of the White.	Sir Richard Hughes, Bart, Rear-Admiral of the Blue.
Comm. Wm. Hotham.	The Hon. Jno. Levison Gore.

Capts.	*Capts.*
John Carter Allen.	John Dalrymple.
John Moutray.	Jonathan Faulknor.
Sir Jno. Jervis, Kt. of the Bath.	Adam Duncan.

The Court in pursuance of an Order from the Commissioners for executing the Office of Lord High Admiral of Gt. Britain & Ireland, etc., dated the 4th Day of this instant September, for enquiring into the Cause and Circumstances of the Loss of His Majesty's Ship the *Royal George* in the morning of the 29th Day of last month, and for the Trial of the Officers and Company of His Majesty's said Ship *Royal George* for their conduct upon that occasion, having proceeded to enquire into the Cause and Circumstances of the Loss of the said Ship *Royal George* and to try her Officers and Company for their conduct accordingly; and having heard the narrative of Captain Martin Waghorn, which was read to the Court, and the evidence adduced, and having maturely and deliberately considered the same, it appears to the Court that the ship was not over-heeled: it also appears to the Court that the Captain, Officers and Ship's

Company used every exertion to right the ship, as soon as the Alarm was given of her Settling; and the Court is of opinion, from the short Space of Time between the Alarm being given and the Sinking of the Ship, that some material part of her Frame gave way, which can only be accounted for by the general state of the Decay of her Timbers, as appears upon the Minutes: The Court doth therefore Adjudge that the Captain, Officers and Ship's Company be acquitted of all Blame on account of the Loss of the said Ship, and they are hereby acquitted of all Blame on account of the loss of her accordingly.

(Signatures of Court here.)

Wm. Bettesworth.

Judge-Advocate on this Occasion.

(Extracts from the evidence of some of the witnesses are given below.)

George Aynon, a shipwright belonging to H.M.'s Dockyard, sent on board to bore, was then called in and sworn.

Court. Were you boring the hole for the cock?

Answer. Yes, I and my brother were.

C. Did you perceive that the ship had a very great heel, or any more than right?

A. No, I did not. I was boring the hole, and my brother sitting down in the tier by me; there was a table that was standing close by me, and that table fell down. I said to my brother the ship was heeling more. He asked me whether I was afraid or not; I told him I was not afraid, but I should like to go upon deck. I stopped, and he immediately found the tier cable going from under him, and he ran to the hatchway, and I stopped and took up my clothes and carried them up on my back, and a man helped me out of the port. Before this, whilst I was boring the hole, the Carpenter came down and said to my brother he had been up upon deck, and the Officers were angry with him for giving the vessel such a heel, and asked him whether there was any danger, and he said he told them none, and he said that the Officers told him, if it could not be conveniently done at that time, to let it alone. My brother made answer and said that it could not be done as it ought to be done, owing to the weather on the outside and the ship not being sufficiently heeled. He mentioned this also when he first slung the grating over the side. The Carpenter asked him, why so, but what farther answer my brother gave I cannot recollect. When we were boring these holes, a man came to us and said there was a deal of water in the hold. We asked him how much, and he said 32 inches.

My brother and I were observing to one another that there must be a deal of water in the bilge, if there were so much in the well.

C. Which way do you apprehend this water came in?

A. I do not know.

C. How was the plank?

A. Sound, but the timbers were rotten.

C. Did you ever perceive any water coming in, till the ship was going down?

A. No, except a very little at the old cock, but that was nothing.

C. Do you know who the person was that told you the water was in the hold?

A. No.

C. Did he appear alarmed, or to intend to give any alarm to you?

A. No.

C. Did he go upon deck?

A. I do not know.

C. Were the timbers of both the holes rotten?

A. Yes, both, and the trunnels.

C. How far were the holes asunder?

A. About 18 inches.

C. Do you know from what cause the ship went down?

A. I do not.

C. Can you form any opinion as to it?

A. No, I cannot.

C. Did you hear anything crack when she went down?

A. No, I did not; but there was such a general cry of the people and noise of things rolling about, that it was impossible to distinguish anything else.

C. Whilst you were boring the holes, did you hear any other observation made, on the situation of the ship, than what you have related, or of any alarm being given to the Officers that there was any water in her, or that she was over-heeled?

A. No; we knew of nothing till we heard the drum beat.

C. Did you happen to make any observations to your brother, or him to you, upon finding the timbers were rotten?

A. None; only the Carpenter, who was present when we found the timbers were rotten, observed that the next time she came home, she must go into dock to be repaired, for they had tied her up with riders as much as they could.

The witness withdrew.

John Smart, late Gunner's Yeoman of the *Royal George*, was then called in and sworn.

C. What part of the ship were you in, when the ship was upon the heel, on the morning of the 29th of last month?

A. In the Gunroom.

C. Did she seem to have a larger heel than usual?

A. I could not observe she had; and I opened the Gunner's cabin to see if everything was fast there, and I saw everything in order, and that nothing had fallen, or slid out of its place.

C. Did you see any water come in at the lower ports?

A. I did not: I was on the starboard side.

C. Did you continue in the Gunroom?

A. I did, till I heard a great crack.

C. What crack did it appear to be?

A. It appeared to be a bodily crack.

C. Was it above or below?

A. Below.

C. What do you mean by a bodily crack?

A. She gave a great jerk or crack first, and within a moment after, another, and went down, and I jumped out of the starboard stern port.

C. Did you observe the heel to be increased before you heard the first crack?

A. No, not in the least.

C. Were there any of the Lower Deck guns over to leeward?

A. None that I know of: the breechings of some of those abaft were cast off, and the guns eased into the combings.

C. Did you ever hear any observation made or alarm given by any person that the ship was over-heeled, or was taking water in, or otherways in danger?

A. I did not. I saw the Armourer jump out of the larboard stern port, just after the second crack, and I then jumped out of the starboard one.

The witness withdrew.

Evidence of Henry Dunbar, late Midshipman of the *Royal George*, quartered on the Lower Gun Deck.

C. Do you know how far the weather guns were run over?

A. Those under my directions were eased in to the combings.

C. How far were the larboard ports from the water, when the ship was heeled?

A. I looked about 7 o'clock, and they were then better than a foot out of the water.

C. Did you ever observe them nearer than that?

A. No. I was below writing in the Orlop[1], from the heeling of the ship to about a quarter of an hour before the ship went down: I observed nothing particular as I went up and down.

C. How long have you belonged to the *Royal George*?

A. About four months.

C. Did you ever see her heeled before?

A. Only just to scrub.

C. Did you perceive anything uncommon in the heel she had that morning?

A. No; nor did it strike anybody as such, to my knowledge.

C. Did you hear any observation made, or alarm given, by any person, that the ship was over-heeled, or was taking in water, or was any otherways in danger?

A. No; not till the drum beat to Quarters to right ship.

The witness withdrew.

Part of Evidence of Mr William Leslie, the Surgeon's Mate.

C. Did she appear to have more heel on the 29th of last month than she had in Torbay, when to pay the bends[2]?

---

[1] MS. 'Hollop.'

[2] *I.e.* to tallow or tar the thickest timbers on the ship's sides.

A. She did not; nor did we at breakfast suffer any inconvenience, or perceive that she was heeled more than she had been usually heeled.

C. Did the tables stand?

A. Yes.

C. Did the table with the medicines and dressings upon it on the Lower Deck stand without support?

A. Yes, to the best of my recollection.

Extract from the evidence of Lieutenant Durham, called in a second time.

C. Did you hear that the provisions were ordered to be stowed on the larboard side of the Main Deck, in order to give the ship a larger heel?

A. No, I did not.

C. How was the wind at the time the ship overset—upon what part of the ship did it blow, I mean?

A. Right ahead.

C. Was the lighter alongside entirely cleared, or only in part?

A. Only in part.

(After all the witnesses had been examined) Vice-Admiral Milbank informed the Court from his place as follows:

When the *Royal George* was docked at Plymouth, I had the honour to command there, and during her being in dock I gave her very constant attendance, saw her opened, and asked many questions; and found her so bad that I do not recollect there was a sound timber in the opening. I asked several of the Officers of the Yard what they intended to do with her, and they said they should be able to make her last a summer, and very bad she was indeed, insomuch that they could scarce find fastenings for the repairs she underwent.

Sir John Jervis from his place confirmed what Vice-Admiral Milbank had related to the Court, respecting the rottenness of the timbers that were exposed to view in her last docking.

The Court was cleared.

After some time spent in deliberation, the Court agreed on the sentence, which was drawn up, and signed by the members and Judge-Advocate.

The Judge-Advocate then pronounced the sentence in open Court. The sentence was then delivered by the Judge-Advocate to the President, to be transmitted to their Lordships.

A true copy, examined with the original minutes by me,

W. BETTESWORTH,

Judge-Advocate on this occasion.

104. CONCENTRATION AT THE VITAL POINT

Extract from Keppel's Speech in the Commons, December 20, 1781. (Keppel, *Life of Keppel*, II, 364.)

Admiral Kempenfelt[1] was a favourite with the Admiralty, and undoubtedly he deserved to be so; but still they had not given him a sufficient force. Upon the expedition from Brest to the West Indies depended the safety of our islands; and all concerns of an inferior nature ought to give way to the most pressing. The safety of our islands ought to be the principal object of our care; we should, therefore, have detached some of our force from the East to strengthen our commander before Brest, as the service he was upon was infinitely more important than was that for which our force in the Downs was stationed. The West Indies might have been preserved. He had said before, and was ready to repeat it, that if a proper use had been made of the force which we actually had, the Comte de Rochambeau would never have been able to land in America; and consequently, the surrender of Lord Cornwallis would never have taken place. He would not say there was treachery, but there was neglect, and an evident want of naval skill in that Board. He, and he believed every man at all acquainted with the nature of a maritime war, held it to be indispensable that, where your force was inferior to that of your enemy, everything depended on the proper direction of it. It was no excuse to say, 'We sent so many ships here, and so many there,' enumerating a parcel

---

[1] On December 12, 1781, Kempenfelt had achieved his brilliant success— the cutting off and capture of 20 prizes in face of a vastly superior French fleet under de Guichen.

of petty occasions. Lesser interests ought to sink before greater. Where the necessity pressed most, there the object should be most attended to, and the preference shown. Admiral Kempenfelt's was a great enterprise; the object was more important than almost any other that had been attempted. It was chiefly from a wise use of our force in Europe that we were to look for success. Had the French design been frustrated on the onset, Sir George Rodney might have taken his time in going to the West Indies. It would have been better to take some of our ships from the East, and send them to assist Mr Kempenfelt, than that his endeavours should have failed.

105. Keppel recommends a Lighter Gun

Keppel to Sandwich. (Keppel, *Life of Keppel*, II, 17.)

Audley Square,
10th March, 1778.

My Lord,—Since I had the honour of conversing with your Lordship upon the equipment of the *Victory*, I recollected that I had omitted giving you my thoughts upon the heavy guns that have been usually put on board ships of the first rate, and which I wish to propose to your Lordship being of a lesser size.

At present the lower deck guns carry a ball of 42 lbs. A gun carrying a ball of 32 lbs. weight seems, to my poor judgment, preferable on many accounts.

First,—Because it may, on board a ship, be fired much oftener than a larger gun.

Secondly,—Because the lesser guns may be used in service at particular times, when guns of 42 lbs. ball cannot be managed at all, and the smaller gun will admit of being traversed more fore and aft.

Thirdly,—Because it will be a considerable ease to a ship at sea.

And fourthly,—Because almost every sea officer of rank that I have conversed with on the matter agrees with these opinions most thoroughly.

I am therefore, my Lord, very desirous that the gun carrying a 32 lb. ball should be directed and established as the lower tier of guns on board the *Victory*.

I have the honour to be, with much respect,
Your Lordship's
Most obedient and humble servant,
A. KEPPEL.

106. JERVIS ON THE INDECISIVE ACTION OFF USHANT, 1778

Jervis to Jackson[1]. (Brenton, *Life of St Vincent*.)

Foudroyant, Plymouth Sound,
July 31st, 1778.

My dear Jackson,—I do not agree with Goodall that we have been outwitted: the French, I am convinced, never would have fought us, if they had not been surprised into it, by a sudden shift of wind; and when they formed their inimitable line, after our brush, it was merely to cover their intention of flight. Four of our ships having got themselves to leeward so far as to be cut off by the enemy, if Admiral Keppel had not judiciously bore down to them, and the shattered state of Sir Hugh's, which disabled him from taking his place in the line, rendered it impossible to renew the attack on the evening of the 27th. I have often told you that two fleets of equal force never can produce decisive events, unless they are equally determined to fight it out, or the Commander-in-Chief of one of them misconducts his line. I perceive it is the fashion for people to puff themselves, and no doubt you have seen, or will see, some of these accounts. For my part, I forbade the officers to write by the frigate that carried the despatches—I did not write a syllable myself, except touching my health; nor shall I, but to state the intrepidity of the officers and people under my command (through the most infernal fire I ever saw or heard of) to my Lord Sandwich, in which particular mention will be made of young Wells.

I am
Most truly yours,
J. J.

[1] Sir George Jackson, Bart. (1725–1822), Secretary to the Navy Board in 1758. Second Secretary to the Admiralty and Judge-Advocate in 1766, in which capacity he served at Keppel's trial in 1778. He was an early patron of Cook, the circumnavigator.

In justice to the *Foudroyant*, I must observe to you that, though she received the fire of 17 sail, and had the *Bretagne*, *Ville de Paris*, and a 74 upon her at the same time, and appeared more disabled in her masts and rigging than any other ship, she was the first in the line of battle, and really and truly fitter for business in essentials (because the people were cool) than when she began. Keep this to yourself, unless you hear too much said in praise of others.

107. KEMPENFELT ON FRENCH GUNNERY

In the scientific study of tactics the French took the lead. English authors lagged behind. No important original work on the subject appeared in English until John Clerk, Esq., of Eldin[1], published his *Essay on Naval Tactics (First Part)* in 1790. Books produced previous to this were translations from the great French authorities. Thus, in 1762, Lieutenant Christopher O'Bryen, R.N., published a partial translation of Hoste's *Treatise*. Then appeared in 1767 a partial translation 'by a sea officer' of Morogues' *Tactique Navale*[2] (1763). In 1782 a few copies of Clerk's *Essay* were printed privately. In 1788 another French 'classic' was translated—de Villehuet's *Le Manœuvrier* (1765). Not until 1797 was Clerk's complete work, in four parts, published.

It is hard to exaggerate the debt owed by the most distinguished of the English tactical thinkers to the great French writers. John Clerk's position is interesting in so far as he had the honour as a civilian to write, in English, the first important work on tactics. It is quite clear that he gave to the service little or nothing that was novel—no problems that had not been deeply pondered many years before his book was published. His plan for breaking the line from to leeward first appeared in 1797, five years after the death of Rodney. Kempenfelt had nothing to learn from Clerk.

The following passages from Kempenfelt's correspondence, though short and miscellaneous, will illustrate the breadth and versatility of his views. Those best qualified to judge, among his contemporaries, recognised his genius to the full. So wonderful an example of the student and the man of action— 'the elements so mixed in him'—has hardly yet been fully appreciated by posterity.

---

[1] Clerk of Eldin (1728–1812) amassed a considerable fortune as a merchant. On retirement from business, he devoted much of his time to drawing and etching in which he was proficient. But his chief interest was in naval tactics, partly perhaps because he had numerous relations in the service.
[2] Referred to by Corbett as 'perhaps the most scientific book on naval tactics ever written.'

Kempenfelt to Middleton[1]. (*N.R.S.* xxxii, p. 290.)

Portsmouth. 28th April, 1779.

Dear Sir,

The course of this court martial[2] has given me a clearer idea of the action between our fleet and that of France last summer than I had before conceived; and the different state the two fleets were in after the action confirms most strongly what I have always thought; that is, that the disabling of your enemy in his masts and rigging should have no small share of your attention and your fire. In this skirmish between the two fleets there was at least as many shot sent from us to them as they sent to us; I should think many more, as several of their ships could not open their lower ports and most of ours could.

Now let us take a view of the conditions of the two fleets after action, owing to the different directions of their fire; ours, except the red division, so totally shattered in masts, rigging, and sails that for the whole evening of that day they could not all form into a line. The French ships, on the contrary, were so little injured in these particulars that they had the perfect command of their yards and sails, and immediately after action ceased formed a regular line on the starboard tack, pointing towards our fleet, and placing those ships in their van which were the van on the other tack, as being fresh ships.

Now consider a fleet dispersed and unable to collect together, whilst the enemy, perfectly capable of manœuvring, is well formed; is not the first, in such circumstances, at the mercy of the last? Suppose you had killed and wounded them five times the number they had you, yet they having the command of motion and direction, which you had not, gave them a decisive superiority. There is no strength and force without motion and direction. Deprive a giant of one of his legs and a stripling shall master him. 'Tis plain to me that our fleet, after that action, for all the first part of the afternoon, was at the mercy of the French. Unconnected to succour and support each other, what defence

---

[1] Sir Charles Middleton (1726–1813); 1778–1790, Comptroller of the Navy; 30 April, 1805–Jan. 1806, First Lord; May 1, 1805, first Baron Barham.

[2] On Sir Hugh Palliser.

could they have made against the attack of a close, well-formed line of ships? Why the French did not profit from this advantage they had, I can't conceive.

In close action such as was between most of our ships and the enemy that day, langridge is certainly the most destructive shot for rigging and sails, much more so than grape. When grape goes through a sail it makes a smooth round hole, but the long and ragged pieces of langridge cut and tear a sail to rags. I think we should make use of this kind of shot. An old ship broke up furnishes ample materials for it.

I am, dear sir,

Your most obedient servant,

RICHARD KEMPENFELT.

108. 'A FLEET IN BEING'; THE INVASION YEAR, 1779

Kempenfelt to Middleton. (*N.R.S.* XXXII, p. 296.)

Victory, Spithead. 5th Sept. 1779.

We don't seem to have considered sufficiently a certain fact, that the comparative force of two fleets depends much upon their sailing. The fleet that sails fastest has much the advantage, as they can engage or not as they please, and so have it always in their power to choose the favourable opportunity to attack. I think I may safely hazard an opinion that twenty-five sail of the line, coppered, would be sufficient to hazard and tease this great, unwieldy, combined armada, so as to prevent their effecting anything; hanging continually upon them, ready to catch at any opportunity of a separation from night, gale, or fog; to dart upon the separated, to cut off any convoys of provisions coming to them; and if they attempted an invasion, to oblige their whole fleet to escort the transports, and even then it would be impossible to protect them entirely from so active and nimble a fleet. I think when the enemy's fleet were off Plymouth, fireships in the night, disguised in the dress of their tenders, as luggers, cutters, &c., might have been applied with success, under the management of some bold, sensible man.

109. THE WESTERN SQUADRON: ARGUMENT AGAINST 'WINTER' BLOCKADE

Kempenfelt to Middleton. (*N.R.S.* XXXII, p. 303.)

Victory, Torbay. 16th Nov., 1779.

Dear Sir,—I mentioned in my last my opinion of the improbability of the combined fleets coming out again this winter; for this reason, that it is morally impossible so numerous a fleet as theirs can keep the sea for any time at this season without receiving great damage. Long nights and heavy gales are formidable enemies to large fleets.

But suppose the enemy should put to sea with their fleet—a thing much to be wished for by us. Let us act wiser, and keep ours in port; leave them to the mercy of long nights and hard gales. They'll do more in favour of you than your fleet can. A large fleet never tacks or wears when it blows hard in a dark night without risking great damage. We have had occasion to do it three times since we have been out, and each time with narrow escapes.

If the wind comes to the eastward we shall proceed westward to our station, and if it should continue a stiff and long-winded wind, we may be drove a 100 or 150 leagues to the westward, and perhaps not able to recover the Channel for six weeks or two months; a pretty situation for the fleet to be in to protect this island! and how much such a circumstance would forward the early equipment of the fleet for spring service! The fleet left Spithead with only two months' provisions. I leave it to you to judge of the prudence of risking their being drove out of the Channel so victualled.

In fine, sir, I don't suppose any person acquainted with naval affairs but sees the necessity of immediately taking in hand to prepare the fleet for the next campaign, to endeavour of having the advantage of being the first in the field.

Let us keep a stout squadron to the westward ready to attend the motions of the enemy. I don't mean to keep them at sea, disabling themselves in buffeting the winds, but at Torbay ready to act as intelligence may direct.

110. Kempenfelt urges Study of Tactical Principles

Kempenfelt to Middleton, January 18, 1780. (*N.R.S.* XXXII, p. 309.)

I believe you will, with me, think it something surprising that we, who have been so long a famous maritime power, should not yet have established any regular rules for the orderly and expeditious performance of the several evolutions necessary to be made in a fleet. The French have long since set us the example. They have formed a system of tactics, which are studied in their academies and practised in their squadrons.

Fleets, as well as armies, require rules to direct their several motions. In the movement of a fleet to perform any evolution, the way of doing it with most regularity, facility and expedition, is to be preferred; and tactics lays down rules for this purpose, by which every ship knows what they have to do when any evolution by signal is ordered, by which the whole fleet act together in concert, to the same end, by the same method; and nothing is left arbitrarily to the captains, who, without some determined rule known to all, by taking different methods for the execution, would embarrass each other.

All general movements, without they are made by established rules known to all, must be disorderly and confused, subject the ships to run foul of each other, be tedious in the performance, and imperfect in the execution. The fleet, therefore, whose motions are regulated by fixed rules, must have greatly the advantage of one whose motions have no rule to regulate them. In the one, when it becomes necessary to change the form or arrangement of it, to re-establish a line of battle disordered by a shift of wind, &c., it is done with order and expedition; in the other, when these things are to be done, there will unavoidably be an awkward slowness in the execution, a long time of confusion before order can be restored, which, if this should happen in the presence of an enemy near, the situation of such a fleet will then be rendered extremely critical and dangerous; for although the enemy may have the same movements to make, yet his motions will be much quicker and more orderly, from the regular rules he acts by, and will therefore be in order before the other is out of confusion; and consequently, if his situation will admit, will lose no time to profit from his advantage, but immediately attack his adversary while in disorder.

Indeed, 'tis too obvious to make any arguments necessary to show that fleets as well as armies require rules for the execution of their movements, and that the one stands in need of tactics as well as the other; without which both are unwieldy masses, where force is lost for want of form and order. Superior address in conduct may make up for the want of numbers, but what is to be expected when skill and address are wholly on the side of numbers?

Oh, but, 'tis said by several, our men are better seamen than the French. But the management of a private ship and a fleet are as different from each other as the exercising of a firelock and the conducting of an army. But don't let us flatter ourselves even with this advantage. The French have a vast navigation trade in which to form seamen; and that industry and genius that leads them to the more sublime part of naval war, we may be assured won't let them neglect the lower parts necessary to the execution of the other.

Enquire of those who were in the fleet with Mr Keppel the summer before last, if the French did not manage their ships like seamen; and as to their frigates, they showed an alertness, I have been told, not equalled by any of ours. When their signals were at any time thrown out to make sail, they were in an instant under a cloud of canvas; when they returned to their admiral, or were called to him, they run close up to his stern with all sail set, when in a moment all disappeared but the topsails. If a ship was but at a small distance, if called to the admiral, she immediately spread all her sail, even to stunsails if they would draw. This appears to be not only seamanship, but the brilliancy of it.

I have heard it said by some that the French out-manœuvred us, or showed more generalship in their conduct than we, the summer before last. I should suppose it to have been so, as they had tactics to direct them and we had not. There is also a vulgar notion prevails amongst us, and that even with our gentry, that our seamen are braver than the French. Ridiculous to suppose courage dependent upon climate. The men who are best disciplined, of whatever country they are, will always fight the best. The Roman troops beat those of all other nations, not because they were Romans, for their legions were composed of people from all countries; but because their discipline was superior to that of all other nations. It is a maxim that experience has ever confirmed, that discipline gives more force than numbers.

In fine, if you will neither give an internal discipline for your ships, nor a system of tactics for the evolutions of your fleet, I don't know from what you are to expect success, when you leave the enemy in unrivalled possession of these advantages. It certainly behoves us at this time to give our navy all the force we can, and no way more speedy, more effectual, and which will be attended with no expense, than establishing and strictly enforcing an internal and external discipline as here recommended; for all military bodies are defective in force in proportion as they are defective in discipline.

We should therefore immediately and in earnest set about a reform; endeavours should be used to find out proper persons, and encouragement offered for such to write on naval tactics, as also to translate what the French have published on that subject. They should enter into the plan of education at our marine academies.

But the most effectual way to obtain every wished for reform in your fleet is to find out a man to place at the head of it, who has genius to comprehend every requisite regulation, and has activity and spirit to enforce their execution. I am sorry to say that wealth, ease, I may add luxury—never favourable to a military character, to assiduity, fatigue, and subordination—show their effect in the fleet, and in a more particular manner call for a disciplinarian to be at the head of it.

III. Discipline of a Fleet

Kempenfelt to Middleton. (*N.R.S.* xxxii, p. 304.)

28th December (1779?).

Without discipline is well planned and strictly supported, a military corps or a ship's crew are no better than a disorderly mob; it is a well-formed discipline that gives force, preserves order, obedience, and cleanliness, and causes alertness and despatch in the execution of business. We want in the navy such a discipline which should be general; and all commanders, &c.,

required to put it strictly in practice. It has been for want of this that such a spirit of insolence and licentiousness has so daringly showed itself of late upon so many occasions. That alarming mutiny the summer before last, on board of the *Prince*[1], in a large fleet, and under the immediate authority of an admiral whose flag was flying on board, was a degree of audacity never heard of before in the annals of our navy. Then the refusal of weighing anchor in the *Defiance*, the *Valiant*, the *Cumberland*. This undisciplined, audacious spirit showed itself upon several occasions in the *Victory* when we first went on board her; however, that is now pretty well suppressed. All these disorders arise from a defect in discipline.

In what order is a military corps kept on shore, when well officered! Certainly the situation of a ship's crew is more favourable to sustain order and regularity than that of a corps ashore, confined within narrow limits, without tippling houses to debauch in, and under the constant eye of their officers. But if six, seven, or eight hundred men are left in a mass together, without divisions, and the officers assigned no particular charge over any part of them, who only give orders from the quarterdeck or gangways—such a crew must remain a disorderly mob, business will be done awkwardly and tumultuously, without order or despatch, and the raw men put into no train of improvement. The officers having no particular charge appointed them, the conduct and behaviour of the men are not inspected into; they know nothing of their proceedings; and the people, thus left to themselves, become sottish, slovenly and lazy, form cabals, and spirit each other up to insolence and mutiny.

The only way to keep large bodies of men in order is by dividing and subdividing of them, with officers over each, to inspect into and regulate their conduct, to discipline and form them. Let the ship's crew be divided into as many companies as there are lieutenants—except the first lieutenant, whose care should extend over the whole. These companies to be subdivided, and put under the charge of mates or midshipmen; and besides this, every twenty-five men to have a foreman to assist in the care of the men, as a sergeant or corporal in the army.

[1] Kempenfelt apparently meant the *Queen*, on board which an outbreak occurred before he joined the fleet.

Each lieutenant's company should be formed of the men who are under his command at quarters for action. These companies should be reviewed every day by their lieutenants, when the men are to appear tight and clean. He is to see that the raw men are daily exercised at arms, and the sails and rigging. The captain should review them himself at least once a week.

When it can be done, the men should always have the full time for their meals and for repose, and certain portions of time in the week allotted for washing and mending; but at all other times they should be kept constantly employed; and whatever they are exercised about, be particularly careful that they do it with attention and alertness, and perfect. Labour to bring them to a habit of this, and suffer nothing to be done negligently and awkwardly. The adage that idleness is the root of evil is with no people more strongly verified than with sailors and soldiers. Motion preserves purity; everything that stagnates corrupts. When you have nothing more necessary for the men to do, let them be exercised at small-arms; it makes the men straight, gives them an easy and graceful motion of the limbs, shakes off the awkward clown, and gives that military air which shows a man to advantage.

This leads me to step a little out of the way to remark that our sea officers should be acquainted with the military art; the seaman and the soldier are two professions that should be united in the former. They should know how to form men for marching; for attacking, or defending themselves when on shore with a body of men; they should know the advantage to be made of ground, by possessing heights, hedges, houses, walls, &c.; the advantage of covering their front or flanks with rivers, ponds, morasses, or woods; how to intrench, or form a redoubt. These are things not very difficult to acquire, and are of infinite advantage to the officer who may command a party ashore in presence of an enemy.

To keep the seamen properly clothed and clean, they should be uniformed, and be obliged to possess a certain quantity of each species of clothing; which that they do, the lieutenant of the company should every Monday make a muster of their clothes. As chests cannot be allowed, haversacks should be provided as other slops, and furnished the purser. This uniformity of the seamen might contribute something to check desertion; I am sure it would keep the men in a more decent appearance. At present, their appearance in general is a disgrace to the service, very shabby and very dirty. This method which I recommend, if strictly pursued, must be attended with the most beneficial effects. The men would be kept sober, orderly, and clean, perfected in all the necessary duties; the officers, by thus daily reviewing the men, would become acquainted with the character and behaviour of each individual; he would find out the turbulent and seditious, and keep a strict hand over such.

An emulation would naturally rise amongst the lieutenants to show their companies perfect in cleanliness, discipline, and all the several manœuvres; the young landmen would very soon be made acquainted with the seamanship and fighting parts of their duty. I am certain that young landmen, with proper attention, may, in three months, if half that time at sea, be made to know every rope in the ship, to knot and splice, hand and reef, and be perfect at the management of the cannon and small-arms.

Divine service should be performed every Sunday; and I think a short form of prayer for mornings and evenings, to be used every day, would be proper. It would take up but a short time. The French and Spaniards, in their ships, have their matins and their vespers every day. Our seamen people are more licentious than those of other nations. The reason is, they have less religion. Don't let anyone imagine that this discipline will disgust the men, and give them a dislike to the service; for the very reverse will be the consequence. Sobriety, cleanliness, order, and regularity, the conveniences resulting from these to them, will convince them that they tend as much to their particular benefit as to the public service.

What I have here recommended I know is not new; I have thought of it many years ago, and I know many others have done the same; but yet it is not adopted. What I want is, that it is commanded, enforced by authority, to be practised in every ship. It is easy and simple, and if strictly observed would very soon produce a most desirable change. With order and discipline you would increase your force; cleanliness and sobriety would keep your men healthy; and punishments would be seldom, as crimes would be rare.

112. On Strategy

Admiral Kempenfelt's observations on the arrangement given to him by Lord S(andwich). (*N.R.S.* XXXII, p. 361.) (Copy in Middleton's hand.)

6th January, 1782.

When the enemy's force by sea is superior to yours and you have many remote possessions to guard, it renders it difficult to determine the best means of disposing of your ships.

When you know the enemy's designs, in order to do something effectual you must endeavour to be superior to them in some part where they have designs to execute, and where, if they succeeded, they would most injure you. If your fleet is so divided as to be in all places inferior to the enemy, they will have a fair chance of succeeding everywhere in their attempts. If a squadron cannot be formed of sufficient force to face the enemy's at home, it would be more advantageous to let your inferiority be still greater, in order by it to gain the superiority elsewhere.

When inferior to the enemy, and you have only a squadron of observation to watch and attend upon their motions, such a squadron should be composed of two-decked ships only, so as to ensure its purpose. It must have the advantage of the enemy in sailing; else, under certain circumstances, it will be liable to be forced to battle, or to give up some of their heavy sailers. It is highly necessary to have such a flying squadron to hang on the enemy's large fleet, as it will prevent their dividing into separate squadrons for intercepting your trade, or spreading their ships for a more extensive view. You will be at hand to profit from any accidental separation or dispersion of their fleet from hard gales, fogs or other causes. You may intercept supplies, intelligence, &c., to them. In fine, such a squadron will be a check and restraint upon their motions, and prevent a good deal of the mischief they might otherways do.

When the enemy are near the Channel, I should suppose the best situation for such a squadron would be to keep without them to the westward. When the enemy perceives your design of keeping the North Sea free by a stout squadron, for your trade to return home that way, it may be supposed they will detach from the grand fleet as many ships as the inferiority of your western squadron will allow, to endeavour, in conjunction with the Dutch, to turn, in that sea, the balance of power on their side.

The enemy I conceive at this time have two grand designs against us. The one, the conquest of our West India Islands; the other, at home, not confined merely to the interception of our trade, but to favour, by their superiority, a formidable descent upon Great Britain and Ireland; and I should suppose the blow would be directed where it would be most felt by us, either against the metropolis or Portsmouth. I should rather think the latter, as less difficult from the nature of the navigation.

They will with some reason conclude that one or other of these designs will succeed; well knowing that we cannot, by our naval power, guard against both; and that, if we employ a force sufficient to defeat their design in one place, we must necessarily leave the other exposed to them.

Mem. by Sir C. M.

As something must be left exposed, it appears to me that Great Britain and Ireland are more capable of defending themselves than our colonies; and that the present year will probably pass over before they discover our design in the North Sea. It behoves us, therefore, to make the best of the time allowed us.

113. A Civilian Critic

Extract from the Introduction to *An Essay on Naval Tactics, systematical and historical*, by J. Clerk, of Eldin. Printed in 1782.

Again, while we remark the wonderful exertions, and constant success, attending the lesser conflicts; while we remark how much, and how often, our ships have been put to severe trial, by being exposed, in all weathers, during the storms of winter, the enemy not daring to set out their heads; when, after recollection, we remark, that, to the numerous, bold, and successful enterprises, *coups des mains*, performed during the last 250 years, and that our enemies have only the single disgrace which befell us at Chatham to counterbalance so great an account, should we not at the same time remark that this boasted intrepidity, this persevering courage of British seamen, has never once been brought to trial where it would have been of the greatest importance; that is, in the greater engagements; of which, because this superiority has never had an opportunity of being displayed, the result has always been the same, namely, that in such actions our fleets, in the two last wars and the present, have been invariably baffled, nay worsted, without having ever lost a ship, or almost a man?

While we remark these circumstances, is it not evident, and will it not be admitted, that one of three things must be the fact, either that our enemy, the French, having acquired a superior knowledge, have adopted some new system of managing great fleets, not known, or not sufficiently attended to by us? or that, on the other hand, we have persisted in following some old method, or instructions, which, from later improvement, ought to have been rejected?

During the course of the wars with the Dutch, much improvement was made, particularly in the invention of signals. But the naval instructions then framed, although founded upon experience and observation, and though they might be admirably fitted for fighting in narrow seas, where these battles were fought; yet, from later experience, it will be found that they have been but ill qualified for bringing on an action with a fleet of French ships, unwilling to stand a shock, having sea room to range in at pleasure, and desirous to play off manœuvres of defence, long studied with the greatest attention.

But, if it were possible that there could have remained a doubt of the truth or force of these observations before the breaking out of the present war, will not this doubt be resolved, if they shall be confirmed by every case that has followed since; whether we consider the intrepidity and exertion so conspicuous in the lesser conflicts, or the defect of conduct and address, so palpable in most of the greater engagements, although, at the same time, our admirals, whether by good fortune, by skilful seamanship, or by permission of the enemy, have never failed, on every occasion, to acquire their wish, viz. the circumstance of being to windward; excepting, indeed, on those occasions where the French have chosen to keep such an advantage, without availing themselves of it; a circumstance which is plainly a confirmation that their system or mode is different from ours, and that they are uniformly determined never to be brought to make the attack, if it can be avoided.

From all which, these three conclusions will naturally follow: 1st, That, in bringing a single ship to close action, and in conduct during that action, the British seamen have never been excelled; 2dly, That the instructions (by which is meant the method hitherto practised of arranging great fleets, so as to give battle, or to force our enemy, the French, to give battle upon equal terms), after so many and repeated trials, having been found unsuccessful, must be wrong; and, lastly, that on the other hand the French having repeatedly and uniformly followed a *mode* which has constantly the effect intended, they therefore must have adopted some new system, which we have not discovered, or have not yet profited by the discovery.

But, it may be asked, Have the French ever effected anything decisive against us? Have they ever, in any of these rencounters, taken any of our ships? Have they ever, presuming upon their superior skill, dared to make the attack?—No. But, confident in their superior knowledge in naval tactic, and relying on our want of penetration, they have constantly offered us battle to leeward, trusting that our headlong courage would hurry us on to make the customary attack, though at a disadvantage almost beyond the power of calculation; the consequences of which have always been, and always will be, the same, as long as prejudices prevent us from discerning either the improvements made by-the enemy, or our own blunders.

114. NELSON'S VIEW OF CLERK OF ELDIN

Sir T. M. Hardy to——(copy sent to Sir J. D. Thomson). (*N.R.S.*xxxix, p. 398.)

5th May, 1806.
Sampson, Hamoaze.

Our departed friend, Lord Nelson, read Mr Clerk's works with great attention, and frequently expressed his approbation of them in the fullest manner; he also recommended all the captains to read them with attention, and said that many good hints might be taken from them. He most approved of the attack from to-windward, and considered that breaking through the enemy's line absolutely necessary to obtain a great victory. I have taken some pains in reading Clerk's Tactics, and I have the highest opinion of the ability of the author of that most excellent work.

115. St Vincent's Views on Clerk of Eldin

Brenton, *Life and Correspondence of Earl St Vincent*, ii, p. 288.

Near Ushant, 2nd June, 1806.

My dear Lord,

Not having Mr Clerk's treatise on naval tactics with me, I am unable to give you a detailed opinion upon the influence it has had in the several victories our fleets have obtained over those of France, Spain and Holland, since its publication. I would not for the world subtract from the merits of Mr Clerk, which I have always admitted; yet on referring to the encyclopaedia, wherein are copious extracts from the pamphlet, I perceive evident signs of compilation from Père le Hoste, down to Viscount de Grenier. In truth, it would be difficult for the ablest seaman and tactician to write upon the subject, without running into one or all the French authors.

Inclosed your Lordship will receive the best judgment I can form on the claim Mr Clerk has of any merit in the battles of the First of June, and the attempts on the preceding days by Lord Howe; the battles of Camperdown and Trafalgar: that fought off Cape St Vincent *is totally out of the question*. I do not see, however, that Ministers can withhold some reward to Mr Clerk.

Yours ever,

St Vincent.

Viscount Howick.

116. Admiral Graves's Account of the Battle of the Chesapeake

Contemporary accounts are here given of the ill-conducted Battle of the Chesapeake (September 5, 1781). In his introduction to *Signals and Instructions* (*N.R.S.* xxxv), Sir Julian Corbett emphasises the fact that Graves was fresh from the Channel Fleet—the school of Howe and Kempenfelt—while Hood was perhaps the ablest exponent of the conservative type.

Rodney's views are specially interesting, since his own attempt to bring on a decisive action (April 17, 1780) had been thwarted by misunderstanding of his plan on the part of his captains. In his own copy of Clerk's *Naval Tactics*, which appeared in 1782, he writes a marginal note to this effect: 'It is well known that attempting to bring to action the enemy, ship to ship, is contrary to common sense, and a proof that that admiral is not an officer, whose duty it is to take every advantage of an enemy by which he will be sure of defeating the enemy and taking the part attacked, and likewise defeating the other part by detail unless they make a timely retreat. During all the commands Lord Rodney has been entrusted with he made it a rule to bring his whole force against part of the enemy's, and never was so absurd as to bring ship against ship.' (*N.R.S.* xxxv, p. 14.)

Graves to Stephens. (*N.R.S.* III, p. 40.)

London, at Sea, 14th of September, 1781.

Sir:—I beg you will be pleased to acquaint the Lords Commissioners of the Admiralty that the moment the wind served to carry the ships over the Bar, which was buoyed for the purpose, the squadron came out, and Sir Samuel Hood getting under sail at the same time, the fleet proceeded together on 31st of August to the southward; my intention being to go to the Chesapeake, as the enemy's views would most probably be upon that part.

The cruisers which I had placed before the Delaware could give me no certain information, and the cruisers off the Chesapeake had not joined; the winds being rather favourable, we approached the Chesapeake the morning of the 5th of September, when the advanced ship made the signal of a fleet. We soon discovered a number of great ships at anchor, which seemed to be extended across the entrance of the Chesapeake from Cape Henry to the Middle Ground; they had a frigate cruising off the Cape which stood in and joined them, and as we approached, the whole fleet got under sail and stretched out to sea, with the wind at N.N.E. As we drew nearer I formed the line, first ahead, and then in such a manner as to bring his Majesty's fleet nearly parallel to the line of approach of the enemy; and when I found that our van was advanced as far as the shoal of the Middle Ground would admit of, I wore the fleet and brought them upon the same tack with the enemy, and nearly parallel to them; though we were by no means extended with their rear. So soon as I judged that our van would be able to operate,

I made the signal to bear away and approach, and soon after, to engage the enemy close: somewhat after four the action began amongst the headmost ships pretty close, and soon became general as far as the second ship from the centre towards the rear. The van of the enemy bore away to enable their centre to support them, or they would have been cut up: the action did not entirely cease until a little after sunset, though at a considerable distance, for the centre of the enemy continued to bear up as it advanced, and at that moment seemed to have little more in view than to shelter their own van as it went away before the wind. His Majesty's fleet consisted of nineteen sail of the line, that of the French formed twenty-four sail in their line. After night I sent the frigates to the van and rear to push forward the line and keep it extended with the enemy, with a full intention to renew the engagement in the morning; but when the frigate *Fortunée* returned from the van I was informed that several of the ships had suffered so much they were in no condition to renew the action until they had secured their masts. The *Shrewsbury*, *Intrepid*, and *Montagu* unable to keep the line, and the *Princesa* in momentary apprehension of the main topmast going over the side; we, however, kept well extended with the enemy all night, and in the morning saw they had not the appearance of near so much damage as we had sustained, though the whole of their van must have experienced a good deal of loss....

The fleets continued in sight of each other for five days successively, and at times were very near. We had not speed enough in so mutilated a state to attack them, had it been prudent, and they showed no inclination to renew the action, for they generally maintained the wind of us, and had it often in their power.

117. Hood's Account of the Battle of the Chesapeake, 1781

Hood to Jackson, September 16, 1781. (*N.R.S.* III, p. 28.)

No. 1 contains my sentiments upon the truly unfortunate day, as committed to writing the next morning, and which I mentioned to Mr Graves when I attended his first summons on board the *London*.

Enclosure 1.

Coast of Virginia, 6th of September, 1781.

Yesterday the British fleet had a rich and most plentiful harvest of glory in view, but the means to gather it were omitted in more instances than one.

I may begin with observing that the enemy's van was not very closely attacked as it came out of Lynn Haven Bay, which, I think, might have been done with clear advantage, as they came out by no means in a regular and connected way. When the enemy's van was out, it was greatly extended beyond the centre and rear, and might have been attacked with the whole force of the British fleet. Had such an attack been made, several of the enemy's ships must have been inevitably demolished in half an hour's action, and there was a full hour and a half to have engaged it before any of the rear could have come up.

Thirdly, when the van of the two fleets got into action, and the ships of the British line were hard pressed, one (the *Shrewsbury*) totally disabled very early from keeping her station by having her fore and main topsail yards shot away, which left her second (the *Intrepid*) exposed to two ships of superior force, which the noble and spirited behaviour of Captain Molloy obliged to turn their sterns to him, that the signal was not thrown out for the van ships to make more sail to have enabled the centre to push on to the support of the van, instead of engaging at such an improper distance (the *London* having her main topsail to the mast the whole time she was firing, with the signal for the line at half a cable flying), that the second ship astern of the *London* received but trifling damage, and the third astern of her (the *London*) received no damage at all, which most clearly proves how much too great the distance was the centre division engaged.

Now, had the centre gone to the support of the van, and the signal for the line been hauled down, or the commander-in-chief had set the example of close action, even with the signal for the line flying, the van of the enemy must have been cut to pieces, and the rear division of the British fleet would have been opposed to those ships the centre division fired at, and at the proper distance for engaging, or the Rear-Admiral who commanded it would have a great deal to answer for. Instead of that, our centre division did the enemy but little damage, and our rear ships being barely within random shot, three only fired a few shot. So soon as the signal for the line was hauled down at twenty-five minutes after five, the rear division bore up above half a mile to leeward of the centre division, but the French ships bearing up also, it did not near them, and at twenty-five minutes after six the signal of the line ahead at half a cable being again hoisted, and the signal for battle hauled down, Rear-Admiral Sir S. Hood called to the *Monarch* (his leader) to keep her wind, as he dared not separate his division just at dark, the *London* not bearing up at all.

118. RODNEY'S VIEWS ON CONCENTRATION

Rodney to Jackson, Bath, October 19, 1781. (*N.R.S.* III, p. 44.)

At present I find myself very much out of order with a very violent pain in my stomach, which has continued these four days and reduced me much, which the news from America and Mr Graves's letter has increased.

Mr Graves, so far from joining Sir Samuel Hood off the Capes, lay idle at Sandy Hook, and suffered the French squadron from Rhode Island to join De Grasse, which by cruising from ten to forty leagues from Sandy Hook or by joining Sir S. Hood he might have prevented, and even, when he afterwards joined him, four of his line-of-battle ships were wanting. Ought any man, after the notice he had received, to have separated his squadron of line-of-battle ships? The whole should have been kept in a body, and always ready to act at a moment's warning, and suffered no repairs, but momentary ones, till the campaign was over.

His letter I cannot understand, and his terms, particularly his 'cut up,' a term neither military or seamanlike; it must have been a mistake in printing; he meant cut off the vans from the centre. The other part of the letter contradicts itself, and his mode of fighting I will never follow. He tells me that his line did not extend so far as the enemy's rear. I should have been sorry if it had, and a general battle ensued; it would have given the advantage they could have wished, and brought their whole twenty-four ships of the line against the English nineteen, whereas by watching his opportunity, if the enemy had extended

their line to any considerable distance, by contracting his own
he might have brought his nineteen against the enemy's fourteen
or fifteen, and by a close action totally disabled them before they
could have received succour from the remainder, and in all
probability have gained thereby a complete victory. Such would
have been the battle of the 17th of April had I been obeyed;
such would have been the late battle off the Capes.

119. 'Breaking the Line': a Criticism

The so-called 'breaking of the French line' by Rodney on the 12th of
April, 1782, in the Battle of 'the Saints,' led to much misconception and has
been often hailed as a new and infallible recipe for decisive victory.

The manœuvre was of course as old as the Dutch Wars, but had fallen
out of favour mainly on account of the ease with which it could be parried
(see pp. 88, 105).

Beatson's view here reproduced is worthy of attention, since it actually
challenges the efficacy of the movement in Rodney's great battle.

Beatson, *Naval and Military Memoirs*, v, 472, 1804 edition.

The whole success of the battle on the 12th of April has been
sometimes attributed to this measure, which has, of course, been
deemed a masterly evolution, worthy of imitation. The British
Admiral has also been supposed to break through a connected
line of the enemy's ships. These representations, however,
appear to proceed from mistakes; for the French line was com-
pletely deranged by the change of the wind *alone*; and so far
was the measure of sailing through the enemy's line with six
ships, unconnected with the rest of the fleet, from being decisive
of victory, that it may be doubted whether it was a fortunate
evolution. If Admiral Rodney's fleet had kept a connected line
of battle ahead sailing large across the bows of the French ships,
which were necessarily forced towards the broadsides of the
British by the wind and totally disordered, it is highly probable
that the fleet of France must, upon the whole, have sustained
much more damage than it did from the fire of the six ships
attached to Admiral Rodney, which had an opportunity of
attacking three or four of the French collected in a confused
manner, and forced to leeward of the British Admiral. And this
is the only real advantage which has been supposed to arise from
Admiral Rodney's weathering the French rear with six ships.

120. CRITICISM OF BRITISH BY 'THE FATHER OF THE AMERICAN NAVY'

Of all the active enemies of Great Britain during the struggle with the American colonies Paul Jones[1] was best qualified to judge her strength and weakness. The view that follows affords an interesting critical summary of the manner in which British and French naval forces were handled.

Memorandum from Paul Jones to the United States Government, 1782. (Quoted by Thursfield, *Nelson and Other Naval Studies*, p. 247.)

There is now, perhaps, as much difference between a battle between two ships, and an engagement between two fleets, as there is between a duel and a ranged battle between two armies. The English, who boast so much of their navy, never fought a ranged battle on the ocean before the war that is now ended. The battle off Ushant was, on their part, like their former ones, irregular; and Admiral Keppel could only justify himself by the example of Hawke in our remembrance, and of Russell in the last century. From that moment the English were forced to study, and to imitate, the French in their evolutions. They never gained any advantage when they had to do with equal force, and the unfortunate defeat of Count de Grasse was owing more to the unfavourable circumstances of the wind coming ahead four points at the beginning of the battle, which put his fleet into the order of echiquier when it was too late to tack, and of calm and currents afterwards, which brought on an entire disorder, than to the admiralship or even the vast superiority of Rodney, who had forty sail of the line against thirty, and five three-deckers against one. By the account of some of the French officers, Rodney might as well have been asleep, not having made a second signal during the battle, so that every captain did as he pleased.

The English are very deficient in signals, as well as in naval tactics. This I know, having in my possession their present fighting and sailing instructions, which comprehend all their

---

[1] John Paul (1747–92)—the name of Jones was assumed in America—was of Scottish birth. He settled early in Virginia where he became a planter, after considerable experience as a master-mariner. On the outbreak of war his ability for administration as well as for active sea-service was at once recognised, and his name soon became famous in both continents.

signals and evolutions. Lord Howe has, indeed, made some improvements by borrowing from the French. But Kempenfelt, who seems to have been a more promising officer, had made a still greater improvement by the same means. It was said of Kempenfelt, when he was drowned in the *Royal George*, England had lost her du Pavillon. That great man, the Chevalier du Pavillon[1], commanded the *Triumphant*, and was killed in the last battle of Count de Grasse. France lost in him one of her greatest naval tacticians, and a man who had, besides, the honour (in 1773) to invent the new system of naval signals, by which sixteen hundred orders, questions, answers, and informations can, without confusion or misconstruction, and with the greatest celerity, be communicated through a great fleet. It was his fixed opinion that a smaller number of signals would be insufficient. A captain of the line at this day must be a tactician. A captain of a cruising frigate may make shift without ever having heard of naval tactics. Until I arrived in France, and became acquainted with that great tactician Count D'Orvilliers, and his judicious assistant the Chevalier du Pavillon, who, each of them, honoured me with instructions respecting the science of governing the operations, etc., of a fleet, I confess I was not sensible how ignorant I had been, before that time, of naval tactics.

121. French Numerary Signals

So long as the old system of Fighting Instructions, conveyed by a limited number of flag-signals, survived, decisive victories were far to seek; and although the existence of Additional Instructions proves that keen and thoughtful officers were alive to the insufficiency of the old code, yet nothing short of its complete abolition could lead to victories in the sense that Nelson understood them. The eighteenth century is full of melancholy examples of half-fought battles, indecisive because the admiral in command had no sanction or means to find solutions for fresh problems undreamt of in the philosophy of the Fighting Instructions. Just as a traveller abroad who is ignorant of the language is powerless to converse beyond the limits of a set and formal phrase-book, so the commanding officer of a fleet in action was dumb when confronted with a situation for which his stock of formal instructions made no provision.

It was obvious that any reform in the direction of 'freedom of speech' must be accompanied by reform in the methods of signalling. The restrictions imposed by the employment of a few flags, sharply distinguished in colour

[1] Jean François du Cheyron du Pavillon, born at Perigueux in 1730; entered French navy in 1748. Edited the official *Tactique navale* in 1778.

and hoisted in the few prominent positions available, would clearly admit of no expansion.

To Admiral Kempenfelt most justly belongs the honour of designing a new signal-book to meet the new needs. He owed much to his close study of French practice. In 1765 de Villehuet had inserted as an appendix to *Le Manœuvrier* the system invented by Mahé de la Bourdonnais. Though first in the field, French seamanship on the whole proved incapable of taking full advantage of this tremendous weapon. If the Phoenicians invented the alphabet, it was the Greeks who wrote; it was the English admirals—not the French—who revelled in their newly-discovered freedom.

Kempenfelt's description of the French system is here reproduced. In 1781 appeared 'General Instructions for the conduct of the ships of war, explanatory of, and relative to the signals contained in the signal-book herewith delivered by Rear-Admiral Richard Kempenfelt.' (Now in R.U.S.I.)

Then appeared sailing and fighting instructions, probably compiled by Lord Howe in conjunction with Kempenfelt in 1782.

Middleton to the Earl of Sandwich, 9 July 1779[1].

My Lord—As your Lordship mentioned his Majesty's inclination to have the subject of signals considered for the use of the fleet, I must inform you that I have had a great deal of correspondence and conversation with Captain Kempenfelt on that head; and it was agreed before he left London to introduce the French system, if practicable, into Sir Charles Hardy's fleet. That gentleman has well considered the subject, but at this juncture it would be dangerous to exchange even a bad set of signals that are generally known for a better which the greatest part of the officers are unacquainted with. Whenever it is his Majesty's pleasure that this subject should be considered and your Lordship can spare Captain Kempenfelt from the service of the fleet, I will engage with the assistance of that gentleman and of some other sea officers which I can name to simplify this very complex business and to reduce it within the practice of the most ordinary understanding.

The materials for this purpose are lying by me, but engaged as I am at present in an office which I own is almost beyond my strength, it would be madness to undertake anything new; and I do assure your Lordship, but for the cowardice of deserting you

---

[1] John Montagu, fourth Earl of Sandwich (1718–1792); 1744 a Lord Commissioner of the Admiralty; First Lord, 1748–1751 (when he delegated his duties to Anson), 1763–1768, and 1771–1782. (*N.R.S. Sandwich Papers*, iii, p. 42.)

and his Majesty's service at a juncture when I see the necessity of keeping together the business of this office, I should certainly withdraw myself from it. The burden, my Lord, is too great for the most able sea officer in this kingdom; and a consciousness of my own inferiority in mind and body has frequently made me wish I had never engaged in it. Important as the office is, I verily believe I shall take my leave of it whenever your Lordship quits the Admiralty.

In the meantime, my Lord, let me have the assistance of Captain Kempenfelt when he can be spared from the use of the fleet. I really want more assistance in my own line, and do not like determining so many things of moment, as I am obliged to do at present, on my own judgment only. Captain Kempenfelt is not merely a sea officer, but a man of deep knowledge in most professions. He will be a great acquisition to his Majesty's service as well as of much assistance to me when he comes to the Navy Board; and if your Lordship could see the multiplicity of Board business which I am every day obliged to go through, you would allow that the Comptroller of the Navy ought to have a sea officer next in authority to himself at the Navy Board. As it now stands I cannot be one hour absent while the Board sits, and if any necessary duty calls me from it, I must sit the longer when I return. You see therefore, my Lord, the necessity of allowing me some further assistance in my own line; and I trust you have that confidence in me to believe I should not press it, if I did not think it necessary and knew that Captain Kempenfelt has had his Majesty's approbation for that appointment. I am [etc.].

122. French Numerary Signals

Kempenfelt to Middleton, March ?, 1781. (*N.R.S.* XXXII, p. 343.)

You have here the numeral signals you desired as near as I can in the words of the author.

Project for signals

Signals should be simple, clear, and easily discernible. I don't know any more perfect than those invented by M. de la Bourdonnais. He made use of broad pennants as more readily fixed to any part than flags. He fixes a number for each pennant; and that several pennants, each designing a particular number, and put one above another, serve as cyphers[1]. By this it is easy to know the number of each signal, because the pennants are numbered by their colours. For example:

A pennant Red signifies	1
White	2
Blue	3
Yellow	4
Red with a white fly	5
Red with a blue fly	6
White with a blue fly	7
White with a red fly	8
Blue with a yellow fly	9
Yellow with a red fly	0

With this arrangement an infinite number of signals may be made. There should be three or four pennants of each sort, in order to express the same number three or four times at once; as, for example, the signal of 33 or 444 or 8888. These signals are made indifferently from any part of the masts or rigging, preferring that part from whence they will be best seen. The uppermost pennant signifies the first number, the second pennant the second number, the third the third number, and the fourth the fourth number. For example, No. 170 is fixed upon to order boats to be manned and armed. This signal is made by throwing out three pennants one above another in the same place; the first red, the second white with a blue fly, and the third yellow with a red fly. The signal will be seen in this manner:

Red pennant		1 ⎫		⎧ Boats
White „	with a blue fly	7 ⎬ 170		⎨ manned
Yellow „	with a red fly	0 ⎭		⎩ and armed.

If you would make several signals at the same time from the same place, you separate each signal with a small red flag, which serves as a comma between the signals.

Care should be taken that the colours of the pennants are bright and striking, as a deep blue, a scarlet red, an orpiment yellow, and a clear white.

[1] Digits.

You form a table of all the signals, placing in the first column the numbers as they stand in their natural order, and in the second column you write in alphabetic order what each signal means. For example:

575 . . abordons l'ennemi.
576 . . abandonnez le vaisseau que vous battez.

You will observe to reserve for the fighting signals the first numbers, as they will then be made with one or two pennants only. As there is frequent occasion at sea to make demands, the ship to whom we make the demand should answer immediately to the question by a signal affirmative or negative, Yes or No, without further preamble.

123. KEMPENFELT'S DESIGN FOR A SIGNAL BOOK

Kempenfelt to Middleton, March 9, 1781. (*N.R.S.* xxxii, p. 340.)

Every article or order in a signal book should be numbered; and then, any ship possessed of eleven flags, different the one from the other, may express signals to any number.

It has been a common saying that it is an advantage to go by signals that we have been used to, and when a new set comes out, to say we have our trade to learn again. This style was very proper with respect to the different signals used by different admirals formerly, when the signals were jumbled together without form or order, and when a long acquaintance with them was necessary to find out the meaning of any signal that was made in the chaotic state in which they were. But when signals are formed upon a proper plan they require no study to comprehend them, and when a signal is made you can immediately turn to the article or order alluded to. If the greatest novice can't do this, the plan is faulty. When in any project for signals they appear intricate and seem difficult to comprehend, you may be sure they are faulty; what is good must be clear and simple.

Had I remained ashore this winter, which my health very much required, I think I should have been able to have rendered the signals much more perfect and useful by the helps I have received from others and my own observations. The plan I followed in the signals I made was not that I most approved of.

That which I would have adopted—though most evidently the best—I could not get any of the admirals or officers of note to approve and countenance. I therefore followed in a great measure Lord Howe's mode, he being a popular character. The night and fog signals we use are almost entirely his, and both extremely defective. I would have used the French night signals, which are by much superior to anything of the kind that has yet appeared, but I was afraid of prejudice, for not an admiral I showed them to but started objections.

124. Medical Reforms

No record of our eighteenth century Navy—however brief—can omit reference to the work of Sir Gilbert Blane (1749-1834). His connection with the service began in 1779, when he went to sea with Rodney as his private physician. He was soon appointed as physician to the fleet, and was present in six general engagements. He presented two Memorials to the Admiralty on the health of the fleet, and the adoption of his suggestions led to very rapid general improvement, shown in a marked decrease of mortality.

His recommendation of the supply of lemon-juice for the prevention of scurvy in 1793 was adopted throughout the Navy in 1795.

Gilbert Blane, M.D., etc., *Observations on the Diseases of Seamen*, p. 323. Third Edition, 1799.

MEMORIAL[1],

Proposing Means for preventing the Sickness and Mortality prevailing among His Majesty's Seamen in the West Indies.

I HAVE for the two last years attended a squadron, consisting seldom of less than twenty ships of the line, in quality of physician to the fleet at Barbadoes and the Leeward Islands. I received, by the order of the Commander in Chief, a monthly return from the surgeon of each ship, setting forth the diseases, deaths, and other circumstances of the respective ships' companies. I also superintended the hospital of the place where the fleet happened to lie when in port. These advantages have afforded me an intimate knowledge of the nature and causes of the sickness and mortality among the seamen, both on board of their ships and in hospitals.

[1] Delivered to the Board of Admiralty in October, 1781.

It appears by my returns that there died in the course of the twelve months preceding July last, on board of ships, seven hundred and fifteen seamen and marines, of whom only fifty-nine died in battle and of wounds. There died in the same time in hospitals eight hundred and sixty-two: so that out of twelve thousand one hundred and nine men, which is the sum total of the complement of twenty ships of the line, there have perished in one year one thousand five hundred and seventy-seven, that is nearly every seventh man.

There were also sent to England in the same year, three hundred and fifty men, disabled by lameness and chronic complaints, the greater part of whom will be for ever lost to the service.

The degree of sickness is very different at different times; but it appears by the returns that, at a medium, there has been one man in fifteen on the sick list.

When it is considered that sickness is almost entirely confined to ships of two and three decks, and that some of these are as healthy as frigates and merchant ships, though in the same circumstances of service with others that are extremely sickly, we are led from hence to infer that sickness is not in its own nature unavoidable, and we are encouraged to hope that the attainment of general health is within the compass of human management.

I humbly and earnestly solicit attention to some of the most material observations and conclusions which have occurred in the course of a service which, though short, has been extensive; and whatever is here proposed has this recommendation, that it is easily practicable, and is no addition to the public charges.

First: I hardly ever knew a ship's company become sickly which was well regulated in point of cleanliness and dryness. It is the custom in some ships to divide the crew into squads or divisions under the inspection of respective officers, who make a weekly review of their persons and clothing, and are answerable for the cleanliness and regularity of their several allotments. This ought to be an indispensable duty in ships of two or three decks; and when it has been practised, and at the same time ventilation, cleanliness, and dryness below and between decks have been attended to, I have never known seamen more unhealthy than other men. The neglect of such attentions is a never-failing cause of sickness.

Secondly: Scurvy is one of the principal diseases with which seamen are afflicted; and this may be infallibly prevented, or cured, by vegetables and fruit, particularly oranges, lemons, or limes. I am well convinced that more men would be saved by a purveyance of fruit and vegetables than could be raised by double the expense and trouble employed on the imprest service; so that policy, as well as humanity, concur in recommending it. Every fifty oranges or lemons might be considered as a hand to the fleet, inasmuch as the health, and perhaps the life, of a man would thereby be saved.

(The rest of Blane's suggestions are given in the summarised form in which he presented them at the end of the memorial.)

Thirdly, The substitution of wine for rum. (Blane's footnote: Had I then known the salutary effects of porter and spruce beer, of which I have since been convinced, I should have proposed them as substitutes for rum.)

Fourthly, The providing of an adequate quantity of necessaries for the sick.

Fifthly, The gratuitous supply of certain medicines.

Sixthly, The curing of certain diseases on board instead of sending them to hospitals; and,

Lastly, The preventing of filth, crowding, and the mixture of diseases in hospitals, by proper regulations, and by establishing hospital ships.

I beg leave again to call to mind that 1518 deaths from disease, besides 350 invalids, in 12,109 men, in the course of one year, is an alarming waste of British seamen, being a number that would man three of His Majesty's ships of the line.

Supplement to the Memorial delivered last Year to the Board of Admiralty (p. 334).

SINCE my return to my duty on this station, additional experience has afforded me farther practical confirmation of the utility of the former proposals.

The great squadron employed on this station has, by the attention of the Commissioners of Victualling, and also of the

Commander in Chief, been supplied with most of the articles recommended, in such quantities as to prove their efficacy; and indeed the small degree of mortality in comparison of former times is a sufficient demonstration of this.

I beg leave to give an instance, in the *Formidable*, of the great and salutary effects of the proposed improvements. This ship left England, furnished not only with sour kraut and molasses, in common with most others in the squadron, but what was peculiar to herself was an entire supply of good wine in place of spirits; and an experiment has been made in this instance, under my own eyes, to ascertain what degree of health it was possible to attain in a great ship in this climate. With the above advantages together with good discipline and medical care, no man[1] died of disease from December, 1781, to May, 1782, and only thirteen were sent to hospitals, whose complaints were small-pox and ulcers. In the months of May and June last, when at Jamaica, there died of disease in this ship three men, and seventeen were sent to the hospital, most of whom had contracted their sickness on board of French prizes.

In the rest of the fleet the health was in proportion to the wine and other refreshments, and the cleanliness, good order, and discipline observed.

In the squadron I attended the last five months, which seldom consisted, during the last three months of that time, of less than forty ships of the line, there have died of disease about 350 men, and about 1000 have been sent to hospitals; a degree of sickness and mortality which, though not greater than what frequently prevails in Europe, I am persuaded would have been still less, had the improvements proposed been complied with in a manner more extensive and complete, and had the general rules of discipline and cleanliness been kept up with due and equal strictness throughout the fleet.

Formidable,

At Port Royal, Jamaica,

    July 16, 1782.

---

[1] The authenticity of this fact, as well as every other assertion in this work relating to the mortality in the fleet, may be proved from the ship's books, deposited at the Navy Office. (Blane's foot-note.)

p. 173.

The sick and wounded of the Navy were first received into Haslar hospital in the year 1754, and it was completed about two years afterwards. Plymouth hospital began first to be occupied in 1760, but was not completed till 1764.

p. 178.

The most remarkable point of comparison exhibited in this table[1] is that of the late war[2] with France, which lasted five years, with the five by-past years[3] of the present war. It appears that in these two hospitals alone, there were upwards of 27,000 more patients admitted in the former than the latter period, though a greater naval force is now kept up than was ever known in this country, and a greater proportion of it on home service than in the late war. The principal causes of this seem to be: 1st, That the navy at the commencement of this war was manned with less impressing than on the like occasions in former wars. The foul air produced by the crowding, and bad accommodation attending the methods of securing impressed men, previous to their distribution, has already been stated as the principal cause of the general infection prevailing in the beginning of wars. 2dly, The greater observance of cleanliness and dryness, and the stricter enforcement of discipline, in consequence of the conviction now entertained by officers, of the indispensable necessity of these to the health of the men under their command. 3dly, The general use of lemon juice, so judiciously and liberally allowed to ships at sea for the three last years. 4thly, The late increase of encouragement to surgeons, and the operation of the regulations established and put in force by the medical board of the navy.

p. 301.

We may consider all water kept in wooden vessels as more or less liable to putrefaction; but there is a substance, which is neither rare nor costly, that effectually preserves it sweet. This is quick lime, with which every ship should be provided, in

---

[1] '[Table showing the number of men admitted, and who have died at Haslar and Plymouth Hospitals, from the year 1755 to the year 1797.'
[2] The American War.
[3] 1793-7, inclusive.

order to put a pint of it into each butt when it is filled. In the year 1779 several ships of the line arrived in the West Indies from England, and they were all afflicted with the flux, except the *Stirling Castle*, which was the only ship in which quick lime was put into the water; nor does it spoil the water for any culinary purpose.

p. 310.

It would certainly be for the benefit of the service that a uniform should be established for the common men as well as for the officers. This would oblige them at all times to have in their possession a quantity of decent apparel, subject to the inspection of their superiors. It would also be less easy to dispose of their clothes for money without detection, and desertion would also thereby be rendered more difficult.

The greatest evil connected with clothing is the infection generated by wearing it too long without shifting, for the jail, hospital, or ship fever seems to be more owing to this than to close air.

p. 137.

The great degree of health at this time[1] enjoyed by the ship's company of the *Agamemnon* deserves particular attention, as it seemed to be owing to a circumstance in the mode of victualling which might, without any expense, and with little trouble, be rendered general in the navy. This consisted in the use of soft bread, that ship having been supplied about this time with flour in place of biscuit. For thirteen weeks the whole ship's company had no bread but what was baked on board, and a certain proportion of it from that time till her arrival in England, in May, 1783, at which time there was not a sick man on the list.

[1] December, 1782.

REVOLUTIONARY AND NAPOLEONIC WARS

In the French Revolutionary and Napoleonic Wars Great Britain speedily regained the prestige lowered so dangerously in the previous war.

As in the preceding sections, no attempt is here made to traverse the whole period historically. The documents selected illustrate partially two crises— the outbreak of the naval mutinies, and the invasion schemes of 1803–5. The selection aims primarily at presenting problems as they appeared to the chief contemporary actors.

Though administration remained far from perfect and abuses survived, British superiority not only in the quality of officers and men but in the number of ships available for service was apparent throughout this period. Only in the black year of mutinies (1797) was public confidence in the service shaken, and even that year witnessed two of our greatest naval victories.

125. THE COPPERING OF SHIPS

Memoranda of Advice. Forethought and Preparation. (By Sir Charles Middleton, almost certainly intended for Lord Melville, on his appointment as First Lord, May, 1804. *N.R.S.* xxxix, p. 24.)

From every information I could pick up for guarding iron bolts in ship's bottoms against the corrosive effects of copper, I was convinced in my own mind that we might with safety copper the bottoms of every ship in the fleet and by that means increase our activity, as far as doubling our force in numbers. The measure to be sure was not only bold, but arduous. I proposed it privately to Lord Sandwich; but he hesitated, and, after several conversations and assurances, he mentioned it to the king. I afterwards accompanied his lordship to Buckingham House and explained the whole process in so satisfactory a manner that he conceived it at once and ordered it to be carried into execution. Having succeeded so far, I authorised our copper contractor to purchase whatever quantity of copper he could procure from the several companies, and which was executed so privately that we secured as much as would cover 40 sail of the line without any increase of price, and actually coppered twenty in six weeks, and, before the war ended, every ship fit for service. The effects of this measure were soon felt; and so much was the activity of the fleet increased that Mr Rigby, in his witty way, observed that, unless the captains were coppered also, we should have none to serve. Admiral Barrington, amongst others, declared that the ships would sink at their anchors. They were ignorant of the means used; and so far were we from meeting accidents, that the enemy had not a line of battle ship of ours in their possession to boast of at the end of the war, while many of theirs had, in consequence of it, been added to ours.

The war being ended and the shattered condition of the fleet well known to me, I saw the necessity of getting forward as fast as possible with our line of battle ships; and notwithstanding we had upwards of thirty new ones in a state of great forwardness, yet, without continued exertion in every part of the department, we should not be able to cope with France and Spain united. The first thing, therefore, was to take in hand, immediately, all the ships that were in want of small repair. We were by this time strong in the number and quality of our shipwrights and caulkers; the stores were greatly increased, and all our store-houses arranged with separate berths for every ship's stores; so that instead of having all the storehouses looked over for single ship's stores, every ship had the power of carrying off her own in 24 hours, instead of weeks, according to the old custom. The general storehouses, instead of having the new stores thrown over the old, as had been customary, to the utter destruction of the latter, were fitted with receiving and issuing rooms for each article, and the oldest expended first. Timber was procured for the several services; and such was Mr Pitt's liberality in the grants, that by the time I quitted the navy board we had upwards of 90 sail of the line fit for service, and all their stores ready for putting on board. Hospital ships, port-admiral's ships, and receiving ships, which were the first wanted, [and which] had been invariably left unprovided, and of course interrupted and kept back our fitting ships for the sea, were all provided; and as many old 40-gun ships coppered and converted into transports as would contain 4 or 5000 men. The advantages arising from these preparations are incredible in the hands of an active administration. The having so many ships prepared for sea, and everything else that belonged to them, ready; the having coppered transports of our own instead of waiting for hired ones, and upwards of £3,000,000 in necessary stores in our arsenals, gave such advantages that the fleet, in my successor's time, was fitted out with a rapidity never known before, and the credit of it imputed to him who had scarcely warmed his seat.

126. Documents Illustrating the Mutinies

A. Spithead

(a) From the Delegates to the Admiralty, April 18, 1797. (Quoted in C. Gill, *The Naval Mutinies of* 1797, p. 362.)

To the Right Honourable the Lords Commissioners
of the Admiralty.

My Lords,

We, the seamen of His Majesty's Navy, take the liberty of addressing your Lordships in an humble petition, shewing the many hardships and oppressions we have laboured under for many years, and which we hope your Lordships will redress as soon as possible. We flatter ourselves that your Lordships, together with the nation in general, will acknowledge our worth and good services, both in the American War as well as the present; for which good service your Lordships' petitioners do unanimously agree in opinion, that their worth to the nation, and laborious industry in defence of their country, deserve some better encouragement than that we meet with at present, or from any we have experienced. We, your petitioners, do not boast of our good services for any other purpose than that of putting you and the nation in mind of the respect due to us, nor do we ever intend to deviate from our former character; so far from anything of that kind, or that an Englishman or men should turn their coats, we likewise agree in opinion, that we should suffer double the hardships we have hitherto experienced before we would suffer the crown of England to be in the least imposed upon by that of any other power in the world; we therefore beg leave to inform your Lordships of the grievances which we at present labour under.

We, your humble petitioners, relying that your Lordships will take into early consideration the grievances of which we complain, and do not in the least doubt but your Lordships will comply with our desires, which are every way reasonable.

The first grievance we have to complain of is that our wages are too low, and ought to be raised, that we might be the better able to support our wives and families in a manner comfortable, and whom we are in duty bound to support as far as our wages will allow, which, we trust, will be looked into by your Lordships, and the Honourable House of Commons in Parliament assembled.

We, your petitioners, beg that your Lordships will take into consideration the grievances of which we complain, and now lay before you.

First, That our provisions be raised to the weight of sixteen ounces to the pound, and of a better quality; and that our measures may be the same as those used in the commercial code of this country.

Secondly, That your petitioners request your Honours will be pleased to observe, there should be no flour served while we are in harbour in any port whatever under the command of the British flag; and also, that there might be granted a sufficient quantity of vegetables of such kind as may be the most plentiful in the ports to which we go; which we grievously complain and lay under the want of.

Thirdly, That your Lordships will be pleased seriously to look into the state of the sick on board His Majesty's ships, that they may be better attended to, and that they may have the use of such necessaries as are allowed for them in time of sickness; and that these necessaries be not on any account embezzled.

Fourthly, That your Lordships will be so kind as to look into this affair, which is nowise unreasonable; and that we may be looked upon as a number of men standing in defence of our country; and that we may in somewise have grant and opportunity to taste the sweets of liberty on shore, when in any harbour, and when we have completed the duty of our ship, after our return from sea; and that no man may encroach upon his liberty, there shall be a boundary limited, and those trespassing any further, without a written order from the commanding officer, shall be punished according to the rules of the navy; which is a natural request, and congenial to the heart of man, and certainly to us, that you make the boast of being the guardians of the land.

Fifthly, That if any man is wounded in action, his pay be continued until he is cured and discharged; and if any ship has any real grievances to complain of, we hope your Lordships will readily redress them, as far as in your power, to prevent any disturbances.

It is also unanimously agreed by the fleet that, from this day, no grievances shall be received, in order to convince the nation at large that we know when to cease to ask, as well as to begin, and that we ask nothing but what is moderate, and may be granted without detriment to the nation, or injury to the service.

Given on board the *Queen Charlotte*, by the delegates of the Fleet, the 18th day of April, 1797.

(Signed by 32 delegates, two from each ship.)

(*b*) The First Project of Reforms. (Gill, p. 368.)

Having taken into our consideration the petitions transmitted by your Lordship from the crews of several of H.M. Ships under your command, and having the strongest desire to attend to all the complaints of the seamen in H.M. Navy, and to grant them every just and reasonable redress, and having considered the difference in the prices of the necessaries of life at this time and at the period when the pay of the seamen was established; we do hereby require and direct your Lordship to take the speediest method of communicating to the fleet that

We have resolved to recommend it to His Majesty to propose to parliament to increase the wages of the seamen in His Majesty's service, in the following proportions, viz.: to add four shillings per month to the wages of petty officers and able seamen, three shillings per month to the wages of ordinary seamen, and two shillings per month to the wages of landsmen; that

We have also resolved that seamen wounded in action shall

be continued in pay until their wounds are healed or until and being declared incurable they shall receive a pension, or shall be received into Greenwich Hospital; and

Having the most perfect confidence in the zeal, loyalty and courage of all the seamen in the fleet, so generally expressed in their petitions, and in their earnest desire of serving their country with that spirit which always so eminently distinguished British seamen,

We have come to this resolution the more readily, that the seamen may have as early as possible an opportunity of shewing their good disposition by returning immediately to their duty, as it may be necessary that the fleet should speedily put to sea to meet the enemies of their country. Given under our hands at Portsmouth the 18th day of April, 1797.

(Signed) SPENCER, ARDEN, W. YOUNG.

To the Rt. Hon. Lord Bridport, K.B., Admiral of the White, Commander in Chief of a Squadron of His Majesty's ships employed in the Channel Soundings, etc.

By Command of their Lordships,

(Signed) W. MARSDEN.

Admiral Lord Bridport delivered to R. Admiral Pole at Portsmouth, 18th April at ½ past 4 p.m.

(c) The 'Total and Final Answer' of the Seamen (April 22). (Gill, *The Naval Mutinies of* 1797, p. 373.)

To the Right honourable the Lords Commissioners
of the Admiralty.

We, the seamen and marines in and belonging to His Majesty's fleet now lying at Spithead, having received with the utmost satisfaction, and with hearts full of gratitude, the bountiful augmentation of pay and provisions which your Lordships have been pleased to signify shall take place in future in His Majesty's royal navy, by your order which has been read to us this morning by the command of Admiral Lord Bridport;

Your Lordships having thus generously taken the prayer of our several petitions into your serious consideration, you have given satisfaction to every loyal and well disposed seaman and marine belonging to His Majesty's fleets: and, from the assurance which your Lordships have given us respecting such other grievances as we thought right to lay before you, we are thoroughly convinced, should any real grievance or other cause of complaint arise in future, and the same be laid before your Lordships in a regular manner, we are perfectly satisfied that your Lordships will pay every attention to a number of brave men who ever have, and ever will be, true and faithful to their King and Country.

But we beg leave to remind your Lordships, that it is a firm resolution that, until the flour in port be removed, the vegetables and pensions augmented, the grievances of private ships redressed, an act passed, and His Majesty's gracious pardon for the fleet now lying at Spithead be granted, that the fleet will not lift an anchor: and this is the total and final answer.

B. The Nore

Earl Spencer to Nepean[1]. (Gill, *The Naval Mutinies of* 1797, p. 379.)

Sheerness,
29th May.

Dear Nepean,

I am sorry I cannot yet give you such a report as I could wish of the state of things here; indeed it is such at present that I have but very slender hopes of its taking a good turn. We lost no time in distributing the King's declaration, with the proper instructions to the several officers to explain very clearly the determination with which we came here, and the object of our coming. The immediate effect of it was pretty good, as about seven ships of those at the Nore hoisted Admiral Buckner's colours, but being frigates and small ships they could not continue to keep them up for fear of the large ships, particularly the *Sandwich* and *Inflexible*, the latter of these two being the most violent and desperate, with her guns loaded up to the muzzle, ready and apparently very desirous of making use of them. The *Clyde* and *San Fiorenzo* were to have slipped and

---

[1] Secretary of the Admiralty.

gone to Harwich in the night, but by some mistake about the captains meeting to concert the plan, and the want of pilots, those here being intimidated and refusing to act, this did not take place. And it is perhaps fortunate that it did not, as today the *Director's* people have communicated with them a promise to support them. Should they keep their word, we shall have to reckon among our friends the *Director*, the *Clyde*, the *San Fiorenzo*, *Iris*, *Ganges*, *Serapis*, *Brilliant*, and *Pylades*, besides the crews of the *Espion* and *Niger* in the harbour, who are disposed (especially the latter) to do anything either afloat or ashore that may be wished of them—a lucky circumstance, as they will, in case of hostilities, be of great use in the dockyard and garrison.

In the evening of yesterday the delegates came on shore headed by Parker, and desired to have a conference with the Lords of the Admiralty, having first enquired whether we were the same Lords who had been at Portsmouth. We sent for answer by the Commissioner that we could only communicate through the Admiral; and accordingly the Admiral went out to them at the door and asked what they had to say. Their first point was that we should go on board the *Sandwich*. This the Admiral said he knew would not be complied with, and after some little time spent in arguing the point with them, they gave it up. They then (Parker always the spokesman) insisted on seeing us, and on our inquiring through the Admiral and Commissioner what they had to say to us, they said they desired the Board would ratify the same terms to them as had been granted at Portsmouth and would promise to take into consideration the other articles which they had since brought forward. We sent them word that we positively refused to concede any other points than those which had already been granted to them in common with the rest of the fleet, and could only see them for the purpose of hearing from them that they had returned to their duty, and had accepted of His Majesty's pardon as offered in his royal declaration. On this they instantly went away, without saying a word more, and soon afterwards took to their boats and went on board. Their behaviour was quiet and orderly: every man's hat was decorated with red or pink ribbon, but there was no huzzaing or music or any other sort of parade or noise. Late last night we sent a message off by Captain Mosse of the *Sandwich*, who went to sleep on board his ship, saying that we expected to hear of the ships having returned to the regular discharge of their duty by twelve o'clock today.

Sir C. Grey is still here to wait the event, and is prepared to take the most vigorous means of *defence* that this situation will afford. He is quite confident of the troops. General Fox seems not so much so.

Yours very sincerely,

SPENCER.

127. PRESSED MEN

Impressment continued until 1833. Defence of such an institution is impossible on any grounds. Yet it is hard to see by what other means the fleets that saved the country could have been manned.

The material provided by the press-gangs is best shown by the descriptions given in 'naval captains' letters extending over a hundred years:

'Blackguards.'

'Sorry poor creatures that don't earn half the victuals they eat.'

'Sad thievish creatures.'

'Not a rag left but what was of such a nature as had to be destroyed.'

'150 on board, the greatest part of them sorry fellows.'

'Poor ragged souls and very small.'

'Miserable poor creatures, not a seaman amongst them, and the fleet in the same condition.'

'Unfit for service and a nuisance to the ship.'

'Never so ill-manned a ship since I have been at sea. The worst set I ever saw.'

'Twenty-six poor souls, but three of them seamen. Ragged and half-dead.'

'Landsmen, boys, incurables and cripples. Sad wretches great part of them are.'

'More fit for an hospital than the sea.'

'All the ragg-tagg that can be picked up.'

(The authors are indebted for the above to *The Press-Gang, Afloat and Ashore* by Mr J. R. Hutchinson [Eveleigh Nash, 1913].)

128. MANNING THE FLEETS, 1803

Rear-Admiral Campbell to Captains Searle, Ferrier, Bedford, Winthrop, and Pearson. (*N.R.S.* XIV, p. 1.)

(Secret)

By George Campbell, Esq., Rear-Admiral of the Blue, &c.

WHEREAS it is intended that a general impress of seamen should take place at the different ports and places along the adjacent coast, and that preparation should be made with the utmost secrecy and caution to perform that service with promptitude and effect, you will, immediately on receipt of these orders, select from the crew of his Majesty's ship under your command a sufficient number of trusty and well disposed men to man three boats, with as many marines and petty officers as you may judge necessary to send in each, under the orders of a lieutenant, to whom you will deliver a press warrant accordingly; and you are likewise to select sixteen steady marines that may be trusted to go on shore to stop the avenues leading up to the country.

And as it is intended that the party from his Majesty's ship under your command should be employed on this service at:

Captain Searle, and *Alarm* lugger	Dartmouth
Captain Ferrier	Paignton
Captain Bedford	Brixham
Captain Winthrop	Torquay
Captain Pearson	Teignmouth and Salcombe;

You will endeavour to have previous communication with one of his Majesty's Justices of the Peace for the district, applying to him to back the warrants, taking especial care to cause as little alarm as possible.

You will direct the officers you may appoint to this service that they are not to regard the protections of any description of persons, excepting those protected pursuant to Acts of Parliament, and all others who by the printed instructions which accompanied the press warrants are forbidden to be impressed; as also such persons as belong to ships and vessels bound to Newfoundland and foreign parts which are laden and cleared outwards by the proper officers of his Majesty's Customs; the crews of transports, storeships, victuallers, or other ships and vessels in the service of the Navy, Victualling, Transport, and Ordnance Boards; ships and vessels laden by the special order and under the direction of the Lords Commissioners of his Majesty's Treasury with provisions and stores for the use of his Majesty's armies, &c.; and vessels and craft in the service of the Corporation of the Trinity House.

On the boats returning to the ships, you will make a return to me of the number and qualities of the men that may have been impressed, and report to me your proceedings on the occasion.

But a very unpleasant and serious circumstance having occurred at Portland, it is my direction that this service is performed with as much caution as possible, to prevent bloodshed and violent measures.

Given, &c., *Culloden* in Torbay, 25th April, 1803.

By command of the Rear-Admiral.

129. A 'HOT PRESS' AT DARTMOUTH

P.R.O., Admiralty, Captains' Letters.

His Majesty's Ship *Venerable*
in Torbay, 26 April, 1803.

Sir,

In pursuance of your order, I went last night to Dartmouth, with the Officers and men previously directed, and made a strict search in all the Public Houses, and in every other place where the Lieutenant of the Rendezvous thought there might be a probability of success. I dispatched at the same time a party to examine all the vessels afloat. I am sorry to say the result of all these endeavours only produced two men; this is, I imagine, to be accounted for by the same duty having been several times performed at Dartmouth since the first breaking out of the Impress, which has made the seamen too wary to be suddenly caught; indeed I am informed that the greater part of them are retired some miles into the country, particularly at the back of

Teignmouth, where nothing but an adequate Military force can insure their being secured for His Majesty's Service.

Inclosed I transmit you a List of the two men impressed and have the honour to remain,

Sir,

Your respectful and obedient Servant,

J. C. Searle.

A list of four Men Impressed by the Boats of His Majesty's Ship *Thunderer*. W. Bedford, Esq., Captain.

Men's Names	Age	Remarks
Thomas Perring	27	Served his time as a rope-maker; has never been at sea; worked in Woolwich yard five years; came to Brixham to see his parents.
Rob Lane	31	Works as a blacksmith at Brixham; never at sea; says he is troubled with fits and sickness.
John Harris	22	Works as a shipwright; has property belonging to him at Newton Abbot.
James Moffett	24	A fisherman belonging to Brixham; says he has a protection for the *Endeavour* sloop now laying at Dartmouth.

130. Weakness of the French at Brest

The lack of offensive spirit on the part of France in the naval operations of the great war was the logical outcome of long adherence to radically unsound principles. In March, 1781, Barras can write to the Minister of Marine: 'Il est de *principe de guerre* qu'on doit risquer beaucoup pour defendre ses propres positions, et très peu pour attaquer celles des ennemis.' The policy is well summed up by a recent French naval historian as 'disdain of the enemy's fleet, geographical or commercial objectives, terror of risks, absence of pursuit, direct coast defence' (Castex).

The outbreak of the French Revolution reduced the French navy to chaos. For many of the brilliant professional officers there was left no choice between exile and the scaffold. It seemed that the very efficiency which dated from the institutions of pre-revolutionary France was itself a crime in 1789. Loud-voiced sentiments of liberty and patriotism now did duty for the discipline and training which Choiseul[1] had designed and in great measure had achieved. Both officers and men, who knew these qualities to be indispensable, would no longer sully reputation and honour by remaining to serve with men 'who had for guide no other principle than that of Nature and a heart truly French.'

Good gunnery and seamanship disappeared with the trained men. The manning of the ships was a perpetual problem; the condition of the men on board was very miserable; and the ships themselves were ill-found and short of spare sails and rigging.

Napoleon was powerless, at short notice, to galvanise his navy into life and vigour, though he often refused to accept the doleful reports of his subordinates.

The following letters well illustrate the Blockade of Brest as it appeared from the French side.

(*a*) Caffarelli[2] to Decrès[3]. (*N.R.S.* XIV, p. 56.)

Brest, 11 messidor, year XI (30 June, 1803).

[Translation]

Our coasts are fortified, it is true, but without troops to defend them, or their number is so small that they do it badly. The general commanding in Finistère begs for at least 2000 men to be sent him. I have asked for at least 1000 more, for our armaments are incomplete, as also our coast detachments.

Our division of four ships cannot put to sea. Its presence in the Goulet would attract the English fleet, and the slightest accident to the ships would involve the certain loss of those which suffered in an action. Accordingly our incapacity for making great efforts permits our enemies to attempt all the small enterprises they can; it is only with diffidence and circumspection that our vessels can sail.

This state of things is distressing, citizen minister.

(*b*) Same to Same. (*N.R.S.* XIV, p. 81.)

[Translation]

Brest, 6 thermidor, year XI (25 July, 1803).

The English are constantly on our coasts; some vessels off Ushant, four or five anchor in the day at the Black Rocks, a

---

[1] Chief Minister of Louis XV, 1758–70; Foreign Minister, 1758–61; Minister of War and of Marine, 1761–66; Minister of War and of Foreign Affairs, 1766–70.

[2] Naval Prefect at Brest.   [3] Minister of Marine.

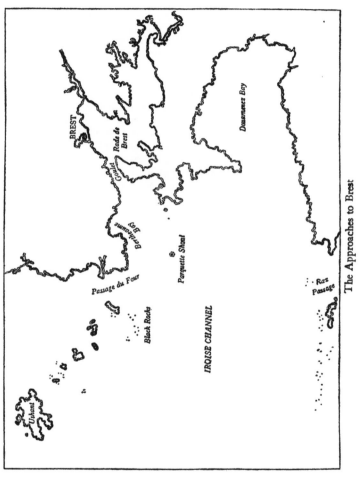

The Approaches to Brest

frigate and a corvette remain under sail at Douarnenez, a corvette and a cutter come right up to the entrance of the Goulet and cruise there constantly. Their boats make descents on the neighbouring islands, where there are no troops; they also go to the coast at a distance from frequented places, and their crews can gather such intelligence as it is possible to extract by intimidation or less direct methods.

An inhabitant of the island of Béniguet has sent me a report, dated the 3rd, which reached me today: the English have landed in arms on Béniguet; they demanded whether there was not, at Conquet, a convoy composed of fifteen luggers coming from the north, and with what they were laden. He replied that he knew nothing about it. They said that they expected to find a further ten ships in this port, in all twenty-five. An English officer has made a bet with this man's wife that before long they will have carried off some of them; the bet was ten louis against one of her cows.

Never, in the last war, did I see such a surrender of Finistère. Brest and the fleet then offered far greater resources for attack or for continuous defence.

131. NAPOLEON URGES ACTIVITY

Napoleon to Ganteaume. (*N.R.S.* XXI, p. 59.)

Aix-la-Chapelle, Sept. 6th, 1804.

Vice-Admiral Ganteaume, Commander-in-Chief of the Brest fleet, I have received your letter of August 27th. I have given orders for the 1273 men wanting to make up the complement of your squadron to be placed at your disposal, viz.: 200 men of the Marine Artillery, 600 dockyard conscripts, and 500 men from infantry of the line. So the *Patriote* is in the roadstead at last! With 21 ships, I hope that you will be in a position to do something.

Your sortie has struck the English with great terror. They know well that, having all the seas to defend, a squadron escaping from Brest could do them incalculable harm; and, if you could carry in Brumaire 16,000 men and 500 horses to Ireland, the result would be fatal to our enemies. Tell me if you think you can be ready, and what are the probabilities of success. See the

Irish General, O'Connor, and discuss with him the possible landing-places. I quite realise that a sortie, like that which you have made, demands favourable circumstances which do not present themselves every day; but I do not understand why your ships do not get under way every day to manœuvre in the roadstead. What possible danger is there in doing that? The fops of the squadron could laugh and gibe at their great expeditions; it would be none the less true that, in these continual exercises, you would give your squadron a deportment and experience of the greatest value, and you would have done everything which depends on you. I do not know the roadstead of Brest well enough to know if a squadron of five ships could manœuvre there, and at your signal put itself in battle order for the different evolutions: if that is practicable, why isn't it done? I have caused these manœuvres to be carried out by the Boulogne flotilla, with excellent results, and it is still doing them; it is an object of encouragement and of instruction the advantage of which no one can deny. We must not look for what we lack; I cannot perform miracles; but we must do what is possible. I have enough experience of the sea to know that, if one were only to weigh anchor, unfurl the sails, and come to an anchor again—I say more, if one were to do no more than clear for action, the result would always be very advantageous. Be frank: how many ships have you which clear for action well? The hammocks are badly stowed, everything is not prepared as it should be; in short, nothing is unimportant for success. Why do you not make, every week at least, the signal to clear for action, and why do you not then visit the ships and see how badly it can be carried out? I will go further: I think that mere practice in signals is useful, and accustoms all the ships to repeat them with the proper smartness and experience. I repeat that these exercises will be laughed at, but none the less the effect will be that the staffs of the ships will get to know the signals well, and will remove the obstacles which are often found in the way of their prompt hoisting and repetition. When the English knew that you were in Camaret Bay, the opinion of the sailors in England was that you were unassailable.

I have no more flag-officers. I should like to make some rear-admirals, but I want to choose the most promising, without regard to seniority. Send me a list of a dozen officers worthy of being made rear-admirals, having the qualities necessary to deserve promotion, and above all still in the vigour of life.

NAPOLEON.

132. INVASION SCHEME DELAYED

Ganteaume's Instructions, March 24, 1805. (*N.R.S.* XXI, p. 215.)

(Telegraphic—Ganteaume to Napoleon.)

The fleet is ready and can set sail tomorrow evening, but there are fifteen English ships in the Iroise, and it is impossible to leave without risking an action.

Success is not doubtful. I await your Majesty's commands.

(Telegraphic—Napoleon to Ganteaume.)

To be transmitted immediately by the telegraph.

A naval victory at this juncture would lead to nothing. Have but one aim, that of accomplishing your mission. Leave port without an action.

He who is to join you has started.   NAPOLEON.

133. NAPOLEON IGNORES THE CLOSE BLOCKADE

Napoleon to Ganteaume. (*N.R.S.* XXI, p. 349.)

Boulogne Camp, 22nd August, 1805.

Vice-Admiral Villeneuve got under way from Ferrol on August 10th, but did not actually leave until the 14th, in order to join you at Brest. From what I can gather from his despatches, it seems to me that he means to go through the Raz. It also seems to me that he is doubtful if, after his junction with you, he will not spend several days revictualling at Brest. I have already informed you, by telegraph, of my intention that you should not allow him to lose a single day, in order that, profiting by the superiority which 50 ships of the line give me, you should immediately put to sea to reach your destination and to enter the Channel with all your forces. I count upon your talents, your firmness, and your character at this all-important juncture. Set out and come here. We shall have avenged six centuries of insults and of shame. Never will my sailors and soldiers have exposed their lives for a grander object.   NAPOLEON.

Between 1793 and 1800 the condition of the French fleet was such that the danger of serious invasion of England was never imminent. A close blockade of Brest was, therefore, considered by Lord Howe to be neither necessary nor desirable. Rather, he aimed at encouraging the French to leave their ports at the least favourable time of year, *i.e.* in winter. In winter, therefore, Brest was left open, and British squadrons withdrawn from the arduous task of close-watching the iron-bound Breton coast. The winter months were spent in training and recruiting the ships' companies at the main depot—Portsmouth. As we have seen, Kempenfelt strongly favoured this husbanding of the ships' strength in winter. Any criticism of Howe's 'open' method of blockade must make full allowance for his motives: he did not design to shut up the enemy in port, but rather to tempt him out and bring him to action. With close blockade there could have been no Glorious First of June.

With the renewal of war and menace of invasion in 1803, the Admiralty at once resorted to the close blockade of Brest, which had been first adopted by Hawke in 1759 and revived by St Vincent in 1800 (see *supra*, p. 139).

Some of the methods suggested and practised, the difficulties encountered, and the objections raised to the close form of blockade are here illustrated.

Towards the end of the critical period from 1803 to 1805 it became actually doubtful to the authorities whether the close blockade of Brest could be maintained. Quite apart from the stress and strain upon the personnel, the wear and tear of ships was causing grave anxiety. It would seem that no absolute judgment can be delivered as to the superiority of the close blockade over the open form. The decision or choice must always be relative to the conditions of time and space, *i.e.* to the condition and strategic position of the enemy's squadrons, and the defence of trade and convoys. In 1805 the French fleet in Brest was regarded by the Admiralty as too close to the Channel to justify the risk of evasion, which was possible, though not probable, had a form of open blockade been adopted.

134. CLOSE BLOCKADE IN 1803

Collingwood to Blackett.

Venerable, off Brest, Aug. 9, 1803.

I am lying off the entrance of Brest Harbour, to watch the motions of the French fleet. Our information respecting them is very vague, but we know they have four or five and twenty great ships, which makes it necessary to be alert and keep our eyes open at all times. I therefore bid adieu to snug beds and comfortable naps at night, never lying down but in my clothes[1].

[1] On August 27 Collingwood writes to Cornwallis: 'It would be desirable to have a cutter here to be some relief to the *Pickle*, whose commander can never be in bed during the night.'

The Admiral sends all the ships to me, and cruises off Ushant by himself; but with a westerly wind it is impossible with one squadron to prevent ships getting into Brest Harbour, for it has two entrances, very distant from each other—one to the south of the Saints, but which, off Ushant, where we are, is entirely out of view. I take the utmost pains to prevent all access, and an anxious time I have of it, what with tides and rocks, which have more of danger in them than a battle once a week.

135. Defence against Invasion

Parliamentary Debates, March 15, 1804: Naval Inquiry brought forward by Pitt (against St Vincent). Extract from a speech by Sir Edward Pellew.

Sir, as I very seldom trouble the House, I hope I may be permitted to make a few observations on a subject of which, from the professional experience I have had, I may be presumed to have some knowledge. From the debate of this night, there is one piece of information I have acquired, that the French have got upwards of a thousand vessels at Boulogne. I am glad to find they are shut up there; we have our advantage in it, we know where they are; I wish we had any means of knowing when they intended to come out. I know this much, however, that they cannot all get out in one day, or in one night either; and when they do come out, I trust that our cockle-shells alone, as an honourable admiral has called a very manageable and very active part of our force, will be able to give a good account of them. Sir, I do not really see in the arrangement of our naval defence anything to excite the apprehensions even of the most timid among us; on the contrary, I see everything that may be expected from activity and perseverance, to inspire us with confidence. I see a triple naval bulwark, composed of one fleet acting on the enemy's coast, of another consisting of heavier ships stationed in the Downs, ready to act at a moment's notice, and a third close to the beach, capable of destroying any part of the enemy's flotilla that should escape the vigilance of the other two branches of our defence.

As to the gun-boats which have been so strongly recommended, this mosquito fleet, they are the most contemptible force that can be employed; gun-brigs, indeed, are of some use, but between a gun-brig and a gun-boat there is almost as much difference as between a man-of-war and a frigate. I have lately seen half a dozen of them lying wrecked upon the rocks.

As to the possibility of the enemy being able, in a narrow sea, to pass through our blockading and protecting squadrons, with all that secrecy and dexterity, and by those hidden 'means that some worthy people expect, I really, from anything that I have seen in the course of my professional experience, am not much disposed to concur in it. I know, Sir, and can assert with confidence, that our navy was never better found, that it was never better supplied, and that our men were never better fed or better clothed. Have we not all the enemy's ports blockaded from Toulon to Flushing? Are we not able to cope, anywhere, with any force the enemy dares to send out against us, and do we not even outnumber them at every one of those ports we have blockaded? It would smack a little of egotism, I fear, were I to speak of myself; but, as a person lately having the command of six ships, I hope I may be allowed to state to the House how I have been supported in that command. Sir, during the time that I was stationed off Ferrol, I had ships passing from the fleet to me every three weeks or a month, and so much was the French commander shut up in that port deceived by these appearances, that he was persuaded, and I believe is to this very hour, that I had twelve ships under my command, and that I had two squadrons to relieve each other, one of six inside, and another of six outside.

136. Wear and Tear of Blockading Squadron

Lord Melville[1] to Cornwallis, November 2, 1804. (*N.R.S.* XXI, p. 117.)

With every disposition to increase your force to the utmost of my power, I do not feel myself warranted to hold out immediately hope of any considerable addition to the number of sixteen I have proposed to be constantly with you.

[1] Henry Dundas, First Viscount Melville (1742–1811). First Lord of the Admiralty from May, 1804, till April, 1805.
List of First Lords of the Admiralty (1788–1805):

1788–97	Earl of Chatham.
1797–1801	Earl Spencer.
1801–4	Earl St Vincent.
1804–5	Viscount Melville.
1805–6	Lord Barham.

To have a force always effective to that amount of course requires several more to supply accidents or replace those who may be obliged, from any circumstance, to come into port. I trust, however, this supernumerary force need not be so large as it must be if the system of unremitting blockade was to be adhered to; but as that, by your orders and instructions as lately transmitted, is considerably relaxed, an opportunity will thereby be afforded to you of furnishing your fleet with those articles of provisions, and replenishing, which might otherwise have rendered it necessary for them to come into port.

I observe what you state relative to the policy of relaxing the strictness of blockade formerly resorted to. I admit the *chances* of what you state; but, on the other hand, I cannot shut my eyes against the *certainty* of what we must all experimentally know, that you have not the means of sustaining the necessary extent of naval force, if your ships are to be torn in pieces by an eternal conflict with the elements during the tempestuous months of winter. And allow me to remind you that the occasions when we have been able to bring our enemy to battle, and our fleets to victory, have generally been when we were at a distance from the blockading station. I am perfectly aware of the peculiar situation of Ireland, and how much it requires to be specially attended to; but I believe it cannot be better done than by keeping your fleet in a sound and effective condition, appropriating (exclusive of the fleet stationed off Brest) at the same time a separate force for the protection of Ireland, to guard against the chance of an invading force, under a detachment from the fleet in Brest harbour, making an abrupt departure from Brest during the time the fleet under your command is obliged from weather to leave the blockading station.

137. The Limitations of the Close Blockade

Collingwood to J. E. Blackett. (G. L. Newnham Collingwood, *Correspondence and Memoirs of Lord Collingwood*, 5th edition, 1837.)

Dreadnought, off Ushant, Feb. 4, 1805.

In the middle of last month we put into Torbay, where we were a week; but the being in Torbay is no great relief, for no person or boat goes on shore. We visit our friends and neighbours in the fleet, but we have no communication with the rest of the world, without they come on board and take the chance of a cruise. The sailing of the enemy's squadron from Rochefort, and evading Sir Thomas Graves, seems to intimate that something is soon to be undertaken by them. It is not yet well ascertained where that squadron is, but by the route in which they were seen, Brest seemed to be their destination, and if they are arrived there, it will be a proof how little practicable it is to block up a port in winter. To sail from one blockaded port and enter another, where the whole fleet is, without being seen, does not come within the comprehension of the city politicians. Their idea is that we are like sentinels standing at a door, who must see, and may intercept, all who attempt to go into it. But so long as the ships are at sea they are content, little considering that every one of the blasts which we endure lessens the security of the country. The last cruise disabled five large ships, and two more lately; several of them must be docked.

If the country gentlemen do not make it a point to plant oaks wherever they will grow, the time will not be very distant when, to keep our Navy, we must depend entirely on captures from the enemy. You will be surprised to hear that most of the knees which were used in the *Hibernia* were taken from the Spanish ships captured on the 14th February[1]; and what they could not furnish was supplied by iron. I wish everybody thought on this subject as I do; they would not walk through their farms without a pocketful of acorns to drop in the hedge-sides, and then let them take their chance.

138. St Vincent maintains the Close Blockade

Brenton, *Life of Earl St Vincent*, II, p. 248.

Off Ushant, 29th March, 1806.

My dear Admiral,

We are between Ushant and the Black Rocks, in the day —stand off at night, and in at 4 o'clock in the morning. The *Mars* anchored off the Black Rocks; *Diamond, l'Agile*, and small craft off the Parquette, and the *Crescent* looks out to the northward of the Ushant. I cannot approve the rendez-vous of my

[1] Cape St Vincent, 1797.

predecessor, 'seven leagues S.W. of Ushant,' and intend to change it to, *well in with Ushant during an easterly wind.*

Upon conversing with an intelligent midshipman of this ship, who was in the *Amethyst* when Sir J. Duckworth fell in with the French squadron off the Canaries, I am convinced it has gone to the Southward, destined either for the Cape of Good Hope or to do us as much mischief as possible at St Helena and Ascension. I send you the young man's observations during the two days they were in sight of the French squadron, because they do him much credit: his name is Pitt; he has lately passed his examination for a lieutenant, and was a shipmate of mine in the *Argo.*

Very truly yours,

Rear-Admiral Markham.

St Vincent.

139. Nelson's Watch off Toulon

Nelson's own description of his watch on the Toulon fleet and Capt. Whitby's commentary thereon are printed below, together with two short letters of Nelson, which though irrelevant in this connection have been inserted, because, like most of his correspondence, they are instinct with his matchless spirit.

It should be remembered that Nelson had neither the requisite number of ships nor facilities for refitting to make any *close* blockade of Toulon possible.

The memorandum of October 9, 1805—the most famous document in naval history—is reprinted as it was originally drafted.

(*a*) Clarke and McArthur, ii, 489.

To Alexander Davidson, Esq.

Victory, Gulf of Palma,
December 12th, 1803.

I care not who is in or out; I shall endeavour to do my duty to my country. I believe I attend more to the French fleet than making captures; but of what I have, I can say, as old Haddock[1] did, *It never cost a sailor a tear, nor the nation a farthing*—that thought is far better than prize-money.

I never saw a fleet altogether so well officered and manned —would to God the ships were half as good! We ought to be amply repaid some day for all our toil. My crazy ships are getting

[1] The words were really Rooke's.

into a very indifferent state, and others will soon follow: the
finest ones in the service would soon be destroyed by such
terrible weather. I know well enough that if I were to go in to
Malta, I should save the ships during this bad season; but if I
am to watch the French, I must be at sea; and if at sea, must
have bad weather; and if the ships are not fit to stand bad
weather, they are useless: unfortunately in bad weather I am
always sea-sick. But, my dear friend, my eye-sight fails me most
dreadfully: I firmly believe that in a few years I shall be stone-
blind; it is this only of all my maladies that makes me unhappy;
but God's will be done.

(b) Nelson to Vice-Admiral Sir Charles Morice Pole, Bart. (Nicolas, *Dispatches
and Letters of Lord Nelson*, VII, Addenda CCXXXIII.)

My dear Pole,   *Victory*, May 25th, 1804.

Where your letter of December 20th has been travelling
to I cannot guess, but it only arrived to me in the *Leviathan* on
the 12th instant. I assure you that I most sincerely wish to
promote Brown, who is an ornament to our Service; but alas!
nobody will be so good as to die, nor will the French kill us.
What can I do? but I live in hopes, as the French keep playing
about the mouth of Toulon harbour, that some happy day I
shall be able to get a blow at them. My system is the very contrary of blockading, therefore I, for one, shall not be entitled to
those thanks which the newspapers say the City of London
mean to give the Blockading Squadrons. I would no more
accept thanks for what I was conscious I did not merit, than I
would refuse them and feel hurt at their not being given for a
great victory, and it is curious I am likely to be placed in both
situations: but such things are.

I am sure Lord St Vincent ought to feel grateful for your
zealous support of his measures; and I hope you will stand by
the Navy against all attempts to have soldiers placed in our
ships independent of the Naval Act of Parliament, from whatever
quarter it may be attempted. When that takes place there is an
end of our Navy—there cannot be two Commanders in one Ship.

We are all as happy as a set of animals can be who have been
in fact more than a year at sea; or rather not going on shore, for

with the exception of anchoring under the North end of Sardinia, not a ship has been to a Naval yard for refitting. Hope keeps us up.

I beg my respectful compliments to Lady Pole; and believe me ever, my dear Sir Charles, most affectionately yours,

NELSON AND BRONTE.

140. NELSON ACKNOWLEDGES LORD HOWE'S CONGRATULATIONS AFTER THE NILE

Nelson to Howe. (Nicolas, *Dispatches and Letters of Lord Nelson*, III, 230.)

My Lord,   Palermo, 8th January, 1799.

It was only this moment that I had the invaluable approbation of the great, the immortal Earl Howe—an honour the most flattering a Sea-Officer could receive, as it comes from the first and greatest Sea-Officer the world has ever produced. I had the happiness to command a Band of Brothers; therefore, night was to my advantage. Each knew his duty, and I was sure each would feel for a French ship. By attacking the enemy's van and centre, the wind blowing directly along their Line, I was enabled to throw what force I pleased on a few ships. This plan my friends readily conceived by the signals, (for which we are principally, if not entirely, indebted to your Lordship) and we always kept a superior force to the enemy. At twenty-eight minutes past six, the sun in the horizon, the firing commenced. At five minutes past ten, when *L'Orient* blew up, having burnt seventy minutes, the six van ships had surrendered. I then pressed further towards the Rear; and had it pleased God that I had not been wounded and stone blind, there cannot be a doubt but that every ship would have been in our possession. But here let it not be supposed that any Officer is to blame. No; on my honour, I am satisfied each did his very best. I have never before, my Lord, detailed the Action to anyone; but I should have thought it wrong to have kept it from one who is our great Master in Naval tactics and bravery. May I presume to present my very best respects to Lady Howe, and to Lady Mary; and to beg that your Lordship will believe me ever your most obliged,   NELSON.

141. NELSON'S WAY WITH THE FRENCH

(a) Nelson to Cornwallis. (*N.R.S.* XIV, p. xvi.)

Victory, December 30, 1804.

My dear Friend,—I always feel happy in hearing from you, for I never, never shall forget that to you probably I owe my life, and I feel that I imbibed from you certain sentiments which have greatly assisted me in my naval career—that we could always beat a Frenchman if we fought him long enough; that the difficulty of getting at them was oftentimes more people's own fancy than from the difficulty of the undertaking; that people did not know what they could do until they tried; and that it was always to err on the right side to fight. I was then at that time of life to make the impression which has never been shaken. But, on the score of fighting, I believe, my dear friend, that you have had your full share, and in obtaining the greatest victory, if it had been followed up, that our country ever saw[1].

I own I should like to see you with the Brest fleet well clear of the land, and from my heart I hope that will happen. There is not, my dear friend, that man breathing who would rejoice more than your most attached and affectionate friend,

NELSON AND BRONTE.

(b) As a complement to this letter may be printed a part of one of Nelson's 'unreserved conversations' with his captains. It is quoted by Clarke and McArthur, II, 413, as having taken place about the 16th June, 1805.

I am thankful that his Enemy has been driven from the West India Islands with so little loss to our Country. I had made up my mind to great sacrifices, for I had determined, notwithstanding his vast superiority, to stop his career, and to put it out of his power to do any further mischief. Yet do not imagine I am one of those hot-brained people who fight at immense disadvantage, without an adequate object. My object is partly gained. If we meet them, we shall find them not less than eighteen, I rather think twenty sail of the line, and therefore do not be surprised if I should not fall on them immediately: we won't part without a Battle. I think they will be glad to let me alone, if I will let them alone; which I will do either till we approach the shores of Europe, or they give me an advantage too tempting to be resisted.

[1] The Saints, April 12, 1782.

142. Nelson's difficulties in the Mediterranean, 1803–1805

Captain Whitby to Cornwallis. (*N.R.S.* xiv, p. 343.)

Newlands, Monday, 11th June, 1804.

By the by, I want to communicate one thing to you which appears to me of great consequence; and but that our seas are so clear, and our posts go so safe, I should have first sent you a cipher, by which it could have come to no one's knowledge but yourself. It, however, may be told in very few words, and I shall do it. Though Lord Nelson is indefatigable in keeping the sea, there are so many reasons that make it possible for the French to escape through the Mediterranean, which, of course, Government are not told by him—and which, perhaps, he does not consider (at least I think so)—that I have been long determined to warn you of the circumstance upon my arrival, not choosing to trust it from the Mediterranean. First, then, he does not cruise upon his rendezvous; second, I have consequently repeatedly known him from a week to three weeks, and even a month, unfound by ships sent to reconnoitre—the *Belleisle* herself was a week; thirdly, he is occasionally obliged to take the whole squadron in to water, a great distance from Toulon; fourthly, since I came away the French squadron got out in his absence, and cruised off Toulon several days, and at last, when he came out, he only got sight of them at a great distance, to see them arrive at their own harbour. From all this I draw one general conclusion—that it is very possible for them to escape him. Upon the last occasion they might have got to the West Indies, or elsewhere, without the possibility of discovery, had they so chosen. And from all this, I draw these particular ones likewise, concurring with other circumstances: they have ten sail of the line at Toulon, one at Cadiz, four, I think, at Ferrol, six at Rochefort, and twenty, you say, at Brest, making in all one-and-forty sail of the line. If they pass Lord Nelson, they can relieve Cadiz (which is only blockaded by two frigates), Ferrol, Rochefort; and if in their way to Brest you meet them some morning, when they are attempting a grand junction, I shall not be surprised. I mention this to you that you may pay what attention you choose to this scheme of probabilities, and have your ships so much in your eye at daylight that you may be prepared for their reception.

I write this in confidence to you, for I would not absolutely dare to give my opinion of the Mediterranean blockade to any other person; for doubtless my Lord Nelson is actuated by a thorough zeal to do right, for he is, indeed, a great and glorious officer. I must add one other thing, however, which is that in gales of wind he drives so far away that the finding him is very difficult, and the enemy have the greatest chance. I have no doubt, therefore, that they *can* come out; the rest, the object, remains to be proved. I must tell you another thing. Gore in the *Medusa* is so inattentive, in my opinion, to his situation at Gibraltar, which I consider the picquet-guard of you and my Lord Nelson, and from which, and which only, you could reasonably hope for intelligence, that I would not advise you to trust to it. When I was there, three ships out of four were stripped for several days; this I think of the very last importance. I may have judged erroneously throughout, but there will be no harm in the hint, which I am convinced you can receive from no other quarter. God bless you, my dear Admiral! I shall say no more than that I am your most sincere and affectionate friend,

J. W.

143. NELSON'S MEMORANDUM

From the original holograph draft in the British Museum. Interlineations are shown in square brackets, deletions in italics, as in the Blue Book on the Tactics of Trafalgar, Cd. 7120.

Memⁿ.   *Victory* off Cadiz,

9 Octr. 1805.

Thinking it almost impossible to bring a Fleet of forty Sail of the Line into a Line of Battle in variable winds thick weather and other circumstances which must occur, without such a loss of time that the opportunity would probably be lost of bringing the Enemy to Battle in such a manner as to make the business decisive.

I have [therefore] made up my mind to keep the fleet in that position of sailing (with the exception of the first and Second in Command) that the order of Sailing is to be the Order of Battle, placing the fleet in two Lines of Sixteen Ships each with an advanced Squadron of Eight of the fasting (*sic*) sailing Two decked ships [which] will always make if wanted a Line of Twenty four Sail, on which ever Line the Commander in Chief may direct.

The Second in Command will *in fact Command* [*his line*] *and* after my intentions are made known to him *will* have the entire direction of His Line to make the attack upon the Enemy and to follow up the Blow until they are Capturd or destroy'd.

If the Enemy's fleet should be seen to Windward [in Line of Battle] *but* [and] *in* that *position that* the Two Lines and the Advanced Squadron can fetch them (*I shall suppose them forty Six Sail* [*in*] *of the Line of Battle*) they will probably be so extended that their Van could not succour their Rear.

I should therefore probably make *your* the 2nd in Commds signal to Lead through about their Twelfth Ship from their Rear (or wherever *you* [He] could fetch if not able to get so far advanced) My Line would lead through about their Centre and the Advanced Squadron to cut two or three or four Ships Ahead of their Centre, so as to ensure getting at their Commander In Chief on whom every Effort must be made to Capture.

The whole impression of the British [fleet] must be, to overpower from two or three Ships ahead of their Commander In Chief, supposed to be in the centre, to the Rear of their fleet. [I will suppose] twenty Sail of the [Enemys] Line to be untouched, it must be some time before they could perform a Manœuvre to bring their force compact to attack any part of the British fleet engaged, or to succour their own ships which indeed would be impossible, without mixing with the ships engaged[1]. Something must be left to chance, nothing is sure in a sea fight beyond all others, shot will carry away the masts and yards of friends as well as foes, but I look with confidence to a victory before the van of the Enemy could succour their *friends* [Rear] and then that the British Fleet would most of them be

[1] Note in margin of original. 'The Enemy's Fleet is supposed to consist of 46 Sail of the Line—British fleet of 40—if either is less only a proportionate number of Enemy's ships are to be cut off; B to be ¼ superior to the E cut off.'

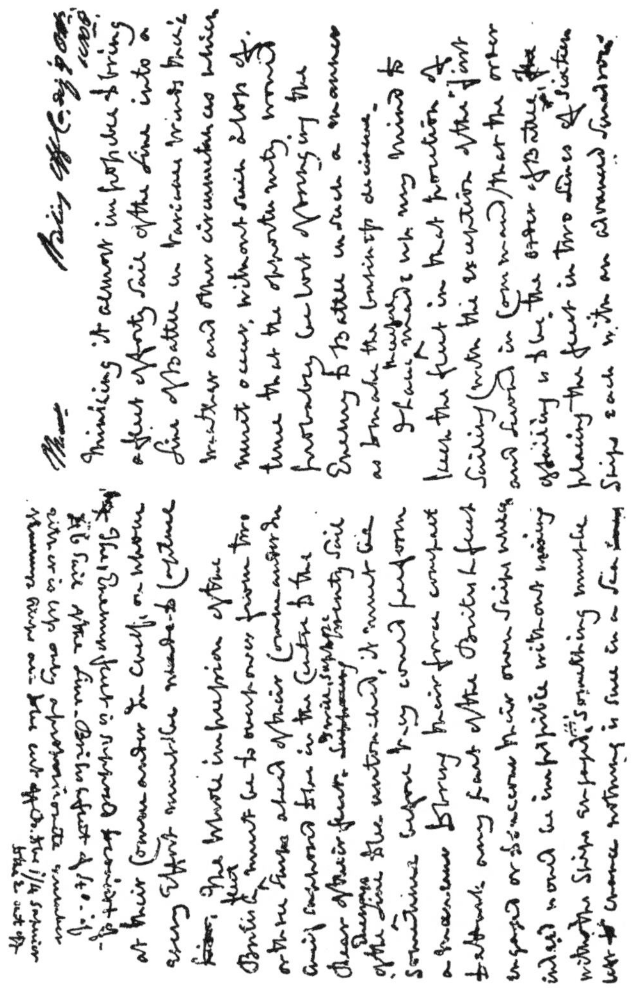

ready to receive their Twenty Sail of the Line or to pursue them should they endeavour to make off.

If the Van of the Enemy tacks the Captured Ships must run to Leeward of the British fleet, if the Enemy wears the British must place themselves between the Enemy and the captured & disabled British Ships and should the Enemy close I have no fear as to the result.

The Second in Command will in all possible things direct the Movements of his Line by keeping them as compact as the nature of the circumstances will admit *and* Captains are to look to their particular Line as their rallying point. But in case signals can neither be seen or perfectly understood no Captain can do very wrong if he places his Ship alongside that of an Enemy.

Of the intended attack from to Windward, the Enemy in Line of Battle ready to receive an attack:

—————————————— B

—————————————E———————————————————

The Divisions of the British fleet will be brought nearly within Gun Shot of the Enemys Centre. The signal will most probably [then] be made for the Lee Line to bear up together to set all their sails even steering sails[1] in order to get as quickly as possible to the Enemys Line and to Cut through beginning from the 12 Ship from the Enemies rear some ships may not get through their exact place, but they will always be at hand to assist their friends and if any are thrown round the Rear of the Enemy they will effectually compleat the business of Twelve Sail of the Enemy. Should the Enemy wear together or bear up and sail Large still the Twelve Ships composing in the first position the Enemys rear are to be [the] Object of attack of the Lee Line unless otherwise directed from the Commander In Chief which is scarcely to be expected as the entire management of the Lee Line after the intentions of the Commander in Chief *is* [are] signified is intended to be left to the Judgement of the Admiral Commanding that Line.

---

[1] Note in margin of original, '*Vide* instructions for Signal Yellow with Blue fly, page 17, eighth Flag Signal Book, with reference to Appendix.'

The Remainder of the Enemys fleet 34 Sail are to be left to the Management of the Commander In Chief who will endeavour to take care that the Movements of the Second in Command are as little interrupted as is possible.

144. Page of Telegraphic Code by which Nelson made his historic Signal[1] on Oct. 21, 1805

Telegraphic Signals;

or

Marine Vocabulary.

By

Captain Sir Home Popham, R.N. 1803.

page 19.   E 5   [Printed.]

238	Each	1238	Either-wise
239	Early	1239	Eligible
240	East-erly-ward	1240	Else-where
241	East-Indies-an	1241	Embay-ed
243	Ease-y-ily	1243	Employ-ed-ing-er-ment
244	Effect-ed-ing	1244	Empty-iness
245	Embark-ation-ed-ing	1245	Enable-d-ing
246	Encamp-ed-ing-ment	1246	Encourage-d-ing-ment
247	End-ing-less	1247	Endanger-ed-ing
248	Endeavour-ed-ing	1248	Enough
249	Enemy-ies	1249	Entirely
250	Enforce-d-ing	1250	Error-oneous-ly
251	Engage-d-ing-ment	1251	Especial-ly
253	England-ish	1253	Esteem-imate-ion
254	Enjoin-ed-ing	1254	Evacuate-d-ing-ion
255	Entitle-d-ing	1255	Even
256	Enter-ry-ance	1256	Evolution-s
257	Erase-d-ing-ment	1257	Evidence-t-ly
258	Essential-ly	1258	Exact-ly-ness
259	Establish-ed-ing-ment	1259	Excellent-ce-cy-tly

[1] This signal was made in twelve hoists, viz.

253	269	863	261	471	958	220	370	4	21	19	24
England	Expects	That	Every	Man	Will	Do	His	D	U	T	Y

260	Evening	1260	Exceed-ed-ing-ly, excess-ive-ly (*sic*)
261	Ever-y-thing-where	1261	Except-ed-ing-ion-able
263	Examine-ation-ed-ing	1263	Exclude-d-ing-sive-ion
264	Example	1264	Expend-ed-ing-ce
265	Exceed-ed-ing	1265	Explain-ed-ing-ation
266	Excuse-d-ing-able	1266	Explode-sion
267	Execute-d-ing-ion	1267	Extend-ed-ing-sive-ion
268	Exert-ed-ing-ion	1268	External-ly
269	Expect-ed-ing-ation	1269	Extinguish-tinct
270	Expedite-ed-ing-ion-ious	1270	Extol-led-ing
271	Express-ed-ing-ion-ly	1271	Extreme
273	Extra-ordinary-ly	1273	Extricate-ed-ing

145. POPHAM'S VOCABULARY CODE

W. G. Perrin, *The Evolution of the Signal Flags*, p. 33.

The present edition[1] is wholly new cast and composed; very considerably enlarged by additional materials; and, as I trust, improved by a distribution of those materials which was intended to increase the facility of reference.

It consists of nearly 6000 primitive words, exclusive of the inflexions of verbs, &c., making in all upwards of 30,000 real words; the sentences have also been extended to about 6000, with 1500 syllables, a Geographical Table, a Table of Technical Terms, a Table of Stores and Provisions, and a Spare Table for Local Significations.

W. G. Perrin, *The Evolution of the Signal Flags*, p. 34.

FA1	Have you an idea
G647	a change of ministers is about to take place
52A	Certainly
8BF	not
G643	ministers are gaining strength
BOE	Your
AC8	sister
852	married
85F	to
C87	a Lord of the Admiralty.

[1] 1812.

INDEX

CAMBRIDGE: PRINTED BY W. LEWIS, M.A., AT THE UNIVERSITY PRESS